剑桥雅思
真题精讲

IELTS13

ACADEMIC

学术类

周成刚 ● 主编

海豚出版社
DOLPHIN BOOKS
中国国际传播集团
CICG

图书在版编目（CIP）数据

剑桥雅思真题精讲. 13. 学术类 / 周成刚主编. —
北京：海豚出版社，2018.4（2023.4重印）
　ISBN 978-7-5110-4181-4

　Ⅰ. ①剑… Ⅱ. ①周… Ⅲ. ①IELTS—题解 Ⅳ.
①H310.41-44

中国版本图书馆CIP数据核字(2018)第049849号

剑桥雅思真题精讲13：学术类
周成刚　主编

出 版 人　王　磊
责任编辑　慕君黎　梅秋慧
特约编辑　刘　畅
封面设计　李　倩
责任印制　于浩杰　蔡　丽
法律顾问　中咨律师事务所　殷斌律师
出　　版　海豚出版社
地　　址　北京市西城区百万庄大街24号
邮　　编　100037
电　　话　010-68325006（销售）　010-68996147（总编室）
邮　　箱　dywh@xdf.cn
印　　刷　三河市良远印务有限公司
经　　销　新华书店及网络书店
开　　本　787mm×1092mm　1/16
印　　张　11.75
字　　数　327千字
印　　数　130001-133000
版　　次　2018年4月第1版　2023年4月第5次印刷
标准书号　ISBN 978-7-5110-4181-4
定　　价　48.00元

我的留学观

留学是当今中国的一个热点话题。所谓热点话题，就是讨论的人多，关注的人多。无论你决心已下还是尚在彷徨犹豫，留学的选择对你的人生来说都将是一个重大决定。它涉及你个人和家庭的许多投入，包括时间、金钱、精力，甚至情感，它关系到你未来的学习、工作和个人生活，它与你的前途息息相关。我相信每一个人在做出最后决定前，一定会一遍又一遍地问自己：

"我到底要不要出国留学？"

"我是否也应该像大多数人一样选择去欧美国家留学？"

首先我想说，决定留学或不留学其实没有对与错，留学只是一种学习方式的选择。而一旦涉及选择，就少不了分析与比较、思考与权衡。来新东方咨询留学的学生和家长，都会向我们提出类似的问题。

从某种意义上说，我们问自己"我到底要不要出国留学"就如同问"我到底要不要上大学"一样。大多数家长不会因为当下大学毕业生就业困难就不支持孩子上大学，也不会因为有一些成功的企业家没有读过大学就不让自己的孩子追求学业。大学生并非个个身怀绝技，也并非都能获得人们期待的那些成功，但大学尤其是名校仍然倍受追捧。为什么？因为大家心中明白，相对于没有上过大学的人，一般来说，大学生的平均综合素质较高，毕业后在职场上具有更强的竞争力和职业发展后劲。也就是说，我们希望通过读大学、读名校，来提高自己的胜出概率。谈到此处，上述的两个问题也就迎刃而解了。欧美国家和名校一样，它们代表着这个世界的先进生产力。无论是科学技术、政治经济，还是文化教育，欧美的大部分国家正在引领世界的发展。换句话说，这些发达国家是大部分发展中国家学习和借鉴的榜样。我们选择留学，选择到发达国家去学习，可以提高自己在世界舞台上的胜出概率，可以获得比其他人更多的成功机会。

那么为什么是否选择留学会在今天成为一个如此紧迫的问题呢？

可以说，这是全球一体化带来的必然社会趋势。所谓全球一体化，就是地区与地区之间，国家与国家之间，经济体与经济体之间的交流和接触日益频繁，障碍逐个被扫除，资源和信息的流动变得前所未有地畅通。一句话，过去因为种种原因，我们隔断了自己和世界绝大部分地区和国家的交流，我们国家的年轻人除了自己不需要和任何国家的同龄人去竞争。但随着国门不断打开，我们国家的年轻人已经和世界各国的年轻人走到了同一个舞台上，需要和全球同龄人去竞争。

今天，一个美国人可以很容易到中国找工作，他们到中国的公司找到一份工作就意味着中国人少了一份工作；相反，一个中国学生很容易到美国去留学，毕业后他们在华尔街谋到一份职业也就意味着抢走了美国人的一个饭碗。

在如此这般的全球同龄人竞争的格局下，越来越多的学生认识到，自己如果要在职场上胜出，就必须掌握当今世界普遍认可的价值观和在全球范围内有竞争力的知识和职业技能。当我们开始去寻找这些东西准备充实自己的时候，陡然发现，这些我们所希望拥有的先进的科学文化知识、有竞争力的核心技术、创新的思维观念，甚至符合人性发展的价值观等，大部分掌握在那些发达国家的手里，至少在目前这个历史发展阶段是如此。过去我们自己和自己比赛，规则和输赢我们自己说了算。但现在，我们要去和世界强队比赛，要按照国际比赛的规则去比，输赢由国际裁判决定。于是，我们不得不开始了解国际比赛，学习比赛规则。这就是为什么今天越来越多的家长要送自己的孩子出国留学，因为家长都希望自己的孩子在比赛中胜出。

事实上，我们背井离乡、负笈海外，或是去留学，或是去进修，或是去游历，都是中国人世代相传的教育理念的延伸和自我实践。几千年来，中国人通过读书改变自己命运的梦想从没有停止过。

过去，许多家庭省吃俭用，用攒下来的钱送孩子进私塾学校，接受教育；书生们则头悬梁、锥刺股，用面壁苦读换来最后的金榜题名，自此改变人生命运。后来我们有了高考，农村的孩子通过上大学或读研究生，进一步提升自己的实力，获取一份比自己的父母更好的工作，去从事教师、工程师、医生和律师这些令人羡慕和受人尊敬的职业。学生通过高考走进了不同的城市，有小城市，也有大城市，当然也有北京、上海等国际大都市。人们渴望走进这些城市，是因为他们知道这些城市更加前卫，人们的思想更加开放，资源更加集中，发展更快，机会更多，实现个人价值的概率更大。

如今，我们出国留学，到伦敦、多伦多、悉尼和纽约这些国际大都市去深造进修，这与当初我们走进县城、省城以及到北京、上海去读书何其相似？长久以来，这些行为和决定背后的核心理念丝毫没有改变，那就是"读书改变命运""教育兴邦"，唯一不同的是地缘和文化意义上的差异。我们只不过是从国内走到了国外，走进了一个不同的文化、语言和价值观的新世界。

当然，我们也不能否认许多中国学生出国留学还有一个目的——把英语学得更好。上两个世纪，英国和美国在文化、经济、军事、政治和科学上的领先地位使得英语成为一种准国际语言。世界上许多重要的社会活动、经济事件和科学发明都是用英语记录的，美、英等发达国家的媒体也在用英语传播他们的信息、知识和观念，影响遍及世界各个角落。我们掌握了英语，就如同掌握了一门世界通用语言，从这个意义上讲，英语之于世界，如同普通话之于中国。当我们在选择学习普通话、方言还是少数民族语言时，大多数人会选择普通话，因为普通话适用范围更广，接受度更高，也更容易习得，更方便和中国各地或各民族背景的人们交流。

有的家长会问，既然英语是一门世界通用语言，那我们是不是早点把孩子送出去更好？我的回答是：如果孩子出去太早，他可能由于长期接受西方文化熏陶，而脱离中国文化的根基，最终成为一个"香蕉人"。反过来，如果孩子仅仅扎根中国，很少与外面的世界接触，那他可能会在和世界对话时缺少应有的准备。

我相信，21世纪的今天，随着全球一体化的深入，无论是世界舞台还是经济高速发展的中国，都需要跨区域、跨文化、跨技能和跨语言的多元化的桥梁性人才。他们往往能够南北迁徙，既受中国文化的熏陶又受西方教育的洗礼；他们深谙世界的发展趋势，知道现在的西方有更多的先进技术，现在的中国有更多的发展机遇；这种"东西合璧"型的人才无论在国内还是国外，都会很容易找到自己的发展空间和职业定位。

写到这里，我不禁想起了过去30年自己的生活、工作、留学和成长的历程。我20世纪80年代上大学，毕业后留校任教10年，虽然是个英语专业的学生，但当时并没有想过要出国留学。突然有一天，我发现周围的朋友和同学都开始出国了，有的在国外大学当了教授，有的回国创业成了成功的企业家，有的把自己的跨国事业越做越红火。人是社会动物，不仅是为自己活着，他的思想、行为和价值观常常要受周围的人的影响，这是我对马克思所言"人的本质就其现实性而言是社会关系的总和"的一个新认识。于是，在这些朋友和同学的影响下，我也出国留学了。10年的大学英语老师生涯为我的澳大利亚留学做好了铺垫，海外的研究生专业学习和优异的考试成绩又为自己赢得了在BBC（英国广播公司）当记者的机会，英国的记者经历又为我日后加盟新东方提供了一份实力保障。今天，我已经把我的职业发展和新东方的发展连在了一起。

如果说，一个留学生只是一个点，那么千千万万的留学生就可以形成一股巨大的社会推动力。纵观中国的近现代史，中国社会每一次重大的社会变革和进步往往都是和留学生以及东西方思想的交汇紧密相关的，中国改革开放30多年所取得的成绩也佐证了这一点。这也许就是当面对21世纪的世界新格局时，中国学生出国留学以及中国留学生归国创业的大潮如此势不可挡的原动力吧！

30年后的今天，我自己的孩子也踏上了他的赴美留学之路。我深知这条路不会平坦，知道他在这条路上有时会倍感寂寞和孤独。但我为他喝彩，为他自豪，因为这是一个90后年轻人自己的选择，因为这是我从前走过的一条路，虽然坎坷崎岖，但路上的风景很美很醉人！

周成刚
新东方教育科技集团首席执行官

目　录

Test 3

Test 4

Listening

Section 1

📖 场景介绍

一位女士电话咨询是否有为游客提供的一日烹饪课。旅游信息咨询中心的工作人员向其介绍了当地三所烹饪学校的特色，包括是否提供一对一课程、是否有特殊需求饮食料理课程、是否有免费体验课、是否有折扣等。

📖 本节必背词汇

cookery	n. 烹饪学；烹饪课	calorie	n. 卡路里（热量单位）
available	adj. 现有的；可获得的	recipe	n. 食谱
focus on	关注；专注于	ingredient	n. 原料；要素
seasonal	adj. 季节性的，随季节变化的	build up	增进，加强
private	adj. 私人的；秘密的	reputation	n. 名声，名誉
deal	n. 对待，待遇；交易	vegetarian	n. 素食主义者
client	n. 客户，顾客	sharpen	v. 磨尖，使锋利
concentrate	v. 关注；集中	chop	v. 切碎，砍
specialist	n. 专家，行家	technique	n. 技术，技巧

📖 词汇拓展

barbecue	n. 烧烤	leaflet	n. 宣传单
brunch	n. 早午餐	perishable	adj. 易腐烂的，易消亡的
budget	n. 预算	reasonable	adj. 合理的
buffet	n. 自助餐	resort	n. 娱乐场所；度假胜地
cancellation	n. 取消	slicer	n. 切片机
discount	n. 打折，优惠	slippery	adj. 滑溜的
entertainment	n. 娱乐	supermarket	n. 超级市场
expense	n. 开销	well-equipped	adj. 装备完善的
facility	n. 设备，设施		

✿ 文本及疑难解析

1. They focus on seasonal products, and as well as teaching you how to cook them, they also show you how to choose them. 他们（指 Food Studio 烹饪工作室）主要教授季节产品的烹饪和选材。注意 as well as 结构后接动名词短语。

2. And could I get a private lesson there? 那里有私教课程吗？指一对一授课形式的烹饪课。

3. They concentrate on teaching you to prepare healthy food, and they have quite a lot of specialist staff. 他们（指 Bond's Cookery School）专注于教你烹饪健康食物，而且那里有很多这个领域的行家。

4. Yes, just key in the name of the school — it'll come up. 是的，把学校名字敲进去，就有了。此处 key 是动词，指可以在搜索引擎中敲出学校名称。

5. And they also offer a special two-hour course in how to use a knife. They cover all the different skills — buying them, sharpening, chopping techniques. It gets booked up quickly though so you'd need to check it was available. 他们提供关于如何使用刀具的两小时特别课程。课程覆盖很多不同的技能，包括如何购买、如何磨刀、切割技术等。课程预定非常快，所以你需要查一下是否还有。

✿ 题目解析

本节全为表格题（table），表格内含少量断句以提示所需答案。

1. 题干词 focus, cook, seasonal 均原文重现，词汇及定位难度不大，答案为直叙。
2. 题干词 small classes 原文重现，答案相对比较容易定位。但原文中的 private lesson 在题干中被替换为 classes，可能造成考生的理解障碍。
3. 题干词 clients, discount 原文重现，定位不难。考生需要对 discount 一词做出快速搭配反应，该词前后可能出现形容词或数字。答案 20% 在 discount 后随即出现。
4. 通过题干语法及基本含义预测本题应填形容词。healthy 为相关答案句中唯一的形容词。
5. 题干词 recipes 原文重现，本题相对较容易定位。build up 和 strengthen 同义替换。
6. 题干词 Thursday 原文重现。从题干中的 free 可以判断应填入名词。lecture 符合题干语法及含义。
7. 本题为直叙。
8. 本题由题干含义可判断需要填与食物相关的名词或形容词。原文 mostly 和题干 mainly 同义替换。dish 可译为"菜"或"食物"。
9. 本题由题干语法可判断需要填名词。locate 一词指"坐落于"，问该烹饪学校离什么位置较近。market 一词符合题干语法及含义。
10. 题干词 special course 原文重现，需填写名词。答案为直叙。

Section 2

▤ 场景介绍

道路委员会主席 Phil Sutton 向民众介绍 Granford 在交通及停车规则方面的一些变化。随着新医院的建立和交通负荷的增加，交通问题的解决变得越来越紧迫。通过对民众的调研，镇政府发现大量需要改造的道路和需要完善的服务，例如红绿灯是否需要增设、人行横道的位置和停车区域的设置是否合理等。

chairman	n. 主席	lorry	n. 卡车，货车
committee	n. 委员会	proposal	n. 提议，提案
inform	v. 通知，告知	budget	n. 预算
regulation	n. 规则，制度	council	n. 委员会，政务会
propose	v. 提议，倡议	representative	n. 代表
summarize	v. 总结，摘要	slide	n. 幻灯片
noticeable	adj. 值得注意的	junction	n. 交叉点，汇合点
overall	adj. 全部的，全体的	pedestrian	adj. 行人的
volume	n. 体积，体量	forbid	v. 禁止，阻止
concern	v. 使担忧；关心	bend	n. 弯道
survey	n. 调研，问卷	disabled	adj. 残疾的；有缺陷的
resident	n. 居民；房客	arrangement	n. 安排；计划
response	n. 回答，答复	widen	v. 使……变宽
visibility	n. 能见度	pavement	n. 便道，人行道
complaint	n. 投诉，抱怨	restriction	n. 限制，限定
congestion	n. 拥挤，拥塞	load	v. 装货，装载
fume	n. 烟雾，烟气	unload	v. 卸货

词汇拓展

convert	v. 改建，改造	redevelopment	n. 再开发
cycling	n. 骑车，骑行	reorient	v. 重定方位
district	n. 区	residential area	居民区，住宅区
drive	n. 机动车道	shade	n. 阴凉
footpath	n. 步行道	shelter	n. 隐避处；遮蔽物
improvement	n. 提高，改进	suburb	n. 近郊，郊区
incorporate	v. 合并，结合	urban	adj. 市区的
intersection	n. 十字路口	vehicle	n. 车辆；交通工具
outskirts	n. 郊区		

文本及疑难解析

1. I'll start by summarizing these changes before we open the meeting to questions. 在谈问题之前，我先总结一下这些变化。open the meeting 可以直接理解为"开始会议"，会议整体是探讨问题，因此说 open the meeting to questions.

2. It's been especially noticeable with the increase in heavy traffic while they've been building the new

hospital. But it's the overall rise in the volume of traffic of all kinds that's concerning us. To date there's not been any increase in traffic accidents, but that's not something we want to see happen, obviously. 非常令人关注的是随着医院的起建，交通变得越来越拥堵。但我们担忧的是各类交通的总体体量的增加。至今交通事故量并没有增加，但显然事故并不是我们希望看到发生的。

3. People were very concerned about the lack of visibility on some roads due to cars parked along the sides of the roads. 人们担心路边停放的车辆阻挡了一些道路的视线。

4. But, of course, it's no good introducing new regulations if we don't have a way of making sure that everyone obeys them, and that's an area we're still working on with the help of representatives from the police force. 但是如果没有办法确保大家能够遵守，那么颁布规定必然是没有意义的，这也是我们和警局代表依然在讨论的。work on 意指正在努力的方向，with the help of... 指 "在……的帮助下"。

5. There'll be a new 'No Parking' sign on School Road, just by the entrance to the school, forbidding parking for 25 metres. This should improve visibility for drivers and pedestrians, especially on the bend just to the north of the school. 在 School Road 上会有一个新的 "禁止停车" 标，正好在学校的入口处，25 米范围之内禁止停车。这应该能让司机和行人的视线更好一些，特别是在学校北边的那条弯道上。

6. As far as disabled drivers are concerned, at present they have parking outside the supermarket, but lorries also use those spaces, so we've got two new disabled parking spaces on the side road up towards the bank. 对于有残疾的司机而言，他们现在可以将车停在超市外面，但大货车也停在这些区域，所以我们在银行旁边的小路上设置了两个新的残疾人停车位。

❀ 题目解析

本节难度适中，由单项选择题 11~13、地图题 14~20 组成。

11. 本题题干 why are changes needed to traffic systems 在原文中高度重现。定位较容易。考生特别需要理解 volume 一词指 heavy traffic，含义为 "体量"。

12. 本题具有一定迷惑性，三个选项在原文中均有提及。考生必须能够注意到 but 之后在强调 parents dropping off their children 不是最大问题，nor 同样在否定 trucks and lorries 带来的问题。lack of visibility 可以理解为 inconvenience。

13. 题干词 regulations 原文重现，定位相对较容易。原文 making sure that everyone obeys them 对应 B. finding a way to make people follow them。

14~20. 这道地图题可以通过题干词定位，按对应原文寻找对应位置，考生必须把握表格第四列中的方位词才能理解并准确找出选项。

题号	题干	对应原文	解题必备方位词
14	New traffic lights	...with Station Road, but we're planning to have another set at the other end, at the School Road junction, ...	a set of, junction
15	Pedestrian crossing	...on the High Street, crossing the road in front of the supermarket.	cross the road, in front of
16	Parking allowed	...parking isn't allowed on the High Street outside the library, but we're going to change that, ...	outside
17	New 'No Parking' sign	...on School Road, just by the entrance to the school, ...	by the entrance to

题号	题干	对应原文	解题必备方位词
18	New disabled parking spaces	...on the side road up towards the bank.	up towards
19	Widened pavement	...manage to get an extra half-metre on the bend just before you get to the school, on the same side of the road.	on the bend, on the same side
20	Lorry loading / unloading restrictions	That's the supermarket on School Road...	on...road

Section 3

📖 场景介绍

两名学生 Emma 和 Jack 在讨论实验主题和细节。Jack 向 Emma 说明为何选择种子发芽作为研究课题，两人同时认为该实验主题所需设备学校实验室都能提供，操作难度不大，所以可行。两人随后确定了实验步骤和注意事项。

🔤 本节必背词汇

germination	n. 发芽，萌芽	modify	v. 修改，改变
eventually	adv. 最终，终于	proportion	n. 比例，占比
optional	adj. 可选择的	impressive	adj. 令人印象深刻的
module	n. 模块，单元	illustration	n. 插图，图解
dissertation	n. 论文	diagram	n. 图表
equipment	n. 设备，工具	procedure	n. 过程，程序
laboratory	n. 实验室	measure	v. 测量，衡量
ambitious	adj. 有野心的，有雄心的	dimension	n. 尺寸；维度
assignment	n. 作业；任务	time-consuming	adj. 消耗时间的
theory	n. 理论，原理	millimetre	n. 毫米
reference	n. 参考；引证	pot	n. 盆，罐
genetically	adv. 从基因方面	label	v. 贴标签，标注

🔤 词汇拓展

abbreviation	n. 缩写	certificate	n. 证书
capacity	n. 能力；容量	critical	adj. 批判式的
catalogue	n. 目录	deadline	n. 最后期限

defend	*v.* 答辩	methodology	*n.* 方法学，方法论
demanding	*adj.* 有难度的	note-taking	*n.* 做笔记
diploma	*n.* 学位	paperwork	*n.* 报告
discipline	*v.* 训练，使有纪律	plagiarism	*n.* 抄袭
draft	*v.* 打草稿	proficiency	*n.* 熟练
eligible	*adj.* 合适的；合格的	prospectus	*n.* 大纲，计划书
field study	实地研究	qualified	*adj.* 有资格的
handwriting	*n.* 书写	respondent	*n.* 受访者
in advance	提前	seminar	*n.* 研讨会
insight	*n.* 洞察力	statistics	*n.* 统计；统计数字
journal	*n.* 期刊	tutorial	*n.*（导师带领的）讨论小组

❀ 文本及疑难解析

1. Yeah, but practically everything we do is going to feed into that. 是的，但实际上我们所有做的（课题实验）都应该在这个范围。feed into 字面含义为"流入，注入，装进"，本句中的 that 指前文中提及的 plant science，因此本句中把 feed into 理解为"归属……范围"。

2. That should be fine if we start now. A lot of the other possible experiments need quite a bit longer. 如果我们现在开始应该没问题。很多其他可以选的实验需要的时间要长得多。

3. Yes, I'd been hoping for something more practical. It does include references to the recent findings on genetically-modified seeds, though. 是的，我一直想要更实用一些的东西，不过（Graves 的著作）里面确实有一些关于转基因种子的最新研究发现。

4. Then we see if our plants have come up, and write down how tall they've grown. 然后看看咱们的植物长得怎么样，再把它们长到多高记下来。come up 字面意思为"上来"，此处意指"植物由下而上得长出来"。

❀ 题目解析

本节由单选题 21~25 及搭配题 26~30 组成。

21. 本题问及做某事的原因，题干中的 why 与原文中的 particular reason 匹配，但选项具有较强混淆性。学生 Emma 引出 B 选项后，Jack 表示确实如此。考生需注意此时 yeah 的含义是 Jack 肯定 Emma 的见解，并不是肯定做该领域实验的原因是为了将来在该领域工作。C 选项中的 dissertation 原文有所提及，但又提到不需要做论文，因此该选项被排除。

22. 本题稍难定位。考生需首先理解题干所指为"目前实验的最大好处是什么？"但题干词在原文中未明显突出。答案关键句 So that'd make it a good one to choose 出现时，正确选项 C 已播放完，容易漏听。本题考查词汇不难，但对短时记忆要求较高。A, B 两项构成混淆，这两个选项虽然都是指好处，但未提及它们是选择该项实验的主要原因。

23. 题干词 tutor 原文重现，本题定位不难。考生需理解 whether anyone else 与 the only ones doing it 为同义替换。

24. 题干词 Graves 在原文中较易定位，该题目仅考核 theory 与 theoretical 的词性替换。

25. 题干词 Lee Hall 在原文中较易定位，该题考查 figure 与 statistics, thorough 与 detail 的同义替换。
26. 由题干词 different 定位。考查 sorts 与 types 间的同义替换。
27. 由题干词 record 及 measure 定位。考查动词 weigh 与名词形式 weight 间的替换。
28. 由题干词 decide 定位。考查形容词 deep 与名词形式 depth 间的替换。
29. 由题干词 different 定位。答案词原文重现，但考查短时记忆能力，答案 pot 出现后才出现定位词。
30. 由题干词 3 weeks 定位。考查形容词 tall 与名词形式 height 间的替换。

Section 4

📖 场景介绍

　　一篇关于动物如何在城市环境下生存并进化的演讲。研究表明，有许多动物在飞速适应着城市生活。其中有一些动物已经在身体构造上产生变化，有一些的"抗压"能力和胆量比郊外的同类物种明显增强。这些差异也表现在一些动物的肢体语言上。

📕 本节必背词汇

evolutionary	*adj.* 进化的	gopher	*n.* 囊地鼠
represent	*v.* 代表，表现	intelligent	*adj.* 聪明的
upheaval	*n.* 突变，巨变	cognitive	*adj.* 认知的；认识的
massive	*adj.* 巨大的，庞大的	reflect	*v.* 反映，反射
adapt	*v.* 适应	adjust	*v.* 适应，调整
adaptable	*adj.* 适应的	anatomy	*n.* 解剖；骨骼
pigeon	*n.* 鸽子	bold	*adj.* 勇敢的，大胆的
perch	*v.* 栖息，停留	threat	*n.* 威胁，恐吓
ledge	*n.* 窗台；房檐的凸起处	counterpart	*n.* 极相似的人或物
immigrant	*n.* 移民；移居者	sensible	*adj.* 明智的；合乎情理的
adaptation	*n.* 适应	stress	*n.* 压力
evolution	*n.* 进化	endocrine	*adj.* 内分泌的；激素的
biologist	*n.* 生物学家	hormone	*n.* 激素，荷尔蒙
specimen	*n.* 标本，样本	squirrel	*n.* 松鼠
urbanise	*v.* 使城市化	intellectual	*adj.* 智力的，智能的
mammal	*n.* 哺乳动物	prevalent	*adj.* 流行的，普遍的
mice	*n.* 老鼠	accustom	*v.* 使习惯

词汇拓展

biodiversity	*n.* 生物多样性	migration	*n.* 移民；迁移
decline	*n./v.* 减少；衰落	mobile	*adj.* 移动的，不定的
endanger	*v.* 使处于危险	predator	*n.* 捕食者
exist	*v.* 存在；生存	preserve	*v.* 保护，保持，保存
feed on	以……为生	prey	*n.* 猎物
generate	*v.* 生产，产出	proliferate	*v.* 扩散，激增
habitat	*n.* 栖息地	proportion	*n.* 比例，比重
inhabit	*v.* 栖息；居住于	survival	*n.* 存活，幸存
investigation	*n.* 调查，调研	turn up	出现
metabolic	*adj.* 新陈代谢的；变化的	wildlife	*n.* 野生动物

文本及疑难解析

1. Another successful species is the pigeon, because they're able to perch on ledges on the walls of city buildings, just like they once perched on cliffs by the sea. 另一个最成功的物种应该是鸽子，因为它们可以像飞落栖息在海边悬崖峭壁上那样停歇在楼房的窗台上。此句中 the wall 在翻译时可以省略。

2. And one thing that researchers are finding especially interesting is the speed with which they're doing this — we're not talking about gradual evolution here — these animals are changing fast. 最让研究者感到有趣的是它们（指这些动物）改变的速度。我们不是在说慢慢的进化，而是它们在飞速变化。with which 引导定语从句。

3. And she found that during that time, these small mammals had experienced a jump in brain size when compared to rural mammals. 而且她发现在那段时间，这些（在大城市生活的）哺乳动物的大脑尺寸比在郊外生活的哺乳动物大了很多。compare to 为固定搭配。

4. So as you might expect, she's found that the urban blackbirds tend to be quite bold — they're prepared to face up to a lot of threats that would frighten away their country counterparts. 因此，正如你所预期的那样，她（德国研究者 Catarina Miranda）发现在城市栖息的黑鸟胆子会更大一些。和在郊外的同类相比，它们更能面对各类威胁而不被吓跑。face up to 意为"面对"。blackbird 指居住在美洲的一种黑鸟，或称为黑鹂，口语中指乌鸦。

5. One possibility is that we may see completely new species developing in cities. But on the other hand, it's possible that not all of these adaptations will be permanent. 一种可能性是我们可能会看到城市里进化出全新物种。但另一方面，可能并不是所有的这些变化都会持续。

题目解析

　　本节为典型的学术报告填空题（连续填空，以句子或笔记形式呈现），整体难度适中。

31. 题干词 adaptability 在原文中以动词形式 adapt 出现，为重要定位线索。另由 31 和 32 题的题干结构可判断需要定位某一名词，且为一种动物。crow 是题干词 pigeon 之前出现的唯一动物名词。

32. 由题干语法可判断需要填写名词。题干词 walls of city buildings 原文重现，just like 与 similar 同义替换。答案 cliffs 为直叙。

33. 本题需理解题干含义，定位某名词符合"城市中的动物正在以非一般的 _____ 适应"。仅有 speed 一词符合词性及含义。

34. 题干词 mammal specimens, Minnesota 原文重现，定位较容易。brain size 与 the size of their brain 仅仅是结构变化。定位词与答案距离非常近。本题难度低。

35. 本题定位稍有难度。考生需要掌握 locate 与 look in 为同义替换，new sources 与 different places 为同义替换。

36. 题干词 Catarina Miranda 及 urban and rural blackbirds 原文重现，定位较容易。考生需要把握在 not...but... 结构中，but 之后为重要信息。

37. 本题通过题干语法可以判断需要定位名词或形容词。考生需把握 brave 与 frighten 呼应，在理解原文中"黑鸟遇到未经历过的新情况会被吓到"的基础上填写答案。

38. 本题通过题干语法可以判断需要定位名词。答案词 stress 出现在题干词 hormones 之前，考查短时记忆。

39. 题干词 squirrel 原文重现，需要定位"松鼠的 + 名词"。答案为直叙。

40. 副标题中的 possibility 及题干词 develop 原文重现，通过题干语法判断需要定位名词或形容词。考生需掌握原文中 not all of these adaptations will be permanent 与题干中 changes may not be 含义相同，答案为直叙。

Reading Passage 1

篇章结构

体裁	说明文
主题	对"新西兰旅游网"的介绍及其对该国旅游业的影响和贡献
结构	第一段：新西兰旅游业概述和"新西兰旅游网"在其中发挥的作用
	第二段："新西兰旅游网"的内容和组成介绍
	第三段：此网站的独特特色
	第四段：此网站的若干新增内容
	第五段：此网站对新西兰旅游业所起的重大作用
	第六段：最为吸引游客的活动类型
	第七段：新西兰旅游业的特殊性及其成功经验的普遍性

解题地图

难度系数： ★★★

解题顺序： TABLE COMPLETION → TRUE/FALSE/NOT GIVEN

友情提示： 本文的叙事线索非常清晰，全文都没有太过艰深曲折的长难句，是一篇比较简单的说明文。一般来说，应对考试的较为合适的阅读顺序是：先读文章标题（副标题），大致了解文章主题；再看所有问题类型，略读题干中的信息，初步进行题型难易的了解和判断；之后才是浏览文章正文开始解题。作为一套试题中的第一篇文章，并且题目基本都是顺序出题的类型，本文还是比较适合使用"平行阅读"这个方法的，也就是：每大致略读一段文章或部分正文，就分别对比两个题型中的前两道，具体来说也就是第1、2题和第8、9题，根据题干进行初步判断，刚刚读过的正文内容是否包含问题中的相关信息。如有对应，则细读相关部分进行解题；如果没有，则继续回到刚才读到的正文处，继续向后略读文章。按照这个推进顺序，稳步进行略读和精读两个动作，即可做到只看一遍文章内容而不落下全部或绝大部分题目信息，从而在考场上更有效率地利用有限的时间进行解题，得到更为满意的做题效果。

必背词汇

1. interactive *adj.* 互动的

   This will make computer games more *interactive* than ever. 这将使电脑游戏比以前更具交互性。
   There is little evidence that this encouraged flexible, *interactive* teaching in the classroom.
   几乎没有证据表明这促进了灵活互动的课堂教学。

2. submit *v.* 提交；屈从（名词形式为 submission）

They *submitted* their reports to the chancellor yesterday. 他们昨天向财政大臣提交了报告。

In desperation, Mrs. Jones *submitted* to an operation on her right knee to relieve the pain.
绝望中，琼斯夫人不得已接受了右膝手术以减轻疼痛。

3. be related to 与……有关

The children, although not *related to* us by blood, had become as dear to us as our own.
这些孩子虽然与我们没有血缘关系，但却变得如同我们亲生的一样亲。

He recognized that Sanskrit, the language of India, *was related* very closely *to* Latin, Greek, and the Germanic and Celtic languages. 他认识到梵语，即印度的语言，与拉丁语、希腊语、日耳曼语和凯尔特语有着密切的同源关系。

4. involved *adj.* 涉及……的，与……有关的

If she were *involved* in business, she would make a strong chief executive.
如果她经商的话，将会是一位很有能力的首席执行官。

During a visit to Kenya in 1928, he became romantically *involved* with a beautiful lady.
在 1928 年到肯尼亚访问期间，他和一位漂亮的女士产生了暧昧关系。

5. unlikely *adj.* 不太可能的，未必会发生的

As with many technological revolutions, you are *unlikely* to be aware of it.
正如很多技术革命一样，你不太可能意识到它。

It's now *unlikely* that future parliaments will bring back the death penalty.
现在看来，今后的议会是不太可能恢复死刑的。

认知词汇

tourism	*n.* 旅游业	evaluation	*n.* 评估
inhabitant	*n.* 居民	interview	*n.* 采访；面试
long-haul	*adj.* 长途的；辛劳的	former	*adj.* 先前的，之前的
currently	*adv.* 目前，当下	rugby	*n.* 橄榄球
gross domestic product 国民生产总值（GDP）		blockbuster	*n.* 电影大片
sector	*n.* 部门；产业	stunning	*adj.* 吸引人的；令人窒息的
launch	*v.* 推出；创立；发射（火箭等）	backdrop	*n.* 背景
campaign	*n.* 大型活动；战役	devise	*v.* 设计
scenic	*adj.* 风景好的	itinerary	*n.* 行程
exhilarating	*adj.* 令人兴奋的，激动人心的	catalogue	*v.* 把……编目分类
authentic	*adj.* 真实的，原汁原味的	route	*n.* 路线
Maori	*n.* 毛利人 *adj.* 毛利人的	highlight	*v.* 突出，强调
potential	*adj.* 潜在的 *n.* 潜力	indicate	*v.* 提示，指示
destination	*n.* 目的地	option	*n.* 选择；选项
presence	*n.* 存在	accommodation	*n.* 住宿
access to	通向……的途径，做……的方法	register	*v.* 注册，登记
participate	*v.* 参加	innovation	*n.* 创新
scheme	*n.* 计划，方案	impressive	*adj.* 令人印象深刻的
undergo	*v.* 经历	expenditure	*n.* 花销
independent	*adj.* 独立的	average	*n.* 平均；平均数 *adj.* 平均的

annual	*adj.* 年度的，每年的	infrastructure	*n.* 基础设施
solely	*adv.* 完全是，仅仅是	underlying	*adj.* 潜在的，暗含的
geographical	*adj.* 地理的	apply	*v.* 适用于
account for	占……百分比	strategy	*n.* 策略
be composed of	由……所组成	unique	*adj.* 独特的，独一无二的
perceive	*v.* 接受，感知	comprehensive	*adj.* 全面的
reliable	*adj.* 可靠的		

❀ 佳句赏析

1. A key feature of the campaign was the website www.newzealand.com, which provided potential visitors to New Zealand with a single gateway to everything the destination had to offer.
   - **参考译文**：这场宣传活动的一个关键特色就是"新西兰旅游"这个网站，它为未来有可能前往新西兰的游客提供了一个一站式端口，在此可以找到新西兰这个目的地所能提供的一切。
   - **语言点**：本句的主干非常简单：A key feature...was the website... 读者在此需要特别注意的地方有两处。(1) 虽然从 which provided... 直到整句结束的部分，与主句之间用逗号隔了开来，然而此句却是修饰前面名词 website 的一个限制性定语从句，而非修饰整个主句的非限制性定语从句。在此温馨提醒所有同学：虽然语法书上对于限制性和非限制性定语从句的主要或者说唯一的区分方式就是有无逗号隔开，但在英美人的语言使用中有时候却并非这么生硬刻板，所以我们在理解的时候也不可完全机械地照搬语法书原则，还是要在阅读材料中灵活地具体问题具体分析为好。(2) 在这个定语从句中又套进了一个省略了连接词 that 的定语从句 the destination had to offer，用来进一步修饰 everything，表明是新西兰这个目的地所能提供的一切。

2. And to maintain and improve standards, Tourism New Zealand organised a scheme whereby organisations appearing on the website underwent an independent evaluation against a set of agreed national standards of quality.
   - **参考译文**：为了维护和不断提升水准，新西兰旅游局还安排了这样一个方案：展示在网站上的所有商家都要按照一套通过决议的国家质量标准来接受一场独立评估。
   - **语言点**：本句的主干依然极其简单：..., Tourism New Zealand organised a scheme... 逗号前面的 to do 结构简明易懂，表示安排这一计划的目的，难点在于 whereby 引导的从句部分。whereby 在雅思阅读文章中远不如 that, which 等连接词的出镜率高，所以可能会让一些考生感到眼生。不妨在此学习一下，一劳永逸：whereby 是一个副词，表示"借此，依靠这个"。whereby 从句表明 organisations 是借由这个 scheme 来完成 underwent 这个动作的。该从句的主干是 organisations... underwent an independent evaluation... appearing on the website 是非谓语动词成分，修饰主语 organisations；against 及后面的内容则是另一个状语成分，表示是按照这套标准来进行评估的。

3. Another feature that attracted a lot of attention was an interactive journey through a number of the locations chosen for blockbuster films which had made use of New Zealand's stunning scenery as a backdrop.
   - **参考译文**：另外一个吸引了大量关注的特色内容是一场互动式旅程，穿越一系列将新西兰令人目眩神迷的风景选作了自己故事背景的电影大片中曾经出现过的地点。
   - **语言点**：本句的主干为 Another feature...was an interactive journey... feature 后面的 that attracted a lot of attention 是一个简单常见的定语从句，不难理解。从 through 开始到整句结束都是修饰这场 journey 的内容，其中 through a number of the locations 这部分是介词词组，表明旅程要"穿越一系列地点"；chosen for blockbuster films 这部分是非谓语动词，修饰 locations，表明这些地点是被一些电影大片选中作为拍摄地的；which had made use of New Zealand's stunning scenery as a backdrop 是一个完整的定语从句，修饰"电影大片"，同时巧妙地再次点题，重点突出了"新西

兰风景美得令人窒息所以才能被选作大片拍摄地"这个信息。

在此，我们也不妨注意一下这个语法现象：英语中更多的修饰说明成分往往出现在所修饰的名词后面，以介词短语或从句的形式存在；而在中文里，则往往把一切修饰说明的成分都堆在修饰对象的前面。此句就是一个很好的例子，在"旅程穿越一系列"和"地点"之间出现了极多修饰信息。假如觉得这样读起来费劲的话，不妨换个语序，说这场旅程"穿越一系列在电影大片中曾经出现过的地点，而这些影片都将新西兰令人目眩神迷的风景选作了自己的故事背景。"

4. To make it easier to plan motoring holidays, the site catalogued the most popular driving routes in the country, highlighting different routes according to the season and indicating distances and times.

- 参考译文：为了帮助用户更简易地规划自驾型假期，网站还分类整理出了新西兰最受欢迎的数条驾车路线，根据季节变化重点推介不同的路线并标注了距离和用时。
- 语言点：本句的理解重点在于，考生要看出并列的两个非谓语动词作状语成分，才能更顺利地把握全句意思。本句主干为 ... the site catalogued..., highlighting...and indicating... 为了方便考生看清，此处省略了主干的宾语部分，也就是 the most popular driving routes in the country。主干之前的 to do 结构依然表示目的，主干后面的两个非谓语动词成分则依次表明，网站在整理出最受欢迎的新西兰自驾路线时，"突出了根据季节而不同的路线"和"标注了距离和用时"。

5. In addition, it appears that visitors to New Zealand don't want to be 'one of the crowd' and find activities that involve only a few people more special and meaningful.

- 参考译文：此外，来到新西兰的游客们好像都不想成为"泯然众人"中的一员，而是觉得那些只有少数几个人参与的活动更为特别而有意义。
- 语言点：本句的主干为 ...visitors...don't want...and find... it appears that 是一个常见的形式主语句型，真正的信息在于 that 后面的内容。这个主干句里，主语 visitors 一共发出了两个并列动作，第一个"不想成为吃瓜群众的一员"很好理解，而第二个动作的完整结构为 find...more special and meaningful，被发现的对象为 activities，也就是发现这样的活动更有意义、更特别，that involve only a few people 则是修饰形容 activities 的定语从句。此处的难点在于，考生有可能在断句方面出现问题，解决办法是培养"预判意识"，对于"find sth./sb. 后面要加形容词补充说明"这个结构更加熟悉，例如 find sth. intriguing（觉得某事有吸引力），find sb. attractive（发现某人很有魅力），等等。这样在读到 find activities 的时候就能明白表述还未结束，进而有意识地去寻找后文中的修饰形容成分。

6. Because of the long-haul flight, most visitors stay for longer (average 20 days) and want to see as much of the country as possible on what is often seen as a once-in-a-lifetime visit.

- 参考译文：由于要进行长途飞行，大部分游客都会在此地待得更久（平均为 20 天）并想要尽可能地到处多看看这个国家，因为他们通常将此行看作一场"一生只来一次"的游历。
- 语言点：本句的主干也是一个主语发出两个动作的结构：most visitors stay...and want to see... 其中逗号前的原因状语成分、第一个动词 stay 后面的补充说明成分，对于考生来说应该都不难理解。稍微长而显得困难一些的地方在于介词 on 后面的名词性从句 what is often seen as a once-in-a-lifetime visit，表明游客抱有"一辈子只来一次"的心理，所以才希望到处多看看这个国家。

✿ 试题解析

Questions 1~7

- **题目类型**：TABLE COMPLETION
- **题目解析**：这几道表格填空题难度都不高。虽然出题范围跨越了文章的第二、三、四段，却不但在题干中包含大写、引号等帮助快速准确定位的信息，对每道题信息的提示关键词也全部都在文章中原词重现，考生只需耐心扫描、找到即可，是可以争取全对而不失分的友好题目。

题号	定位词	文中对应点	题目解析
1	database, information, regularly	第二段第五句： In addition, because participating businesses were able to update the details they gave on a regular basis, the information provided remained accurate.	此题可先根据信息类型，旅游服务的database，粗略定位到第二段第二句话。阅读题干句可知，需要寻找的细节信息是：允许商家对信息规律性地发出一个什么样的动作，空内需填动词，以此来精准定位则可找到本段第五句里的regular提示，对比原文可知，答案为update。
2	evaluation, impact	第二段最后两句： And to maintain and improve standards, Tourism New Zealand organised a scheme whereby organisations appearing on the website underwent an independent evaluation against a set of agreed national standards of quality. As part of this, the effect of each business on the environment was considered.	通过阅读题干可知，空格中需填企业对什么产生的影响，空格中应为名词。用evaluation可以定位到第二段倒数第二句，关于此句的详细分析，可以参见前文"佳句赏析"的第二句；但此句其实并未提及任何与impact相关的信息，因此读者需继续往下再读一句，即可看到同义词effect，就此对比可知，答案为environment。
3	special features, interview, former, sports	第三段第二句： One of the most popular was an interview with former New Zealand All Blacks rugby captain Tana Umaga.	本题的定位非常容易：即使不靠分类信息中的special feature来寻找，也能利用题干空格前的interview或former找到原文中一模一样的对应处。即使考生并不认识题干中的sports在文章里的对应词语rugby（即"橄榄球"这种体育项目），也能根据题干中要求"只填一个词"的说明，分析出在rugby captain这个结构中，必然是由前词修饰后词，对应于题干中的"sports _____"，从而得出答案为captain。
4	interactive, various locations	第三段第三句： Another feature that attracted a lot of attention was an interactive journey through a number of the locations chosen for blockbuster films which had made use of New Zealand's stunning scenery as a backdrop.	本题与上一题题干用and相连接，应是在原文中位置也接近的同类信息。考生仍可直接利用interactive和locations定位到出题句；关于本句的细节分析，可以参见前文"佳句赏析"中的第三句。阅读题干可知，需要寻找"在什么中用到的若干地点"；与上一题同理，即使不认识blockbuster这个单词，也能利用词组的修饰和先后关系，锁定答案为位置靠后的films。
5	driving routes, depending on	第三段最后一句： To make it easier to plan motoring holidays, the site catalogued the most popular driving routes in the country, highlighting different routes according to the season and indicating distances and times.	本题可用driving routes粗略定位到第三段的最后一句话，本句的具体解析可以参见前文"佳句赏析"中的第四句。解题关键在于考生需认识according to和depending on这两个同义替换表述，但这个认知要求绝对不高，因为二者都是雅思考试中非常高频出现的核心用法。对比二者，可以顺利得出答案为season。

题号	定位词	文中对应点	题目解析
6	Travel Planner, public transport, local	第四段第二和第三句：The Travel Planner offered suggested routes and public transport options between the chosen locations. There were also links to accommodation in the area.	本题中的大写Travel Planner可以帮助考生迅速粗略定位到第四段句首，不过离空格更近的定位词public transport却出现在第二句里，且此句仍未提及可以和公共交通相并列的信息，考生需耐心看到第三句，才能找到与local进行同义替换的in the area，进而顺利得出答案为accommodation。
7	'Your Words', link to	第四段最后一句：The website also had a 'Your Words' section where anyone could submit a blog of their New Zealand travels for possible inclusion on the website.	本题也有大写信息 'Your Words' 来帮助考生直接定位到出题句，通过阅读题干可知，空格内需要填写"游客可以发送一个自己什么的链接"，答案应为某个名词。如果考生认识原文句中的动词 submit，当然很好；如若不然的话，其实分析该句的句型，也可知道 could 后面所跟的生词必为动词，而接下来 a 后面所跟的当是名词，从而得出答案为 blog。

Questions 8~13

- **题目类型**：TRUE/FALSE/NOT GIVEN
- **题目解析**：这几道判断题难度适中：除第一道题可能会出现定位困难的情况外，其他题目大多集中在文章的第六、第七段内；题干中的定位词要么原词重现在文章里，要么对应的同义替换也并不困难，是相对比较友好的判断类型题目。

题号	定位词	文中对应点	题目解析
8	itineraries and packages, travel companies, individual tourists	第三段第四句：As the site developed, additional features were added to help independent travellers devise their own customised itineraries. 或 第六段第一句：The website was set up to allow both individuals and travel organisations to create itineraries and travel packages to suit their own needs and interests.	题干：The website www.newzealand.com aimed to provide ready-made itineraries and packages for travel companies and individual tourists. 译文："新西兰旅游"网站旨在为旅游公司和个人游客提供定制好的行程和旅行套餐。本题在定位上颇有迷惑性，可能许多考生看到题干以后都会欢天喜地，马上用网站名称回原文去定位，找到了第二段段首。然而稍微细读一两句就会发现，这里完全没有包含题干中的任何其他相关内容。且结合文章标题并往下略读部分文章可知，本文全篇都是在讲这个网站的相关内容，因此网址名称实际上没有帮助定位的作用。如改为用itineraries这个相对不易被替换的名词来寻找，则可分别在文章的第三段和第六段中找到相关信息，两处都是说"这个网站也要帮助个人游客来定制专属自身需求的行程"，这与题干信息ready-made"事先定制好的"相抵触，由此可得出正确答案为FALSE。

题号	定位词	文中对应点	题目解析
9	geographical location	第六段第二句： On the website, visitors can search for activities not solely by geographical location, but also by the particular nature of the activity.	题干：It was found that most visitors started searching on the website by geographical location. 译文：经发现，大多数访问者都开始按照地理位置在网站上进行搜索。 本题的定位倒是非常容易，可以直接在原文中找到一模一样的题干关键词 geographical location。细读定位句可知，此网站既可以按照地理位置，也可以按照项目属性来进行信息检索，并没有给出"到底哪种为更多的访问者使用"这个内容；如果再向后略读几句，会发现文章开始进入"游客满意度"的新话题，仍未提供题干相关信息，由此可得出正确答案为 NOT GIVEN。
10	26%	第六段第三句： This is important as research shows that activities are the key driver of visitor satisfaction, contributing 74% to visitor satisfaction, while transport and accommodation account for the remaining 26%.	题干：According to research, 26% of visitor satisfaction is related to their accommodation. 译文：根据研究结果，26% 的游客满意度与其住宿有关。 本题的难度比较低，既可以直接根据 26% 这个数字来定位，所找到的句子也提供了足够的信息帮助解题，无需再向后文继续阅读。根据原文句的信息，交通和住宿一共占游客满意度的 26%，则住宿这一项的所占比例绝对不可能是 26% 而必定小于这个数值，与题干信息构成了矛盾，因此答案为 FALSE。
11	local culture	第六段第四和第五句： The more activities that visitors undertake, the more satisfied they will be. It has also been found that visitors enjoy cultural activities most when they are interactive, such as visiting a marae (meeting ground) to learn about traditional Maori life.	题干：Visitors to New Zealand like to become involved in the local culture. 译文：来新西兰的游客们喜欢参与当地文化。 本题的定位并不困难，可直接通过题干中的 culture 在原文中找到同根词 cultural，根据原文信息可知"游客最享受的是互动型的、可亲身参与的文化活动"，本句承接上一句内容，同为表述"游客满意度"的贡献因素这个话题，综合两句意思，不难得出 like 与 enjoy 的同义替换关系，进而可判断此题答案为 TRUE。
12	small hotels, larger ones	无	题干：Visitors like staying in small hotels in New Zealand rather than in larger ones. 译文：游客更喜欢待在新西兰的小型旅馆而不是大酒店里。 判断题的绝大多数题目为顺序出题，考生可从上一题对应的原文处向后略读寻找，同时提醒自己不时浏览下一题的题干关键词，直到文中已出现13题的相关内容，仍无法找到关于旅馆大小的表述，便可得出本题答案为 NOT GIVEN。

题号	定位词	文中对应点	题目解析
13	unlikely, return	第七段倒数第二句： Because of the long-haul flight, most visitors stay for longer (average 20 days) and want to see as much of the country as possible on what is often seen as a once-in-a-lifetime visit.	题干：Many visitors feel it is unlikely that they will return to New Zealand after their visit. 译文：很多游客感到，他们这次游览过新西兰以后很可能不会再来一次了。 本题的解题关键在于，考生需认识unlikely这个多次出现在阅读文章中的高频词，从而明白题干的意思为"游客仅来一次、不会重返"，回到原文中，由若干个简单词通过连字符组合成的once-in-a-lifetime应该不是生词，不会阻碍考生的理解。原文此句的详细解析请参见前文"佳句赏析"中的第六句。对比两句可知答案为TRUE。

✍参考译文

—————— 案例研究："新西兰旅游"网站 ——————

　　新西兰是个有着400万居民的小国家，距离世界上所有的大型游客市场都隔着一场辛苦的长途飞行。旅游业目前占这个国家国民生产总值的9%，是其最大的出口行业。不同于其他的出口行业是要制造产品再将其销售到海外，旅游业会将顾客带到新西兰来。产品就是这个国家本身——其人民、其地点和身处其中的体验。在1999年，新西兰旅游局推出了一场大型宣传活动，旨在向全世界展示出一个全新的品牌地位。这场宣传集中突出了新西兰的优美风景、各种激动人心的户外项目和原汁原味的毛利文化，它将新西兰塑造成了世界上最强有力的国家品牌之一。

　　这场宣传活动中的一个关键特色就是"新西兰旅游"这个网站，它为未来有可能前往新西兰的游客提供了一个一站式端口，在此可以找到新西兰这个目的地所能提供的一切。此网站的核心内容在于一个由各路旅游服务经营者信息所组成的数据库，其中既有位于新西兰本土的商家，也有驻扎海外的提供前往此国旅游服务的公司。任何与旅游相关的经营者都可以通过填写一张简单的表格而获准加入。这就意味着：即使是最小型的住宿加早餐旅馆或特色活动的提供者都能在此网站上获得一席之地，从而接触到所有打算远道而来的游客。此外，由于参与的商家可以定期更新自己放上去的各项细节，因此网站信息就能始终保持准确。为了维持并不断提升水准，新西兰旅游局还安排了这样一个方案：展示在网站上的所有商家都要按照一套通过决议的国家质量标准来接受一场独立评估。作为这种做法中的一项，每个企业对于环境产生的影响都要受到考量。

　　为了充分传播这场新西兰体验，该网站还推出了与名人和知名地点有关的特色介绍。其中最受欢迎的内容之一是对新西兰全黑橄榄球队前队长Tana Umaga的访谈。另外一个吸引了大量关注的特色内容是一场互动式旅程，穿越一系列将新西兰令人目眩神迷的风景选作故事背景的电影大片中曾经出现过的地点。随着网站的发展，又有一些额外特色被补充增加了进来，帮助自助型游客借此规划自身专属的特色行程。为了帮助用户更简易地规划自驾型假期，网站还分类整理出了新西兰最受欢迎的数条驾车路线，根据季节变化重点推介不同的路线并标注距离和用时。

　　后来，又增加了一项"旅行规划助手"特色，网站访问者可以点击他们感兴趣的地点或景点并标注"书签"，然后在地图上查看结果。"旅行规划助手"会提供往来于各个选定地点之间的推荐路线和公共交通方式选择。同时还有查看当地住宿信息的链接。只要在网站上进行注册，用户就可以保存他们的旅行计划、稍后返回查看，或者把计划打印出来一路携带。网站上还有一个"听你说说"的版块，任何人都可以把自己有关新西兰旅游的博客记录提交上来，这些游记内容将有可能展示在网站页面上。

新西兰旅游局的这个网站因其线上成就和创新赢得了两次威比奖（Webby Awards 被称为"互联网界的奥斯卡奖"）。也许更重要的还在于：新西兰旅游业的兴旺发展是令人惊叹的。总体旅游消费在1999 年到 2004 年期间平均每年增长 6.9%。仅从英国一地，在 2002 年到 2006 年之间，前往新西兰的旅游量就有平均每年 13% 的增长，而同期内英国的总体海外旅游增长率只有 4%。

之所以成立这个网站，是为了让个人和旅游公司都能据此创建出适合他们自身需求和兴趣的行程和旅游套餐。在此网站上，访问者并非仅仅只能以地理位置为线索来搜寻各项活动，而是还可以按照旅游活动的特定属性来查找。这一点是很重要的，因为研究显示：各种活动项目是游客满意度的关键驱动因素，为总体游客满意度贡献了 74% 的份额，而交通和住宿一共才占那余下的 26%。游客参与的活动越多，他们就会越对自己的旅行感到满意。研究同时发现的还有：游客最享受的文化相关活动是那些有互动性质的，例如参观一处"毛利会堂"（会议场所）来了解传统的毛利人生活。许多远道而来的游客都非常享受这样的学习体验，这为他们提供了故事素材，可以带回去与朋友和家人分享。此外，来到新西兰的游客们好像都不想成为"泯然众人"中的一员，而是觉得那些只有少数几个人参与的活动更为特别而有意义。

我们当然可以说，新西兰并不算一个典型意义上的旅游目的地。它是一个小国家，游客经济主要由小型商家所组成。它被大众普遍视为一个安全的讲英语的国家，有着可靠的交通基础设施。由于要进行长途飞行，大部分游客都会在此地待得更久（平均为 20 天）并想要尽可能地到处多看看这个国家，因为他们通常将此行看作一场"一生只来一次"的游历。然而，其旅游业兴旺发展背后的经验却可放之四海而皆准——一个强有力品牌的效应，一项基于独特体验的策略，以及一个全面而十分照顾用户体验的网站。

Reading Passage 2

篇章结构

体裁	说明文
主题	对"厌烦"这种情绪的研究与讨论
结构	A 段："厌烦"情绪难以定义，也难以定性好坏
	B 段：对"厌烦"情绪的进一步分类
	C 段：一种观点认为，"厌烦"情绪也许有助于启发创造力
	D 段：另一种截然相反的关于"厌烦"情绪的看法
	E 段：性格特征与"厌烦"情绪之间的关联
	F 段：一种新的厌烦感的来源和应对之道

解题顺序： LIST OF HEADINGS → MATCHING FEATURES / SUMMARY COMPLETION →
LIST OF HEADINGS

友情提示： 本文中包含一个出镜率相对较低、许多考生都不熟悉或不喜欢的题型："为段落选
出大意概括句"。这种题主要考查考生对全段大意内容的理解和总结，有时候无法
单纯依靠题干和段落中词汇的匹配来解题，而是需要考生能快速读懂每句大意，同
时掌握一段内句子之间所构成的顺承、转折、进一步解释说明等关系，从而得出全
段大意的总结。不过，由于本篇是一套试题中的第二篇文章，考生的答题时间仍比
较充分，想要全面照顾所有题型的阅读策略仍然应是平行阅读：先大致浏览一段内容，
对比 headings 选项中哪一条是针对本段的提炼总结；再查看匹配题中作为选项出现
的大写人名，如刚才读过的段落里提及了某个人名，就迅速回到刚才读过的段里，
找到具体细节，对比做题；如果完全没有提及任何题干中的人名，则本段与解答匹
配题无关，进而对比摘要填空题的第一道题干，按照"有相关信息解题、无相关信
息不必回看"的原则，稳步向后文进行速读和精读的交替动作。按照这种顺序逐段
推进，即可比较理想地达成"文章只看一遍而查看过所有题型中的所有题目"这个
目标。

📖 必背词汇

1. end up doing... 最终结果是……

   请格外注意：这个词组容易引起误解，因为 end 有"终结"的意思，而鉴于 stop doing sth. 表示的是"停
   下正在做的事情"，所以看似相似的 end up doing sth. 往往容易被误解为"终结做某事"；实则恰好相反，
   它表示"最终的结果是 doing sth."。这个表达在剑桥雅思阅读文章中有过若干次出镜。

   Which of the following is mentioned by the writer as a reason why children *end up living* on the streets?
   以下的哪一项是作者提及的、造成儿童最终流落街头的原因？

   What's more, your efforts to improve the situation can *end up making* you feel worse.
   更有甚者，你挣扎着改善这种状态的努力有可能最终令你感到更加糟糕。

2. approach *n.* 方法 *v.* 接近

   We will be exploring different *approaches* to gathering information. 我们将探索收集信息的不同方法。

   When I *approached*, they grew silent. 当我走近时，他们就不说话了。

3. classify *v.* 分类（名词形式为 classification）

   Rocks can be *classified* according to their mode of origin. 可根据岩石的成因对其进行分类。

   The coroner immediately *classified* his death as a suicide. 这名验尸官立刻将他的死亡定性为自杀。

4. productive *adj.* 有成果的，创造性的

   Training makes workers highly *productive*. 培训使工人们的工作效率很高。

   He was hopeful that the next round of talks would also be *productive*.
   他对下一轮会谈也会富有成效充满了希望。

5. outcome *n.* 结果

   Mr Singh said he was pleased with the *outcome*. 西恩先生说他对结果感到满意。

   It's too early to know the *outcome* of her illness. 现在还不知道她病情的结果。

6. potential *adj.* 潜在的 *n.* 潜力

We are aware of the *potential* problems and have taken every precaution.

我们意识到了潜在的问题，已经采取了一切防范措施。

The meeting has the *potential* to be a watershed event. 这次会议有可能成为一次分水岭事件。

7. arise *v.* 产生，出现

The birds also attack crops when the opportunity *arises*. 有机会的时候，鸟儿也会破坏作物。

This serenity *arose* in part from Rachel's religious beliefs.

这种平和状态在某种程度上源于雷切尔的宗教信仰。

8. identify *v.* 确认，辨认

There are a number of distinguishing characteristics by which you can *identify* a Hollywood epic.

通过其诸多与众不同的特点，你可以识别出好莱坞的史诗影片。

Police have already *identified* 10 murder suspects. 警方已经确认了 10 名谋杀嫌疑犯。

9. damaging *adj.* 破坏性的（动词和名词形式为 damage）

The weakened currency could have *damaging* effects for the economy.

货币贬值可能会对经济造成破坏性的影响。

The blast had serious effects with quite extensive *damage* to the house.

爆炸造成了严重影响，房屋被大面积损坏。

10. threshold *n.* 门槛；界限，临界点

He stopped at the *threshold* of the bedroom. 他在卧室门口停了下来。

Moss has a high *threshold* for pain and a history of fast healing.

莫斯的忍痛能力很强，而且有迅速愈合的经历。

认知词汇

stimulating	*adj.* 有刺激性的，令人兴奋的	specialise	*v.* 专注于；以……为专业领域
stretch	*v.* 拉伸，延伸	explosive	*adj.* 爆发性的
frustration	*n.* 挫败感	trait	*n.* 特质，特点
apathy	*n.* 漠不关心	predict	*v.* 预测
apathetic	*adj.* 无动于衷的	prone to	更容易……的；更倾向……的
depression	*n.* 抑郁	psychologist	*n.* 心理学家
indifference	*n.* 无所谓	creative	*adj.* 有创意的
agitated	*adj.* 焦虑的，激动不安的	control group	对照组
restless	*adj.* 躁动不安的	wander	*v.* 漫游，漫步
disgust	*n.* 厌恶，恶心	convince	*v.* 说服，使确信
motivate	*v.* 驱动，激发	undesirable	*adj.* 不受欢迎的，不好的
infection	*n.* 感染，传染	adaptive	*adj.* 适应的
infectious	*adj.* 有传染性的；会感染的	evolve	*v.* 进化
distinct	*adj.* 分明的；完全不同的	survive	*v.* 生存，幸存
calibrating	*adj.* 调准的，校准的	toxic	*adj.* 有毒的，有害的
reactant	*adj.* 对（刺激等）有反应的	fester	*v.* 恶化，溃烂
axis	*n.* 轴（复数形式为 axes）	irritability	*n.* 易怒
arousal	*n.* 激发；觉醒	personality	*n.* 性格；个性
intriguingly	*adv.* 有趣地	suffer	*v.* 受苦，感到痛苦

curiosity	*n.* 好奇	snack	*n.* 零食
detrimental	*adj.* 有害的	distraction	*n.* 分心
alleviate	*v.* 减轻，缓解	speculate	*v.* 推测；思索
get stuck in	陷入，卡住	overstimulation	*n.* 过度刺激

佳句赏析

1. There isn't even agreement over whether boredom is always a low-energy, flat kind of emotion or whether feeling agitated and restless counts as boredom, too.
   - 参考译文：其至连"厌烦是否总是一种低能量的、平淡的情绪"或者"感到躁动不安、坐立不宁是否也能算作厌烦"这样的问题，都还不曾达成过共识。
   - 语言点：本句的主干极其简单：There isn't even agreement... over 后面表示的都是争论的对象和内容，即 whether...or whether... 这个结构所分别引导的两种情况。只需看清楚这个选择式结构，再分别阅读 whether 后面的两句内容，就能很好地理解整句的意思了。

2. These can be plotted on two axes — one running left to right, which measures low to high arousal, and the other from top to bottom, which measures how positive or negative the feeling is.
   - 参考译文：这些类型可以排列在两条轴线上——一条从左到右，表示的是从低到高的感受激发程度，另一条是从上到下，衡量的是这种感受有多么积极或消极。
   - 语言点：本句的结构依然简单，就是破折号前面的句子部分：These can be plotted on two axes... 读者请特别注意：破折号后面的内容虽然长，但根本不是完整句子结构，而是 one...and the other... 的简单成分。之所以如此之长，是因为 one 后面用了 running left to right 的非谓语和 which measures low to high arousal 的定语从句两个修饰成分；the other 后面也用了介词词组 from top to bottom 和定语从句 which measures how positive or negative the feeling is 这样两个修饰成分。

3. However, it remains to be seen whether there are any character traits that predict the kind of boredom each of us might be prone to.
   - 参考译文：然而，是否存在着任何性格特质，能预示我们每个人也许更倾向于感受到哪一种厌烦情绪，还有待于再等等看定论。
   - 语言点：本句虽然篇幅比前两句都短，从语法结构上来看却更为复杂一些。it remains to be seen 是句子的主干，但 it 是形式主语，真正有待于仔细看的是由 whether 引导的内容：首先是 there be 句型 there are any character traits，之后的 that predict the kind of boredom 是修饰 traits 的定语从句，再之后的 each of us might be prone to 则是另一个修饰 boredom 的定语从句。

4. In experiments published last year, Mann found that people who had been made to feel bored by copying numbers out of the phone book for 15 minutes came up with more creative ideas about how to use a polystyrene cup than a control group.
   - 参考译文：在去年发表的一些实验中，Mann 发现：与对照组相比，那些被要求从电话簿里连抄 15 分钟数字号码、从而感到无聊厌烦的实验对象关于如何使用一个聚苯乙烯杯子想出了更多颇有创意的点子。
   - 语言点：本句的主干是 Mann found that... that 后面的部分全部都为宾语从句，而在任何包含宾语从句的长句中，真正的实际信息表达都是在从句中进行的。从句的主干为 people...came up with more creative ideas...than a control group。people 后面的 who had been made to feel bored by copying numbers out of the phone book for 15 minutes 是一个较长的定语从句，注意此从句中使用的是被动形式 had been made，意在强调这些人是"被外界因素弄得感到厌烦"而非自发主动地感到无聊，由 by 所带领的部分则表示"令这些人觉得厌烦的方法是让他们连续 15 分钟抄电话簿里的数字号码"；ideas 后面的 about how to use a polystyrene cup 修饰说明这些人是关于什么对象而产生更多创意的。

5. Perhaps most worryingly, says Eastwood, repeatedly failing to engage attention can lead to a state where we don't know what to do any more, and no longer care.

- 参考译文：也许最令人担忧的是，Eastwood 说，反复地失去专注力可能会导致这样一种状态：我们不知道还能做什么、并且也不再在乎了。

- 语言点：本句其实不算长难，只是在句子主干出现之前先给了比较零碎的两个部分，一个是状语的开场白 Perhaps most worryingly，用来为后面的情况作出评价；另一个则是 says Eastwood 的插入成分。句子的主语是 failing to engage attention 这个动名词形式，一旦看出这个成分，考生应该不难继续找到 can lead to 的谓语部分，进而抓住"不能做什么可能导致某种状态"这个句子主干，where 引导的定语从句部分则是对这种 state 的进一步修饰说明。

6. Working with teenagers, they found that those who 'approach' a boring situation — in other words, see that it's boring and get stuck in anyway — report less boredom than those who try to avoid it by using snacks, TV or social media for distraction.

- 参考译文：通过对青少年的观察研究，他们发现那些"主动靠近"一个无聊场合的人们——换句话说，明知这是令人无聊厌烦的，但还是投身其中——要比那些试图用零食、电视或社交媒体来转移注意力的人们更不容易感到厌烦。

- 语言点：本句同样包含宾语从句结构，但比第四句更为复杂一些。第一个逗号前面的 Working with teenagers 为状语部分，用来表示后面主句 they found... 的信息来源。宾语从句的主干为 those...report less boredom than those...，是将两种人群进行了比较。第一个 those 后面的定语从句之所以显得格外复杂，是因为从句中又补入了一个由一对破折号进行解释说明的部分，如果感觉一次看完有困难的话，不妨先忽略破折号部分，直接将定语从句读为 who 'approach' a boring situation，然后再回头来看 in other words 的解释部分；第二个 those 后面是常见的 who 引导的定语从句，不难理解。

✿ 试题解析

Questions 14~19

- **题目类型**：LIST OF HEADINGS
- **题目解析**：此类型题目考查考生对于段落大意进行总体理解和把握的能力，切记不可只凭文中某个句子、某几个单词就仓促"对应"于选项中的同样或类似词汇而得出结论，而是应当把注意力更多地放到句子与句子之间的并列衔接、起承转合关系上来，才能更加准确地做答。

14. Problems with a scientific approach to boredom

参考译文	想找到一个科学地研究分析厌烦情绪的方法所产生的问题
定位词	problems, scientific approach

文中对应点	本题首要的解答难点在于考生需能够正确理解这个对应选项本身的意思。problems with 的意思是"伴随或由于 with 之后的行为动作所产生的问题",而 approach 作为名词指"方法"这个用法在雅思阅读文章中比比皆是,理论上来说不应成为认知障碍。a scientific approach to boredom 指"研究厌烦情绪的科学方法"。将两个部分组合在一起,题干的意思是说:人们试图找到科学方法去研究厌烦这种情绪,而要这么做会存在或产生若干问题。 A 段的第二句话就用句首的 But 点明了此句是本段的主题,即"很难对厌烦情绪下一个可以放在实验室里研究(也就是进行实证性的科学客观研究)的定义"。接下来的段落部分则细节列举了之所以不好定义、研究的各种原因,对应正确选项为 iv。

15. Creating a system of classification for feelings of boredom

参考译文	创立一个体系来为厌烦的感觉进行分类
定位词	system, classification
文中对应点	本段是典型的"总分总"结构。在第一句话里就交代了段落主旨:Goetz 及其团队最近区分出了五种各有不同的厌烦情绪。本句的句子虽然长,修饰说明成分也多,但结构清楚不难理解,考生只需找准 have identified 这个谓语部分即可轻松看懂。接下来的段落内容分别展开细说其中的几种厌烦情绪好坏各不相同,结尾再来一句 however,表示研究尚不成熟、还不能太早得出"哪种性格特点对应哪类厌烦情绪"的确定结论,也为行文留下余地、显得客观。综合来看,还是在围绕着"厌烦情绪的进一步分类"展开的,对应正确选项为 vi。

16. The productive outcomes that may result from boredom

参考译文	厌烦感有可能引向的创造性结果
定位词	productive outcomes, result from
文中对应点	本段如果采用掐头去尾、只看前两句和最后一句的办法,表达的主题并不明确。第一句承接上一段结尾,表明有学者进行了更多的研究;第二句则是泛泛而谈"之所以会厌烦必有原因",至于这个原因是什么,读者还需继续向下阅读。所幸紧跟其后的第三句就点明了段落主旨:有学者发现厌烦感会让我们更有创意,读到此处答案已经呼之欲出。而假如考生懒于多读,直接跳到段尾最后一句:学者建议人们主动寻找厌烦状态,则对这样做的原因和好处仍为一知半解,未必能顺利得出正确选项为 i。 特此温馨提示广大雅思考生:虽然确实有非常"规则"的段落,能只读首尾就得出其主旨大意,但毕竟提供雅思阅读文章的作者们文风不同,各有各的写作习惯,未必个个遵循"总分总"这个套路。在段落篇幅不长、句子结构不难的情况下,还是收起惰性、运用快速阅读大意的 skimming 技巧更为可靠。

17. A potential danger arising from boredom

参考译文	厌烦情绪有可能导致的潜在风险
定位词	potential danger
文中对应点	本段开宗明义,第一句就指出:有学者不信服上一段里的看法。接下来的内容都是在以具体细节的方式论述这位学者之所以不赞同上一段理论的原因。虽然本段篇幅相对较长,一些句子里也出现了诸如 toxic(有毒的)、gear(齿轮)等考生也许不太熟悉的词汇,但却到处可见并不生僻的表达负面意义的词汇和短语,行文意图仍是非常清晰的,对应正确选项为 v。

18. Identifying those most affected by boredom

参考译文	找出那些最受厌烦情绪困扰的人群
定位词	identify, most affected
文中对应点	本段的前三句和最后一句话是比较有总结性的内容，考生从第二句话的阅读中即可得到"厌烦情绪与人的个性有关"这条信息，假如耐心看到第三句，便可进一步加深"本段重点在于讨论厌烦与人的性格特征之间的关系"这种印象；假如直接跳到最后一句，会发现还是在说"不同性格的人感受厌烦的难易程度并不一样"。最后这一句的句式结构略复杂，具体解析可以参见前文"佳句赏析"的第六句。无论是略读段落首尾还是耐心读完全段，对比 headings 选项范围，都能找出最合适的选项应为 viii。

19. A new explanation and a new cure for boredom

参考译文	对厌烦情绪的一种新解释和新疗法
定位词	new explanation, new cure
文中对应点	本段的难度极低，不仅篇幅短小，且在第一句里就点明了主题，直接给出了 new source 这一直接对应选项 new explanation 的信息，对应正确选项为 iii。

Questions 20~23

- **题目类型**：MATCHING FEATURES
- **题目解析**：这道匹配题的难度比较低，不但因为这是一个人名匹配观点的、容易定位的题目，而且因为四个人名对应五个选项，迷惑选项不多、阅读量也不算大。考生只需找到每个人名在文章中的位置，读懂此人的观点表达，再认真耐心分析题干，进行比对，就能比较顺利地解题。

题号	定位词	文中对应点	题目解析
20	Peter Toohey	A 段最后两句： In his book, *Boredom: A Lively History*, Peter Toohey at the University of Calgary, Canada, compares it to disgust — an emotion that motivates us to stay away from certain situations. 'If disgust protects humans from infection, boredom may protect them from "infectious" situations,' he suggests.	这道题出得颇为巧妙，可以很好地体现"上下文语境"能够如何帮助考生减少也许不认识的生词所带来的阅读困难。人名所在的句子先是将厌烦与厌恶情绪进行了对比，指出后者能使人们远离某些场合；由于本句并不直接包含能对应选项内容的解题信息，所以考生需继续向后文阅读。下一句继续用对比的句式点出：厌烦可以保护人们远离"有感染性"的社会场合。即使考生并不认识此处的 infectious 一词，也不难从上一句中的 infection 和两句之间的对比关系中猜出：infectious 在这里与"需要 stay away 的"形成了同义替换关系，从而找到包含 avoid 同义关系的对应答案 E. Boredom may encourage us to avoid an unpleasant experience. （厌烦情绪也许能激励我们去避开一场不愉快的经历。）

题号	定位词	文中对应点	题目解析
21	Thomas Goetz	B 段第四句：Of the five types, the most damaging is 'reactant' boredom with its explosive combination of high arousal and negative emotion.	此题的人名集中出现在文章 B 段中，因此考生需要拿出耐心来，在第一个包含人名 Goetz 的句子里没能找到对应任何选项的答案时，继续向后文阅读，同时不忘对比选项内容，则可找到对应选项为 B. One sort of boredom is worse than all the others. （有一种类型的厌烦情绪比其他所有种类都要更糟。）
22	John Eastwood	D 段倒数第三句：What's more, your efforts to improve the situation can end up making you feel worse.	本题的难度最高，主要原因在于 Eastwood 这个人名广泛分布在文章的 D 和 E 两个最长的段落里，难免给考生造成不小的定位困难。如果实在觉得通读效率不高，不妨跳过这里去寻找下一个人名及其对应答案，缩小剩下的选择范围。其实如果考生浏览过文章的全部题型和大致看过题干，就会发现下一个摘要填空题型也是围绕 Eastwood 这个人展开提问的，因此只要在平时练习 skimming 能力、提升阅读句子大意的能力，每读几句原文就对比一下剩余选项，也不难找出对应答案为 D. Trying to cope with boredom can increase its negative effects. （应对厌烦情绪的努力尝试有可能会加重其消极效果。）
23	Francoise Wemelsfelder	F 段第一句：Psychologist Francoise Wemelsfelder speculates that our over-connected lifestyles might even be a new source of boredom.	本题的难度明显远低于上一题，考生只需找到人名所在句即可轻松判断对应答案为 A. The way we live today may encourage boredom. （我们今天的生活方式有可能助长了厌烦情绪的滋生。）

Questions 24~26

- **题目类型：** SUMMARY COMPLETION
- **题目解析：** 此题虽然开篇就有 John Eastwood 这个比较好找的大写人名，但定位回原文却会发现此人名遍布 D, E 两段，考生仍需耐心读懂题干、看清所要寻找的答案是何词性，再依据题干中给出的定位词找到表达类似意思的原文句，才可顺利解答。

题号	定位词	文中对应点	题目解析
24	John Eastwood, central feature, cannot, due to, failure, 'attention system'	D 段第八、九句： For Eastwood, the central feature of boredom is a failure to put our 'attention system' into gear. This causes an inability to focus on anything, which...	本题的定位不算困难，因为不仅有 Eastwood 这个人名，而且还有带引号的 'attention system' 作为帮助；难点之一来自题干比较长，考生需仔细阅读包含空格的句子，明白此句的意思是"在 Eastwood 看来，厌烦情绪的核心特征在于人们不能_____，而原因是他称为'注意力系统'的失调"，可知答案应为动词词性；另有一个小问题在于，包含 Eastwood 和 'attention system' 的句子本身确实没有符合题意的答案，因此考生需耐心向后再读一句，通过题干中 cannot 和原文中 inability 的对应锁定答案为：focus。
25	important aim, may have problems	E 段第四句： People who are motivated by pleasure seem to suffer particularly badly.	题干的意思是："那些觉得_____是人生中一个重要目标的人可能会在应对厌烦情绪时出现问题"，可知答案应为名词，且有明确指向是针对某个人群。读懂这个题干对于定位来说至关重要，因为文章的 D 段和 E 段都是 Eastwood 观点的表达，而本题距离上一题的位置比较远，要求考生在每读几句原文后，都对比题干信息、辨析是否有可以对应的地方，在找到 suffer 与 may have problems 这个比较隐晦的对应后，才能确认答案为：pleasure。
26	characteristic of, can...cope with	E 段第五句： Other personality traits, such as curiosity, are associated with a high boredom threshold.	本题与上一题通过 whereas 一词形成了比较明显的对比，因此在找到了上一题答案后，本题的定位就会轻松很多。题干说："那些有着_____性格的人通常都能应对厌烦情绪"，通过题干中的 characteristic 与文章中的 personality traits 的明确对应关系可知，答案应为：curiosity。

参考译文

为什么感到厌烦会是令人兴奋的——而且也是有用的
这种最常见不过的情绪正在逐步显现出远比我们以为的更有趣

A 我们都知道它是种什么感觉——你根本没法让自己的心思集中在任何事上，时间好像过得格外迟缓，而且无论你做什么好像都无法让自己感到好受一些。然而要对"厌烦情绪"下个定义，以便于可以将它置于实验室里接受研究，却被证明是很困难的。首先，它可以涵盖一大堆其他精神状态，例如挫败感、冷漠、压抑或满不在乎，甚至连"厌烦是否总是一种低能量的、平淡的情绪"或者"感到躁动不安、坐立不宁是否也能算作厌烦"这样的问题，都还不曾达成过共识。在其著作《厌烦：一段鲜活的历史》中，加拿大卡尔加里大学的 Peter Toohey 将它与"厌恶"——这种情绪会促使我们规避某些场合或情况——进行了对比。"如果说厌恶保护人类不受到感染，那么厌烦也许就保护了我们不受到一些'有感染性'的社会场景的影响。"他这样提议。

B 通过要求人们描述自己感到厌烦的体验，德国康斯坦茨大学的 Thomas Goetz 及其团队最近区分出了五种不同的类型：全无所谓、摇摆不定、有所期待、应激反应、无动于衷。这些类型可以排列在两条轴线上———一条从左到右，表示的是从低到高的感受激发程度；另一条是从上到下，衡量的是这种感受有多么积极或消极。极为有趣的一点是，Goetz 发现，尽管人们能体验到各式各样的厌烦情绪，他们往往都更经常地感受到其中的某一种。在这五个类型中，最有破坏力的是"应激反应型"厌烦情绪，它综合了高应激反应和消极情绪的爆发式力量。最有用的类型是被 Goetz 称为"全无所谓型"的厌烦感觉：某个人并没有从事任何能带来满足感的活动，但仍然觉得放松和平静。然而，是否存在着任何性格特质，能预示我们每个人也许便倾向于感受到哪一种厌烦情绪，还有待于再等等看定论。

C 英国兰卡斯特中央大学的心理学家 Sandi Mann 走得更远。"所有情绪之所以会出现都有原因，厌烦情绪也不例外"，她这样说。Mann 发现厌烦的状态会让我们更有创造力。"我们都不愿自己处于厌烦情绪之中，然而实际上，它能把我们带向各种各样奇妙的结果"，她这样提出。在去年发表的一些实验中，Mann 发现：与对照组相比，那些被要求从电话簿里连抄 15 分钟数字号码、从而感到无聊厌烦的实验对象关于如何使用一个聚苯乙烯杯子想出了更多颇有创意的点子。Mann 得出的结论是：一项消极被动、令人厌烦的活动最有利于启发创意，因为它让思维得以飘散游荡。实际上，她甚至还进一步提出：我们就应该在生活中寻找更多的厌烦状态。

D 加拿大多伦多约克大学的心理学家 John Eastwood 对此论调并不信服。"如果你正处在一种神游状态，那你就并不是在感到厌烦"，他这样说道。"在我看来，厌烦从定义上来说就不是一种令人欣悦的状态。"那也并不一定意味着它就不是可适应性的，他又补充说。"疼痛就是可适应性的——如果我们没有物理痛感的话，就会遇上各种糟糕的境况。难道那就意味着我们应当积极主动地去引起疼痛吗？并非如此。但是即使厌烦感已进化到帮助我们生存下来，如果我们任由它发展蔓延的话，它也仍然可以是毒害无穷的。"在 Eastwood 看来，厌烦情绪的核心特质是无法将我们的"注意力系统"挂档启动。这造成了无法专注在任何事上，从而令时间流逝的速度似乎慢得令人痛苦。更有甚者，你挣扎着改善这种状态的努力有可能最终令你感到更加糟糕。"人们总是在尝试与周遭世界建立起联系，如果他们没能成功，就会感到那种挫败和易怒"，他这样说道。也许最令人担忧的是，Eastwood 又说，反复地失去专注力可能会导致这样一种状态：我们已经不知道还能做什么、并且也不再在乎了。

E Eastwood 的团队目前正在尝试着探索注意力系统之所以失效的原因。时日尚浅，不过他们认为，其中至少有部分原因在于个人性格。易于厌烦的状态与一系列各种各样的性格特征有关，那些受追寻快乐所驱动的人们似乎格外深受其苦。其他的性格特质，例如好奇，通常构成了一个很高的厌烦情绪门槛（也就是说，好奇心重的人更不容易感到厌烦）。关于厌烦会产生有害影响的更多证据来自于对那些或多或少容易感到厌烦的人群的研究。似乎那些更容易厌烦的人们在教育、职业、甚至是整体人生中面临着更为惨淡的前景。但是当然了，厌烦情绪本身并不会杀人，是那些我们用来应对它而做出的行为可能会给我们带来危害。在事情走到那一步之前我们能做些什么来缓解它呢？ Goetz 的团队给出了一个建议。通过对青少年的观察研究，他们发现那些"主动靠近"一个无聊场合的人们——换句话说，明知这是令人无聊厌烦的，但还是投身其中——要比那些试图用零食、电视或社交媒体来转移注意力的人们更不容易感到厌烦。

F 心理学家 Francoise Wemelsfelder 认为，我们当下这种交互联结过于紧密的生活方式有可能是一种新型的产生厌烦情绪的源头。"在现代人类社会里，存在着大量的过度刺激，但仍有许多因寻找意义感而产生的问题"，她这样说道。因此，与其去寻找更多的精神激励，也许我们更应该放下自己的手机，利用厌烦感来驱动我们去以一种更有意义的方式来参与这个世界的运转。

Reading Passage 3

📖 篇章结构

体裁	说明文
主题	人工智能是否可以进行艺术创作
结构	第一段：人工智能在艺术领域中已有的成就
	第二段：人工智能创作挑战了人的特殊性
	第三段：早期人工智能只是实施人类创意的工具
	第四段：某个人工智能体现出了类人的创造力
	第五段：另一个人工智能的创作曾引起了极大争议
	第六段：一项研究证明无论专家还是普通人都对机器创作怀有偏见
	第七段：对产生这种偏见原因的一种解释

🌐 解题地图

难度系数： ★★★★★
解题顺序： MULTIPLE CHOICE → MATCHING SENTENCE ENDINGS → YES/NO/NOT GIVEN
友情提示： 本文中的三个题型都是基本遵循顺序规律的类型，位列第一的选择题直接在题干中指明了去第一段、第四段等帮助快速定位的信息，考生不妨就按照这个大体顺序依次阅读文章各段，不时回到题目中对比寻找帮助做题的信息。综合来看，本篇虽然长难句不多，但信息前后照应、互相关联，往往需要考生在定位到某句具体信息后还要在附近多看几句或联系前文已读过的内容，才能更准确答题，确是全套试题中最难的一篇。

🔤 必背词汇

1. **attain** *v.* 取得（成就），获得
   Jim is halfway to *attaining* his pilot's licence. 吉姆快要拿到他的飞行员执照了。
   Business has yet to *attain* the social status it has in other countries.
   商业（在这个国家）还没有获得它在其他国家所取得的社会地位。

2. **supersede** *v.* 超越，取代
   Hand tools are relics of the past that have now been *superseded* by the machine.
   手工工具是历史的遗物，现在已被机器取代。
   Future tests of general relativity by radio observations of this system will *supersede* the best Solar System available. 未来将通过对该系统的射电观测来测试相对论，这将取代最好的太阳系测试。

3. **undermine** *v.* 损害，破坏
   Offering advice on each and every problem will *undermine* her feeling of being adult.
   就每个问题向她提出建议将会逐渐让她觉得自己不是个成年人。

Popular culture has helped *undermine* elitist notions of high culture.
流行文化能够动摇高雅文化的精英观念。

4. deteriorate *v.* 退化，衰落（名词形式为 deterioration）
There are fears that the situation might *deteriorate* into full-scale war.
人们担心局势会恶化为全面战争。
concern about the rapid *deterioration* in relations between the two countries 对两国关系迅速恶化的担忧

5. inferior *adj.* 较差的，劣于的
This resulted in overpriced and often *inferior* products. 这就导致产品标价过高而往往质量较次。
If children were made to feel *inferior* to other children, their confidence declined.
如果令儿童感觉到自己不如其他孩子，他们的自信心会下降。

6. source *n.* 来源，出处
Over 40 per cent of adults use television as their major *source* of information about the arts.
40% 以上的成年人把电视作为他们获取艺术信息的主要途径。
Tourism, which is a major *source* of income for the city, may be seriously affected.
作为该市主要收入来源的旅游业可能会受到严重影响。

7. dismiss *v.* 不予理会；解雇，开除；驳回
Mr. Wakeham *dismissed* the reports as speculation. 韦克厄姆先生把这些报道当作臆测而不予理会。
I *dismissed* the problem from my mind. 我不再想这个问题了。

8. criterion *n.* 标准（复数形式为 criteria）
The most important *criterion* for entry is that applicants must design and make their own work.
最重要的参赛标准就是申请人必须设计并制作自己的作品。
British defense policy had to meet three *criteria* if it was to succeed.
英国防御政策要想成功必须满足三项标准。

9. resemble *v.* 类似，像
Some of the commercially produced venison *resembles* beef in flavour.
一些商业化养殖的鹿肉味道像牛肉。
It is true that both therapies do closely *resemble* each other. 真的，这两种疗法太相像了。

10. highlight *v.* 突出，强调 *n.* 最精彩部分
Last year Collins wrote a moving ballad which *highlighted* the plight of the homeless.
去年柯林斯写了一首感人的叙事诗，突出描写了无家可归者的苦境。
This incident *highlights* the care needed when disposing of unwanted plants.
这一事件凸显出了处理废弃植物时所需的慎重。

11. striking *adj.* 惊人的，打动人的
The most *striking* feature of those statistics is the high proportion of suicides.
那些统计数据最引人注目之处就是高自杀率。
He bears a *striking* resemblance to Lenin. 他与列宁有着惊人的相似之处。

12. reveal *v.* 透露，揭示
She has refused to *reveal* the whereabouts of her daughter. 她拒绝透露女儿的行踪。
No test will *reveal* how much of the drug was taken. 没有化验能显示出该药物的摄入剂量。

✿认知词汇

artificial	*adj.* 人工的		gallery	*n.* 美术馆，画廊
enrapture	*v.* 使狂热，使着迷		sophisticated	*adj.* 复杂的；完善的
trick	*v.* 糊弄，蒙骗		core	*n.* 核心
prestigious	*adj.* 有声望的		humanity	*n.* 人性

computational	*adj.* 计算机的	pseudoscience	*n.* 伪科学
scare	*v.* 吓唬，使恐惧	condemn	*v.* 谴责
exhibit	*v.* 展览	deliberately	*adv.* 故意地
canvas	*n.* 帆布，画布	vague	*adj.* 模糊的
impressive	*adj.* 令人印象深刻的	replica	*n.* 复制品，仿制品
keen	*adj.* 热情的，热心的	impulse	*n.* 冲动
criticism	*n.* 批评	outraged	*adj.* 狂怒的，被激怒的
minimal	*adj.* 最少的	punch	*v.* 击打
trawl	*v.* 查阅，搜索	amid	*adv.* 在……中间
scratch	*n./v.* 潦草涂写；刮擦	controversy	*n.* 争议
original	*adj.* 原创的，有创意的	recoil	*v.* 退缩
fuzzy	*adj.* 模糊不清的	clue	*n.* 线索
landscape	*n.* 风景	participant	*n.* 参与者
depict	*v.* 描绘	tune	*n.* 乐曲
mechanical	*adj.* 机械的	rate	*v.* 评分
bug	*n.* 漏洞，故障；小虫子	tend to	倾向于
glitch	*n.* 小故障，小毛病	objective	*adj.* 客观的
eerie	*adj.* 诡异的，怪诞的	analysis	*n.* 分析（复数形式为 analyses）
renowned	*adj.* 著名的	prejudice	*n.* 偏见
laud	*v.* 赞美，称赞	reckon	*v.* 认为
palette	*n.* 调色板	stem from	来自于
millennium	*n.* 千禧年，一千年（复数形式为 millennia）	essence	*n.* 精华
		speculation	*n.* 深思
prospect	*n.* 前景	complex	*adj.* 复杂的
subtle	*adj.* 微妙的	precisely	*adv.* 恰好地，精确地
composition	*n.* 作曲	tap into	探索，发掘
revered	*adj.* 受尊崇的	inspiration	*n.* 灵感，启发
genuine	*adj.* 真正的	theme	*n.* 主题
blast	*v.* 抨击，严厉批评		

❀佳句赏析

1. Classical music by an artificial composer has had audiences enraptured, and even tricked them into believing a human was behind the score.

   - 参考译文：由人工智能作曲家所创作的古典音乐曾经令观众听得如痴如醉，甚至让他们误以为这首乐曲是人类的杰作。

   - 语言点：本句的主干结构是 Classical music...has had audiences enraptured, and even tricked... 这是由一个主语 classical music 发出两个动作、带两个谓宾部分的结构。其中需要读者格外注意的是第一个谓宾部分：has had audiences enraptured。这个结构类似于 have sth. done "让别人来完成做某事"的用法，由于 classical music 不是有主观能动性的"人"，不能主动去 enrapture 吸引观众，所以 have audiences enraptured "使观众被吸引而沉醉其中"这种结构的表达是更为准确的；在第二个谓宾结构中，believing 后面跟着的是一个省略了 that 的宾语从句，表明让人们所相信的内容。

2. Unlike earlier 'artists' such as Aaron, the Painting Fool only needs minimal direction and can come up with its own concepts by going online for material.

- 参考译文：不同于诸如 Aaron 这样的早期"艺术家"，"绘画愚人"只需要极少量的指令，就能通过上网搜索材料而产生它自己的创作理念。

- 语言点：本句也是一个主语带领两个谓宾的结构，主干为 the Painting Fool only needs...and can come up with...，与上句相比显得更加简单。主干前面的 unlike 引导的部分是状语，表明 Painting Fool 与前者的不同之处；第二个谓宾部分则是略长的 do sth. by doing sth. 结构，表明是依靠做 by 后面的事情来取得 come up with 后面的结果，考生只需看清楚这个结构，即可准确理解本句。

3. Researchers like Colton don't believe it is right to measure machine creativity directly to that of humans who 'have had millennia to develop our skills'.

- 参考译文：像 Colton 这样的研究者们并不赞成将机器创造力直接与人类创造力相提并论互相比较，因为人类"已有几千年的时光来发展我们的技巧了"。

- 语言点：本句主干为 Researchers...don't believe it is right to do sth.。其实这个主干本身足够简单，不难理解，难点在于考生需掌握 measure sth. to sth.，这个结构表示"把某事与某事放在一起进行衡量比较"，并理解 that of humans 中的代词 that 指代的是 creativity，也就是，衡量比较的双方是"机器的创造力"和"人类的创造力"。humans 后面由 who 引导的是一个常规常见的定语从句，难度不高。

4. The participants weren't told beforehand whether the tunes were composed by humans or computers, but were asked to guess, and then rate how much they liked each one.

- 参考译文：这些参与者并没有被事先告知这些曲目究竟是由人类还是电脑所创作的，但是被要求去进行猜测，然后给出自己对每一首曲子喜好程度的评价。

- 语言点：本句的主干是 The participants weren't told..., but were asked to... 这是一个主语加两个被动结构的形式，第一个被动结构虽然长，但由 whether 引导的从句非常清晰好辨认，应该不会给读者造成太大理解困难。需要重点注意的是在第二个被动结构中，动词 asked 后面其实跟着两个被要求完成的动作，一个是比较明显的 to guess，另一个则是按照语法惯例省略了 to 的动词 rate。也就是说，参与者被要求完成的是两个动作，一为猜测，二为评价自己的喜好程度。

5. Paul Bloom of Yale University has a suggestion: he reckons part of the pleasure we get from art stems from the creative process behind the work.

- 参考译文：耶鲁大学的 Paul Bloom 提出了一个见解：他认为我们从艺术中得到的愉悦有一部分来自于作品背后的创作过程。

- 语言点：本句虽然不长，但由于带了两个省略了 that 的从句而显得有些复杂。冒号前面的总述不难理解，冒号后面的主干结构是 he reckons... reckons 后面的所有部分都是省略了连接词 that 的宾语从句，表明此人的看法；宾语从句自己的主干是 part of the pleasure...stems from...，而 pleasure 后面的 we get from art 则是省略了 that 或 which 的一个定语从句。读者如果能正确找到宾语从句的谓语动词为 stems，则可顺利读懂句意。

✿ 试题解析

Questions 27~31

- **题目类型**：MULTIPLE CHOICE
- **题目解析**：此部分题目难度相当之高。虽然题干问题要么明确指点了答案出自哪一段，要么也会提及人名大写等帮助迅速定位的关键词，但考生却基本无法只靠阅读包含关键词的单独一句话来确定答案，而是需要比较准确地大致通读全段或一段的大部分内容、甚至要对比前文，才可以准确锁定正确选项。单选题考查考生理解细节信息和通读句子大意的双重能力，考生也因此需要同时提升单词认知基础和速读理解能力来提升这种题型的解答正确率。

题号	定位词	文中对应点	题目解析
27	first paragraph	第一段	题干：What is the writer suggesting about computer-produced works in the first paragraph? 译文：作者在第一段里对电脑创作的作品提出了什么看法？ 一般来说，直接告知答案位于哪一段的选择题都无法只靠段中某一句的内容来作答，而是要通读全段内容、反复对比选项意思，进行正确选择或排除错误选项。好在第一段篇幅并不长，一共只有四句话，主题也比较统一，都是在说由人工智能创作的音乐和绘画作品已经取得了哪些成就，对应的正确答案正是 B 项：在这个领域中已经取得了相当多的成就。 A项说"人们对它们的接受度可以有相当大的差别"；C项说"它们在某些艺术类型上取得了比另一些类型上更多的成功"；D项说"这些进步并没有公众所相信的那样巨大"；都是原文中并未提及的信息，没有太大的混淆性。
28	Geraint Wiggins	第二段最后三句: 'This is a question at the very core of humanity,' says Geraint Wiggins, ...'It scares a lot of people. They are worried that it is taking something special away from what it means to be human.'	题干：According to Geraint Wiggins, why are many people worried by computer art? 译文：按照Geraint Wiggins的说法，为什么有许多人会对电脑艺术感到担忧？ 利用Geraint Wiggins人名大写可以比较快速地按照顺序定位到第二段里。此人一共说了三句话，大意比较一致，都是在说电脑创作挑战了人之所以为人的本质性、核心性地位，对应正确选项为C：它损害了一种基本人性属性。 A项说"它就审美角度而言不如人类艺术"；B项说"它也许最终会超越人类艺术"；D项说"它会导致人类能力的退化"；这些都不是Wiggins表达的意思，可以依次排除。

题号	定位词	文中对应点	题目解析
29	Aaron, Painting Fool	第四段第二句：Unlike earlier 'artists' such as Aaron, the Painting Fool only needs minimal direction and can come up with its own concepts by going online for material.	题干：What is a key difference between Aaron and the Painting Fool? 译文：Aaron 与"绘画愚人"之间最关键的差别是什么？ 本题的定位比之前两道题显得略简单一些，可以根据题干中的两个大写名称找到文章中的相应句子。关于本句的详细解析，考生可以参见前文"佳句赏析"中的第二句。本题解题难度依然不低，首要原因就在于考生有可能不熟悉 subject matter 这个词组的意思是"题材，主题"；再者，仅根据定位的这一句话，意思其实并不非常明确，似乎并不能直接靠关键词对应出正确选项，考生需结合前文阅读到的文章大意，再对比后文接下来的进一步细节描述，明白 Painting Fool 与之前各种软件的区别正是在于"并非只是执行创造者的编程指令，而是有了一定的搜索筛选的自主性"这一点，才能准确锁定正确选项为 C：其创作主题的来源。 A 项说"其编程者的背景"；B 项说"公众对其作品的反应"；D 项说"其作品的技术标准"；这些内容都未在文章中提及过。
30	Simon Colton, fourth paragraph	第四段第六、八、九句：..., Colton argues that such reactions arise from people's double standards towards software-produced and human-produced art. ... 'If a child painted a new scene from its head, you'd say it has a certain level of imagination,' he points out. 'The same should be true of a machine.'	题干：What point does Simon Colton make in the fourth paragraph? 译文：Simon Colton 在第四段中提出了什么观点？ 本题的难度在于 Simon Colton 此人在整个第四段里多次发表看法，考生需耐心正确读懂多句话的句意、反复对比四个选项，才能最终找到正确答案为选项 D：人们往往会按照不同的标准来评判电脑艺术和人类艺术。 A 项说"电脑软件创作的艺术经常被轻视为是孩子气和幼稚的"；B 项说"创造性的相同概念不应当被运用在所有艺术形式上"；C 项说"期待一台机器像人类那样富于想象力是不合理的"；这些描述中虽然似是而非地提及了几个在第四段中出现过的词汇，但细看其意思都不符合文中 Simon Colton 的观点表达。

题号	定位词	文中对应点	题目解析
31	chair	第四段倒数第二、三话：Some of the Painting Fool's paintings of a chair came out in black and white, thanks to a technical glitch. This gives the work an eerie, ghostlike quality.	题干：The writer refers to the paintings of a chair as an example of computer art which... 译文：作者提到了关于一把椅子的绘画作品，是想作为哪种电脑艺术的例子？ 要找到 chair 在原文中的定位并不困难，且前面的两道题也都是定位在同样的第四段里，考生对本段前文的信息有一定了解，可以帮助解题；然而此题难度还是较高，主要原因在于选项信息的迷惑性比较大，尤其是 C 项和 D 项。考生需非常仔细地对比题干意思和段落信息，才能逐步排除其他选项，最终确定正确答案为 A：取得了尤其令人震撼的效果。 B 项说"展示出了一定水平的真正艺术技巧"，这在文中并没有提及，因为电脑的自主性是体现在搜索素材方面而非创作技巧；C 项说"与一位著名艺术家的作品非常相似"，由于段中确实也提到了一位著名人类艺术家善于只使用调色板中的少数颜色来进行创作，因此本项的确具有相当大的迷惑性，但仔细阅读对比的话还是能够辨析出，文章里提及这位著名艺术家主要是想为"人们应当对电脑创作和人类创作一视同仁"这个观点作为佐证，二者之间的相似处并不是作者想要强调的"电脑艺术的特点"；D 项说"突出显示了软件的技术局限性"，虽然文章中确实提及之所以创作出这组黑白椅子画作是由于软件故障，但这也依然并非是"电脑艺术特征"这个问题的对应答案。

Questions 32~37

- **题目类型**：MATCHING SENTENCE ENDINGS
- **题目解析**：这种句首配句尾的完成句子题之所以令许多考生感到困难，在很大程度上来源于反复对比匹配的需要，也就是先利用题干句首部分、回原文定位答案，再阅读每个选项、找出最合适的对应；其中回原文定位的时候，也许需要阅读若干句内容才能最终确定有和其相匹配的选项答案，对考生的阅读速度、理解能力以及耐心都提出了比较高的挑战。

题号	定位词	文中对应点	题目解析
32	Simon Colton, long-term view	第五段第一句：Researchers like Colton don't believe it is right to measure machine creativity directly to that of humans who 'have had millennia to develop our skills'.	本题的定位对考生来说有一定困难，原因在于Colton此人在文章的第四和第五段中多次出现，考生需耐心确认到底是哪一句话对应了此处的句首信息。不过，由于之前的选择题已经集中在第四段里出了三个问题，考生已经出于解题需要比较全面地阅读了该段内容，因此继续向第五段寻找Colton的其他看法帮助解题就成为了比较顺理成章的动作。本题对应句的详细解析可以参见前文"佳句赏析"中的第三句。题干问"Simon Colton认为什么时候要考虑长久观点是很重要的"，通过对比选项内容可知，正确答案应为D项：比较人类和电脑的艺术成就时。

题号	定位词	文中对应点	题目解析
33	David Cope, EMI	第五段第六句： Audiences were moved to tears, and EMI even fooled classical music experts into thinking they were hearing genuine Bach.	本题的题干问 "David Cope的EMI软件是如何令人们吃惊的"。定位基本紧跟上题，又有大写名称辅助，唯一的麻烦在于考生不能仅凭包含David Cope和EMI的一句话就找到答案，而是应该耐心读过三句，才能顺利对比选定正确答案为A项：创造出了与人类艺术实际上真假难分的作品。
34	Geraint Wiggins, Cope	第五段第八句： Some, such as Wiggins, have blasted Cope's work as pseudoscience, and condemned him for his deliberately vague explanation of how the software worked.	本题有两个大写人名帮助定位，且定位到的句子即是出题处，无需向前向后多读其他内容，只需专心读懂定位句即可。题干问 "Geraint Wiggins 批评 Cope 没有做什么"，回到原文考生即使不认识 blast 和 condemn 这两个与题干 criticise 形成同义替换关系的动词，也可以借助 for 这个相同的结构确定答案的出处，对比选项可知正确答案为 E 项：透露他的程序的技术细节。
35	Douglas Hofstadter, EMI	第五段第九句： Meanwhile, Douglas Hofstadter of Indiana University said EMI created replicas which still rely completely on the original artist's creative impulses.	题干问 "Douglas Hofstadter宣称EMI是在做什么"。本题定位紧跟上题，且也有大写帮助定位，考生只需找到原文句，即使不认识诸如replica这样略显生僻的词汇，应该也能凭借雅思阅读中高频出现的rely on与dependent on的同义替换关系，找到正确选项C：创作出的作品要完全依赖其创造者的想象力。
36	audiences, EMI, angry	第五段第十句： When audiences found out the truth they were often outraged with Cope, and one music lover even tried to punch him.	题干问 "听过EMI所创作音乐的观众在什么之后感到了愤怒"。本题的定位不难，考生只需从上题位置继续向后文阅读一句，即可凭借关键词定位到答案相关处；但有趣的是，这句话里的相关信息只是简单提到了found out the truth（发现了真相），却并没有明确说出这个 "真相" 到底是什么。不过一路读来段落内容其实一直在讲 "电脑创作" 这个主题，因此仍是不难找到正确答案为G项：发现它是电脑程序的产物。
37	David Moffat, participants	第六段第三、四句： He asked both expert musicians and non-experts to assess six compositions. The participants weren't told beforehand whether the tunes were composed by humans or computers, but were asked to guess, and then rate how much they liked each one.	题干问 "David Moffat研究中的参与者们不得不在没有做什么的情况下去评估音乐"。本题最明显的定位帮助是大写人名，但人名所在的原文句并不包含解题内容，考生需继续向下阅读两句才能确定答案。其中最直接对应答案的第六段第四句略复杂，本句详细解析可以参见前文 "佳句赏析" 中的第四句。正确答案为B项：知道作品到底是人类还是电脑创作的。

Questions 38~40

- 题目类型：YES/NO/NOT GIVEN
- 题目解析：判断题考查考生对文章细节信息的理解精确程度，所以在定位以后往往需要耐心对比题干信息，并且不可匆忙根据一句话来作出判断，而是需要在定位句附近根据具体情况向前或向后再读若干句，才能做出最准确的选择。本篇文章中的判断题均包含人名大写帮助定位，句意表述也并不晦涩曲折，是相对比较友好的判断题类型。

题号	定位词	文中对应点	题目解析
38	Moffat, EMI	第六段第一、二句：But why did so many people love the music, yet recoil when they discovered how it was composed? A study by computer scientist David Moffat of Glasgow Caledonian University provides a clue.	题干：Moffat's research may help explain people's reactions to EMI. 译文：Moffat的研究也许有助于解释人们对EMI的反应。 本题有人名大写帮助定位，虽然包含Moffat本身的句子并没有直接提及EMI，但内容直接与前一段对EMI的描述相关，对于做完了上一个句子匹配题的考生来说，不难得出正确答案为YES。
39	non-experts, Moffat, predictable	第六段	题干：The non-experts in Moffat's study all responded in a predictable way. 译文：Moffat研究中的非专业人士全都做出了预料之中的反应。 本题与上一道题共用同样的大写人名定位，不难寻找。但考生需比较耐心地看懂接下来的几个句子，了解到在此实验中，无论专家还是门外汉都做出了类似的反应，而人们却本来期待专业人士会给出更为客观的判断评估的。在这个描述内容中，始终没有提及过是否对非专业人员的反应做出过预期，由此可得正确答案为NOT GIVEN。
40	Justin Kruger, Paul Bloom	第七段第二、四句：Paul Bloom of Yale University has a suggestion: he reckons part of the pleasure we get from art stems from the creative process behind the work. ... Meanwhile, experiments by Justin Kruger of New York University have shown that people's enjoyment of an artwork increases if they think more time and effort was needed to create it.	题干：Justin Kruger's findings cast doubt on Paul Bloom's theory about people's prejudice towards computer art. 译文：Justin Kruger 的发现对 Paul Bloom 关于人们对待电脑艺术存在偏见的理论提出了质疑。 本题中的两个人名位于同一段的前后位置，虽然文中并未直接提及这两人的观点到底是一致还是彼此矛盾冲突的，但考生在认真看过两人的观点表达后，不难看出两人提出的理论大同小异，是互相支持赞同的关系，这与题干信息相抵触，因此可得出正确答案为 NO。

参考译文

人工智能艺术家
电脑真的能创造艺术作品吗？

　　"绘画愚人"是数目正在与日俱增的——按照它们的创造者所宣称的说法——拥有创作才华的电脑程序之一。由人工智能作曲家所创作的古典音乐曾经令观众听得如痴如醉，甚至让他们误以为这首乐曲是人类的杰作。由机器人绘画的艺术作品曾经卖出过数千美元的价格并挂在声名卓著的画廊中展览。还有一些这样的软件，它们创作出来的艺术是其编程者事先根本不曾想象过的。

　　人类是唯一能够常规性地完成复杂艺术创作行为的物种。如果我们可以将这个过程分解成为电脑编码，那又将把人类创造力置于何处呢？"这是一个关乎人性最核心的问题"，伦敦大学金史密斯学院的一位计算机创造力研究学者 Geraint Wiggins 这样说。"它让许多人感到恐惧，他们担忧这会从人之所以为人的意义中剥夺走某些特殊的东西。"

　　在某种程度上，我们对电脑参与创作的艺术都很熟悉。问题在于：艺术家的工作是在何处止步，而电脑的创作力又是从何处开始的呢？不妨想想最老牌的机器艺术家之一：Aaron，这个机器人创作的绘画作品展览在伦敦泰特现代美术馆和旧金山现代艺术博物馆里。Aaron 可以拿起一支画笔，自行在画布上作画。也许确实令人惊叹，但它也仍然无非就是一台用来实现编程者自己创意理念的机器罢了。

　　"绘画愚人"的设计者 Simon Colton 非常热切地想要确保他的产品不会引来同样的批评。不同于诸如 Aaron 这样的早期"艺术家"，"绘画愚人"只需要极少量的指令，就能通过上网搜索材料而产生它自己的创作理念。这个软件启动其自身的网页搜索功能，浏览各个社交媒体页面。它现在也开始展示出了某种想象力，能从寥寥数笔的初稿中创造出完整画作。它的原创作品之一是一系列朦胧风景画，描绘的是树木与天空。虽然有些人也许会说这些画作有一种机械感，Colton 却反驳说，这样的反应是出于人们对待软件创作和人类创作艺术的双重标准。毕竟，他这样说，要考虑到"绘画愚人"是在没有参照一张照片的情况下画出了这些风景。"如果一个孩子从自己的头脑中描绘出一副新的景象，你就会说这小东西是有一定的想象力水平的"，他指出。"放在一台机器上应当也是一样的道理。"软件漏洞也有可能会造成意想不到的效果。"绘画愚人"描绘一把椅子的一些作品成了黑白色，多亏了一个技术故障。这赋予了画作一种怪诞、诡异的感觉。有一些如 Ellsworth Kelly 般著名的人类艺术家就因为非常克制地运用自己调色板上的色彩而广受传颂——那么放在计算机身上为什么就应当有所不同呢？

　　像 Colton 这样的研究者们并不赞成将机器创造力直接与人类创造力相提并论互相比较，因为人类"已有几千年的时光来发展我们的技巧了"。另一些人则颇为着迷于这样的前景：一台电脑也许能比肩于我们最好的艺术家，创作出同样富有创意而精致细巧的作品。到目前为止，只有一位接近这个目标。作曲家 David Cope 发明了一个程序，称作"音乐智能实验"，简称 EMI。EMI 不仅创作出了 Cope 风格的乐曲，而且还仿制出了最受尊崇的古典音乐作曲家们的作品，包括巴赫、肖邦和莫扎特。观众被打动得泪流满面，EMI 甚至骗过了古典音乐方面的专家，让他们以为自己听到的是真正的巴赫作品。然而并非所有人都对此表示了惊叹。有一些人，例如 Wiggins，就猛烈抨击 Cope 的这项创造为伪科学，还斥责他对这个程序到底如何运行的解释刻意说得含糊其辞。与此同时，印第安纳大学的 Douglas Hofstadter 认为，EMI 创作的这些仿制品仍然要完全依赖于原创艺术家的创作灵感。在观众们发现了真相以后，他们常常会对 Cope 感到异常愤怒，有一位乐迷甚至想要痛揍他。在这样的一片争议声中，Cope 销毁了 EMI 的关键数据库。

　　但是为什么会有这么多人热爱那些音乐本身，在发现了它是如何被创作出来的之后却畏惧退缩呢？格拉斯哥卡利多尼亚大学的计算机科学家 David Moffat 进行的一项研究提供了一条线索。他让专业音乐家和非专业人士同时去评估六首乐曲。这些参与者并没有被事先告知这些曲目究竟是由人类还是电脑所创作的，但是被要求去进行猜测，然后给出自己对每一首曲子喜好程度的评价。那些认为创作者是电脑的人们通常会比那些认为其创作者是人类的听众更不喜欢这支乐曲。即使是在专家们之中情况也是如此，而人们原本期待这些人的分析评估会更客观。

这种偏见到底来自何处？耶鲁大学的 Paul Bloom 提出了一个见解：他认为我们从艺术中得到的愉悦有一部分来自于作品背后的创作过程。这能为它赋予一种"不可抗拒的精髓感"，Bloom 这样说。与此同时，纽约大学的 Justin Kruger 所进行的实验也显示：人们如果认为创作某件艺术品需要更多的时间和精力，就会更加欣赏它。类似地，Colton 认为当人们去体验艺术时，他们会不禁去好奇艺术家当时正在想什么或者艺术家正在试图向他们表达什么。因此，这一点似乎就很明显了：当创作艺术的是电脑时，这种遐思就被打断了——因为没有什么可探索的。但是随着技术变得越来越复杂，在电脑的艺术创作中找到那些更意义深邃之处可以逐渐成为可能。正是因此，Colton 才会指示"绘画愚人"去搜索各社交媒体网页来获取灵感：希望通过这种方式，它将会选取那些对我们来说已经具有意义的主题。

Writing

Task 1

📖 题目要求

（见《剑桥雅思官方真题集 13：学术类》P29）

🖋 审题

题目翻译：下面的两幅地图显示了 2007 年和 2010 年一家城市医院的道路设施。选取并汇报主要特征，总结信息，并在相关处进行对比。

☕ 考生作文

（见《剑桥雅思官方真题集 13：学术类》P126）

☯ 参考译文

两幅地图表现了两个不同年份（2007 和 2010）前往一家城市医院的方式。

根据这两幅地图，主要内容，即城市医院，被环路包围着。在这两幅图里，有两个内容保持不变。这两个内容是城市医院和员工停车场。除了这两个内容以外，有的内容在 2010 年地图出现，但没在 2007 年地图出现。呈现在 2010 年地图上的额外内容是位于城市医院东边的公共停车场。其他的额外内容是位于医院路上、可通往公交车站的两个交通环岛。

总之，有两个主要内容在 2007 年和 2010 年的地图上没有任何变化。它们是城市医院和员工停车场。不过，有一些额外内容没有出现在 2007 年地图但出现在 2010 年地图上。这些内容是公共停车场、公交车站和两个环岛。

> 注：本书中作文部分的"参考译文"与《剑桥雅思官方真题集 13：学术类》中的"考生作文"对应，采取直译的方式，保留了原文中的错误及不当之处，方便读者参考对照。有关文中错误的订正，详见后文的具体分析。

☕ 考官点评

（见《剑桥雅思官方真题集 13：学术类》P126）

✍参考译文

  考生呈现了所有的核心内容（医院、环路，以及 2010 年的新公共停车场、员工停车场和公交车站），但描述有不准确之处（比如 two features that still remained. This two features are City Hospital and staff car park "有两个内容保持不变。这两个内容是城市医院和员工停车场"），然而员工停车场过去是供员工和公众共同使用的停车场，而公交车站则没有展开介绍。不过组织清晰，衔接手段运用得当（According to 根据，Apart from 除了，The further additional features 其他的额外内容），虽然代词使用有错误（This two features 应为 These two features）。词汇量足够符合任务的要求（two different years 两个不同年份，features 内容，remained 保持，additional 额外的），虽然 features 一词使用过度。第二行有个明显的拼写错误（sourrounded 包围，应为 surrounded），不过这并没有给读者理解造成困难；类似的是，around-turn 可以很容易理解为 roundabout 环岛。综合使用了简单句式和复杂句式，大体运用正确。

⚙分析

  本文得分为 5.5 分，在 task achievement, coherence and cohesion, lexical resource, grammatical range and accuracy 四个方面得分分别为 5、6、6、6。具体分析如下：

写作任务完成情况

  得分 5 分。5 分作文与 6 分作文在内容方面的最大区别在于 5 分作文缺乏清晰的概述或缺少数据支持。其次，5 分作文往往描述核心特点不够全面，而 6 分作文对于核心特点的描述相对完整。本文非数据图，不涉及任何数据，概述方面也相对完整，主要失分点在于描述不够准确，有些内容没有展开介绍。

  本文为地图描述，涉及对象是 2007 年和 2010 年的城市医院。既需要描述两个年份中保持不变的特征，更重要的是要描述哪些地方是 2007 年存在而 2010 年消失了的以及 2010 年新增加的内容。

  文章描述的核心内容（key features）：医院、环路，以及 2010 年的新公共停车场、员工停车场和公交车站。

  不变的部分：城市医院和员工停车场。

  新增的部分：位于城市医院东边的公共停车场，以及位于医院路上、可通往公交车站的两个交通环岛。

  文章结尾的概述（overview）：简单总结了不变的内容和新增的内容。

  如果要在内容方面有所改进，需要对核心特征进行更准确和充分的描述。

<u>描述中不准确的地方</u>

  第二段："有两个内容保持不变。这两个内容是城市医院和员工停车场"。事实上，2007 年地图中 city hospital（城市医院）东南方的是 staff and public car park（供员工和公众共同使用的停车场），而在 2010 年该处改建为 staff car park（员工停车场）。

<u>描述中未展开的地方</u>

  文中在描述 2010 年新建地方的时候，描述了医院东边的公共停车场和南边的两个环岛，但只是简单提到环岛通向公交车站。比较好的写法可以是指出 2007 年直接设置在 Hospital Rd 两旁的六个 bus stops 被去除，在道路西边建造了较大的 bus station，并有道路通往北边和南边的两个环岛，分别与围绕医院的 ring road（环路）和 city road（城市道路）相连。

连贯与衔接

  得分为 6 分。一般说来，5 分作文往往缺乏整体的连贯性和逻辑性，而 6 分作文能连贯地组织信息，并有效使用衔接手段。但 6 分作文一般会在衔接手段和指代方面存在一些问题。

使用得当的衔接手段

第二段第一句：According to both maps, the main features... 本句中的介词 according to（根据）后接上一句中提到的 maps，起到了衔接作用。

第二段第四句：Apart from these two features... 本句中的 apart from（除了……以外）表示对比关系。

第二段第六句：The further additional features are... 本句表示补充说明关系。

第三段第一句：Overall, there are two major features... 本句中的 overall 表示总结。

指代错误

指示代词（this/these 等）是重要的句内及句间衔接手段。本文用了多处正确的指示代词，但也出现了错误。

第二段第三句：This two features are City Hospital and staff car park. 本句中单数形式的指示代词 this 应改为复数形式的指示代词 these，因为后跟复数名词 two features。

词汇丰富程度

6分。本文使用的词汇量足够符合任务的要求，但之所以没有能够达到 7 分，主要是因为灵活性和准确性不够。

本文中使用较好的词汇表达

two different years 两个不同年份 features 内容 remained 保持

located 位于 additional 额外的 lead to 通往 major 主要的

灵活性

features 一词使用过度，短短的一篇 170 字小作文就出现了 11 次。其实可以换用一些同义词，比如 characteristics, traits, points 等。

准确性

拼写错误：sourrounded 应为 surrounded。

用词错误：around-turn 应为 roundabout。值得注意的是，考生为了词汇的丰富多样，避免使用图例中的 roundabout，自创了 around-turn。虽然这个错误不影响读者的阅读，但考试的时候，如果考生没有把握改写，不如沿用原有表达。当然，词汇量比较丰富的考生会想到环岛的其他表达：circle, traffic circle, road circle, rotary, circular intersection 等。

语法多样性及准确性

语法方面，本文为 6 分。5 分作文特点是句子结构有限，虽然有写复杂句的尝试，但错误多，且给读者造成阅读困难。而 6 分作文则能综合使用简单句式和复杂句式，大体运用正确。虽然有一些语法错误，但不至于影响交流。

第二段第一句：According to both maps, the main features which is city hospital is sourrounded by Ring Road. 本句的语法错误比较明显，主谓不一致，复数名词 features 后不能跟单数动词 is，但想表达的意思"根据这两幅地图，图中的主要内容是被环路包围着的城市医院"还是显而易见的。本句可改为：According to both maps, the main feature is the city hospital, surrounded by the ring road.

第二段第二句：In these two maps, there have been two features that still remained. "在这两幅图里，这两个内容保持不变。"本句可改为：In these two maps, the two features remain unchanged.

第二段第五句：The additional features that appear on the map of 2010 are public car park which located on the east-side of the city hospital. 根据上下文，本句可改为 One of the additional features that appear on the map of 2010 is the newly-built public car park located on the east side of the city hospital.

Task 2

📖 题目要求

（见《剑桥雅思官方真题集 13：学术类》P30）

🖋 审题

题目翻译：生活在一个你必须讲外语的国家会带来严重的社会和现实问题。你在何等程度上同意还是不同意这一说法？

☕ 考生作文

（见《剑桥雅思官方真题集 13：学术类》P127）

🔄 参考译文

显而易见，生活在国外有利有弊。我同意这个说法，但我认为任何前往另一国家的人都应该尊重该国文化。我将在本文中略述社会和现实问题。

社会问题是语言障碍，也就是说从另一个国家来的人不一定能说和理解当地语言，这对生活和来到这个国家的人来说可能是个问题。另一个问题和语言障碍有关，但可能会影响其他人的行为。来到这个国家的人可能会因为他们的行为或语言而冒犯别人。比如说，一些文化像英国人倾向于非常礼貌，和其他文化相比说话的方式会不一样。因此一个不知道在某个特定文化下如何表现得体的人可能会冒犯他周围的人。

实际问题是对于文化的误解。这意味着一个去其他国家旅游的人不理解其他文化，按自己的想法来做事。

第二个实际问题是找工作。一个在外国工作的人可能对他的服务对象来说不合适。比如说，如果一个人在餐厅工作，生活在这个国家和出生在这个国家的人可能不尊重也不喜欢这个在餐厅工作的人，这可能是因为文化的差异。

总之，我们可以说人们去外国的时候会有很多误解。从我个人经验来说，我认为为了知道如何在不同文化的不同处境下行为处事，人们应该教育自己。

☕ 考官点评

（见《剑桥雅思官方真题集 13：学术类》P127）

🔄 参考译文

考生处理了题目要求中的两方面情形，回应了在外语环境下可能经历的一些社会和实际问题。观点有例证的支持，虽然还有进一步展开论证的空间。文章组织符合逻辑，清晰的行文推进发展贯穿全文。衔接手段使用恰当（Another problem, For example, Therefore, That means..., The second...problem, To summarize）。词汇量足够，体现出一定的灵活性和准确性，对语体和搭配有认知（language barrier, linked to, influence the behaviour, offend, misunderstanding, misconceptions）。综合使用简单句和复杂句式，包括从句（which means that, a person who）、情态动词（should, might, would）和分词（finding a job）。语法掌握和标点使用较好，虽然第二段第一句不完整。

⚙分析

本文得分 6.5 分。在 task achievement, coherence and cohesion, lexical resource, grammatical range and accuracy 四个方面得分分别为 6、7、7、6。具体分析如下。

写作任务回应情况

本文在内容方面得分为 6 分。6 分作文的特点是文章涉及题目中的所有内容，不像 5 分作文经常会部分跑题。而与 7 分作文相比，6 分作文往往有论证不够充分的现象。

本文内容方面没有任何遗漏。文章需要分析生活在必须讲外语的国家的社会和现实问题。考生根据题目要求从社会和现实两方面进行了回应。第一段考生提出自己的基本观点，同意题目的说法。第二段分析社会问题，即语言障碍。不会说当地语言会导致理解和行为方面的问题。第三和第四段分析实际问题，从文化误解和找工作两方面展开。结尾段简单总结，提出误解经常产生，需要依靠自我教育学习在不同文化和语境下的行为方式。

本文在内容上的确从社会和现实两个方面进行了分析，但除了第二段相对例证充分，其他主体段落只是提出观点，稍加论证，不够充分和全面。

连贯与衔接

本文在连贯与衔接方面得分为 7 分。文章组织逻辑性强，行文清晰，层层推进。主体段落从题目要求的社会和现实两个层面分别分析。在分析社会影响的时候，先分析语言障碍对外来者的不利影响，然后分析语言障碍对本地居民的负面伤害。分析现实层面的时候，先是从抽象角度分析导致误解的原因，然后分析在找工作方面对外来者的具体影响。

衔接手段的运用
表因果关系：therefore
表列举关系：another problem, the second...problem
表对比关系：however, but
表解释说明：which means..., that means...
表举例关系：for example
表总结：to summarize
代词：this, that

词汇丰富程度

词汇方面得分为 7 分。本文词汇的使用体现出一定的灵活性和准确性，使用不常见词汇（less common lexical items）的时候，对语体和搭配有认知。

词语搭配（collocation）
名词 / 形容词与名词的搭配：language barrier（语言障碍）
动词与介词的搭配：be linked to（与……有关）
动词与名词的搭配：influence the behavior（影响行为）

语体意识（style）
offend（冒犯）
misunderstanding（误解）

misconception（误解）

这三个单词都比较正式，而且多用于书面语体。

个别拼写错误

第一段：agre 应为 agree

语法多样性及准确性

本文在语法方面得分为 6 分。文章既有简单句，又有复杂句，这是 6 分作文与 5 分作文的重要区别。和 7 分的差距主要在复杂句式的多样性和准确度上。

从句（subordinate clauses）

第一段第一句：it 引导形式主语句。

第二段第一句：以 which means 开头的非限定性定语从句。

第二段第三句：An individual who... who 引导定语从句，修饰 an individual。

第二段第五句和第三段第二句：a person who... who 引导定语从句，修饰 a person。

第四段第二句：An individual who... who 引导定语从句，修饰 an individual。people who... who 引导的定语从句，修饰 people。

第五段第一句：misconceptions which people have... which 引导定语从句，修饰 misconceptions。

情态动词的使用

第一段第二句、第五段第一句中的 should，表示态度和观点。

第一段第三句、第二段第一句、第三段第一句中的 would，表示推测。

第二段第一句、第二段第二句、第二段第五句、第四段第二句、第四段第三句中的 might，表示语气委婉的推测。

分词结构（gerunds）

第一段第一句：living in a foreign country 作主语。

第一段第二句：coming... 作定语，修饰 anybody。

第二段第一句：coming from... 作定语，修饰 a person。

第四段第一句：finding a job 作表语。

文中有一些不影响理解的语法错误，比如第一段第二句：

I agre with this statement, however I think that anybody coming in another country should respect national culture. 本句中的 however 为副词，不能连接主谓结构，应改为 but；coming in another country 应改为 coming to another country。

本句应改为：I agree with this statement, but I think that anybody coming to another country should respect its national culture.

Speaking

Part 1

在第一部分，考官会介绍自己并确认考生身份，然后打开录音机/笔，报出考试名称、时间、地点等考试信息。考官接下来会围绕考生的学习、工作、住宿或其他相关话题展开提问。

🔍 话题举例

Television programmes

1. **Where do you usually watch TV programmes/shows [Why?/Why not?]**

Well I think nowadays I *hardly ever* watch live TV on the actually TV set. I have *subscribed to* a few *online TV streaming sites* so I can easily watch the shows I like wherever I want, on my phone or laptop, totally *commercial free*, which of course is another important advantage.

hardly ever 几乎没有	subscribe to 订阅
online TV streaming sites 网络电视	commercial free 无广告

2. **What's your favorite TV programme/show? [why?]**

Much as I hate to admit it, I am a *reality TV junkie*! I also watch stuff like *comedies* and *crime TV programmes*. But you *could burn the house down around me* while my favorite reality show is on! I know most of the shows are of little value but I just *can't help it*!

reality TV 真人秀	junkie [俚语] 比喻对某事痴迷的人
comedy 喜剧	crime TV programme 犯罪剧
could burn the house down around me [比喻] 完全无视周遭	can't help it 无法自拔

3. **Are there any programmes/shows you don't like watching? [Why?/Why not?]**

Well, it would have to be *soaps*. They are just so *predictable* and boring. I prefer shows like the British TV series *Black Mirror*. There's always a *twist* at the end which will leave you wanting more. And I like those *dystopian* stories; they really *make you think*.

soaps 肥皂剧	predictable （情节）可以预测的
twist 情节反转	dystopian 反乌托邦的
make you think 引人思考	

4. **Do you think you will watch more TV or fewer TV programmes/shows in the future? [Why?/Why not?]**

I'd like to say fewer! I mean, I know I'd be *better off* spending time on something more *productive*. In fact, whenever I *binge-watch* some hit shows I feel guilty. But I don't think I could simply quit it because if I did, I'd *miss out on* so many things that my friends would be talking about.

better off 更好	productive 产生价值的
binge-watch 一次看很多集	miss out on [习语] 错过

Part 2

考官给考生一张话题卡（Cue card），考生有 1 分钟准备时间，并可以做笔记（考官会给考生笔和纸）。之后考生要作 1~2 分钟的陈述。考生讲完后，考官会就考生阐述的内容提一两个相关问题，由考生作简要回答。

> Describe someone you know who has started a business.
> You should say:
> > who this person is
> > what work this person does
> > why this person decided to start a business
> and explain whether you would like to do the same kind of work as this person.

➡️话题卡说明

本题看似是描述人物，但更核心的话题是 business，本题意味着考生需要展现出对描述人物和商业相关词汇的掌握。使用以下策略可以有意识地增加语法结构的丰富度。

开篇介绍	In recent years, there has been *a surge in entrepreneurship* in China and it seems that everybody is thinking about starting a business of some kind. But this person I'd like to talk about is truly a pioneer. His name is Mr. Luo.
选择要点	First, I think I'll explain what he does. Originally he was an *anchor* at Chinese Central Television, a job many *people would kill for*. But he saw an opportunity when more and more Chinese people started to use Wechat, an *instant messaging* and *social networking* app, so he quitted and started his own business. He started off by opening an account sharing book reviews and mini lectures on Wechat. And gradually he had *had* such *a huge following* that he opened up his website to well-known writers and professors to offer online courses for a price.
比较对比	Contrary to *popular belief* that people won't pay for anything they read online, Mr. Luo's business has *gone from strength to strength*. Not only have people been willing to "pay for knowledge", they have also *stayed* very *loyal to* his website and seemed very happy to *gobble up* everything that was *on offer*.
解释原因	Of course, Mr. Luo's success was *no accident*. He didn't get attention right away but he *made a name for himself* by delivering a high-quality mini lecture every single morning for two years straight. And another reason for his success is his *keen insight into* the needs of China's *rising middle class*, who is hungry for the information and knowledge that they believe would help them increase their wealth or improve the quality of their lives.

使用否定	I wouldn't say that he is my role model because I think I lack the *business acumen* and *charisma* he possesses. However, I do admire his persistence and courage to challenge *the status quo*.
作出推测	I don't think I would be able to do the same kind of work as he, but I'd love to start a course of my own on his website one day if I had the chance. Although I think *there's little likelihood of* this happening because I don't think I've got *what it takes to be* a lecturer!

重点词句

a surge in entrepreneurship 创业的热潮

anchor 主播

something people would kill for
　[习语] 很多人梦寐以求的……

instant messaging 即时通讯

social networking 社交网络

have a huge following 有众多粉丝

popular belief 一般大众的想法

go from strength to strength [习语] 不断壮大

stay loyal to 对……非常忠实

gobble up 狼吞虎咽

on offer 提供的，出售中的

no accident 绝非偶然

make a name for oneself as... 建立起……的名声

keen insight into 对……敏锐的认识

rising middle class 崛起的中产阶层

business acumen 商业头脑

charisma 人格魅力

the status quo 现状

there's little likelihood of... 几乎不可能……

what it takes to be...
　[习语] 成为……需要的东西

Part 3

第三部分：双向讨论（4~5分钟）。考官与考生围绕由第二部分引申出来的一些比较抽象的话题进行讨论。第三部分的话题是对第二部分话题卡内容的深化和拓展。

话题举例

Choosing work

1. **What kinds of jobs do young people not want to do in your country?**

Well, I guess it really *depends on one's circumstances*. But generally, I think *the younger generation* have received better education than their parents' generation so they tend to *have higher opinions of themselves* and refuse to do the jobs that they think are *beneath them*, such as *blue collar jobs* or service jobs. On the other hand, I suppose most young people today would prefer to *go see the world* and work in a big city rather than be stuck in the small town where they were born, even though their parents may have *had a good life all planned out for them* — working as a *civil servant* in the local government, marrying early and buying a house near the best school in town. I guess it's fortunate that not every child chooses to *follow in their parents' footsteps*! After all, this is how the society progresses, isn't it?

depend on one's circumstances 取决于个人境遇

have high opinions of oneself 自视甚高

a white/blue collar job 白领／蓝领工作

have a life planed out for them 为他们设计好了人生

follow in one's footsteps [习语] 追随某人的足迹

the younger generation 年轻一代

beneath them 配不上他们的

go see the world 去看世界

civil servant 公务员

2. **Who is best at advising young people about choosing a job: teachers or parents?**

Well, it's a tough question because I think *ultimately* it's *up to* young people themselves to decide what they want to do with their lives, but I guess both teachers and parents have some useful *perspectives to offer*. A teacher may know more about the student's academic performance thus could *make a reasonable prediction about* their potential in the field, while a parent may be *a better judge of* their children's *character*, and they could also be good *role models* if they have had *fulfilling careers* themselves. However, both teachers and parents could be *biased*, so I believe it's best to listen to different opinions so that you can *make a well-informed decision* yourself.

ultimately 最终

offer perspectives 提供不同的视角

a good judge of character 善于识人的人

a fulfilling career 有满足感的职业

make a well-informed decision 做出明智的选择

up to [习语] 取决于

make a prediction about 作出预测

role model 榜样

biased 偏颇的，片面的

3. **Is money always the most important thing when choosing a job?**

Definitely not! I mean even if you believe in *materialism* and think more money will bring more happiness, it will still be very *short-sighted* to *prioritize* money *over* other factors like your passion, *career path*, *work-life balance*, etc. Because *in the long run*, it is those factors that will make sure you're enjoying your life. In fact, *I'd argue that* money should probably come last when choosing a job, especially for a new graduate. I think it's very important to *think long term* and remember that everybody has to *pay their dues* if they want to be successful. There's a saying that goes "do what you love and the money will follow". I think it makes sense because if you really find your passion, you'll *be highly motivated* to work hard and think creatively and eventually be more successful at what you do.

materialism 物质主义

prioritize A over... 把 A 置于……之前

work-life balance 工作和生活的平衡

I'd argue that 我认为

pay one's dues [习语]（在成功之前）付出相应的努力

short-sighted 短视的

career path 职业发展

in the long run 从长远来看

think long term 从长计议

be highly motivated 有极大的动力

Work-Life balance

1. **Do you agree that many people nowadays are under pressure to work longer hours and take less holiday?**

Totally. It seems that overwork is *the norm* in most of the big cities around the world. Some may do it voluntarily, but I guess most people *feel compelled to* do so because of the *fierce competition* — they are constantly worried about being replaced if they don't work hard enough. Technology is not *doing us any good* either because now we are expected to respond to emails and messages *at all hours*, even when we're on holiday, which means *the line between* work life *and* personal life *is increasingly blurred*, *putting us in a position* where we find it impossible to *take time off*.

the norm 常态
fierce competition 激烈的竞争
at all hours 任何时间
put...in a position... 把某人置于某种境地
take time off 休息

feel compelled to 被迫做某事
do someone good 对某人有好处
the line between...and...is increasingly blurred
　……之间的界限越来越模糊

2. **What is the impact on society of people having a poor work-life balance?**

Well obviously people's health will suffer if they are constantly *overloaded*. Not only will *fatigue* lead to *reduced productivity* at work, but working late every night will also *put a strain on* people's relationships with their family and friends, which will certainly *have* serious *repercussions* on people's social life and the wider community. For example, children of an overworked couple are usually *at risk of underachieving* at school.

overloaded 超负荷的
reduced productivity 降低的生产力
have repercussions 带来（通常是负面的）影响
underachieve 表现不佳

fatigue 劳累
put a strain on 给……带来压力
at risk of 面临……的风险

3. **Could you recommend some effective strategies for governments and employers to ensure people have a good work-life balance?**

Well, this all sounds a bit *paradoxical*, doesn't it? Forcing people to take more holiday? But I guess the government does need to make sure that employees have their *legal entitlement to* a break from work. Now exactly how this could be done is really *beyond my knowledge* but *as far as I know*, I think it's really *down to* the employers to ensure they improve efficiency in the workplace rather than overload their staff. I think it's really important to establish a company culture that *sends the right message*, such as "work hard, play hard" so the employees will know that they won't *be penalized for* taking time off, instead they will be rewarded for coming up with creative solutions that allow them to finish work early.

paradoxical 矛盾的
beyond my knowledge 超过我的认知范围
be down to [习语]……的责任
be penalized for 为……受到惩罚

legal entitlement to 对……的合法权利
as far as I know 据我所知
send the right message 传递正确的理念

Listening

Section 1

📓 场景介绍

一位女士刚刚搬到新地区居住，打电话询问当地自行车俱乐部的活动细节和加入会员的费用及要求。俱乐部秘书 Jim 向女士介绍了不同的会员服务条款、常规活动安排，以及关于装备的注意事项。

📖 本节必背词汇

membership	n. 会员；会员资格	kit	n. 装备，成套用品
adult	n. 成人	cyclist	n. 骑行者
cycling	n. 骑行	ride	n. 短途旅行，骑乘
recreational	adj. 娱乐的，消遣的	fitness	n. 健康；适当
quarterly	adv. 按季度，一季一次地	novice	n. 新手，初学者
upgrade	v. 升级，优化	stadium	n. 体育场
insurance	n. 保险	afterwards	adv. 之后
activity	n. 活动；活跃	similar	adj. 相似的
permit	v. 允许，同意		

📖 词汇拓展

advert	n. 广告	expense	n. 开销
annual	adj. 每年的	explore	v. 探索，探究
brochure	n. 小册子，手册	leaflet	n. 宣传单
campsite	n. 营地	scenery	n. 风景，景色
energetic	adj. 精力充沛的	self-drive	n. 自驾
excursion	n. 长途旅行	trek	n. 艰难的行走；长途跋涉

🌸 文本及疑难解析

1. Well, I'm not really up to that standard. 我还没到那种标准。up to 此处理解为"到达"。

2. It's paid quarterly, and you can upgrade it later to the Full membership if you want to, of course. 这是按季度收费的，当然你之后如果想升级到正式会员也是可以的。

3. No, it's made to order by a company in Brisbane. 不是，这是布里斯班的一家公司定制的。it's made to order 意为"定制"。

4. And the members often go somewhere for coffee afterwards, so it's quite a social event. 会员们经常在（活动结束）之后去一些地方喝咖啡，所以这其实是个社交活动。social event 可以理解为"社交活动"，event 一词经常被用作"活动"，可以说 we're having an event tonight。

5. If you check the club website, you'll see that the route for each ride is clearly marked. So you can just print that out and take it along with you. It's similar from one week to another, but it's not always exactly the same. 如果你查一下俱乐部的网站，你会看到每一条骑行路线都是清晰标好的。所以你可以打印出来带着。每周之间变化不大，但不会总是一样的。

⚙️ 题目解析

本节为典型的个人信息表。难度低。

1. 本题用题干数字 $260 较易定位。答案为直叙。无难度。
2. 本题为直叙。无难度。
3. 本题为直叙。无难度。
4. 由题干结构可判断本题所填信息为数字。原文出现混淆内容，考生小心分辨所需数字一定与 Level B 匹配。
5. 本题用题干数字 5.30 较易定位。答案为直叙。无难度。
6. 注意题干数字 5.30 在原文中替换为 at the same time，entrance 替换为 gate。替换难度不大。
7. 题干词 members 及 afterwards 均原文重现，较易定位。答案为直叙。
8. 本题由题干语法判断需定位名词，含义需匹配"经常没有 ____"。leader 一词符合含义。
9. 题干词 website, check and print 原文重现。答案为直叙。考生需注意 route 一词的拼写。
10. 本题为直叙。无难度。

Section 2

📓 场景介绍

慈善会向新员工和从未参与过慈善活动的新成员介绍已经举办并获得大量好评的活动，例如办公技能和表达技能提升、读书活动等。主讲人另外特别介绍了帮助老年人学会使用现代科技和社交媒体的活动。已经举办的该类活动确实帮助老年人提高了使用社交媒体与家人进行联系的信心。在之后的活动中还有更多改良内容会陆续加入。

🔤 本节必背词汇

volunteering	n. 志愿活动	participate	v. 参与，参加
charity	n. 慈善；慈善机构	commitment	n. 承诺；承担义务
benefit	v. 对……有好处	feedback	n. 反馈，反应
community	n. 社区；团体	overwhelmingly	adv. 压倒性地

positive	adj. 积极的，正面的	participant	n. 参与者
motivate	v. 鼓励，激发	outdated	adj. 过时的
potential	adj. 潜在的	keen to	热衷于做某事
customer	n. 顾客	dismissive	adj. 拒绝的；轻蔑的
applicant	n. 申请者	update	v. 更新；与时俱进
conservation	n. 保护，保存	impress	v. 为……留下深刻印象
digital	adj. 数字的，数码的	grocery	n. 杂货
inclusion	n. 包含；内含物	handy	adj. 方便的，手边的
relevant	adj. 相关的，有关联的	tablet	n. 便签簿

词汇拓展

arrangement	n. 安排，约定	equipment	n. 设备，器材
cheque	n. 支票	legal	adj. 合法的，法定的
credit card	信用卡	licence	n. 执照，许可证
deposit	n. 押金，订金	organization	n. 组织，机构
donate	v. 捐赠，捐献	premises	n. 地点，场地
enquire	v. 咨询，询问		

文本及疑难解析

1. Participating doesn't necessarily involve a huge time commitment. The company will pay for eight hours of your time. That can be used over one or two days all at once, or spread over several months throughout the year. 参与活动一般不需要太多时间投入。公司会付给你八小时的报酬。这八小时可以在一两天内用完，也可以在一年中的几个月内用完。

2. But we've also agreed to help out on a conservation project in Redfern Park. 我们还答应在 Redfern 公园搞一个保护项目。此处 conservation project 可以理解为保护公园环境的活动。

3. And this year, instead of hosting the event in our own training facility, we're using the ICT suite at Hill College... 今年我们不在自己的培训场地搞活动，而是在希尔学院的 ICT 套房举办…… facility 字面指设备，也可以指场地设备。

4. The feedback was very positive. The really encouraging thing was that participants all said they felt much more confident about using social media to keep in touch with their grandchildren, who prefer this form of communication to phoning or sending emails. 反馈非常积极。让我们感到倍受鼓舞的是所有的参与者都说他们在使用社交媒体与孙辈交流的时候更加自信了，与打电话和发邮件相比他们更喜欢这种沟通方式。

5. They weren't that impressed with being able to order their groceries online, as they liked going out to the shops, but some said it would come in handy if they were will or the weather was really bad. 他们（老年人）对在网上购买生活用品不觉得什么，因为他们都喜欢亲自去商店。但有些人说在生病或者天气不好的时候（网上采购）还是比较方便。

题目解析

本节由单选题 11~16 和多选题 17~20 组成。

11. 本题定位较直接。通过题干及选项可以判断需要定位时间。仅 C 选项符合原文，无干扰项。

12. 题干词 feedback 原文重现，定位较易。选项 B 中 job satisfaction 与原文 motivated at work 同义替换。A, C 具有混淆性。但 A 选项指晋升机会，原文 a good thing to have on their CVs 单纯指在简历上比较好看，两者间无直接联系。C 选项指与同事间的关系，原文 relationship with people in the local community 指与同一社区的人之间的关系，两者间亦无联系。

13. 题干词 last year 原文重现。定位后需注意提高的是失业人员的 telephone skills，与 C 选项中的 communication 相符，writing down messages 和 speaking with confidence 均为 telephone skill 的举例。

14. 题干词 this year 原文重现。答案为直叙。

15. 本题由题干中的专有名词 Digital Inclusion Day 定位。答案为直叙。

16. 本题由题干词 take part 定位，答案 A 为直叙。选项 B, C 具有混淆性。但原文中 won't provide any training 与 B 冲突，don't forget to tell your manager 指不要忘记告诉经理，未提及需要 permission from their manager，切忌进行多余推理。

17~18. 本题定位较易，考生需掌握 old-fashioned 与 outdated 为同义替换，little interest 与 dismissive 为同义替换。A 选项具有混淆性，但原文提及不是所有人都是 70 多岁，有的人要年轻些，有的则已经 90 多岁了，与 they were all over 70 冲突。B, D 选项为断章取义。

19~20. 本题容易受上题影响而漏听。考生需掌握 communicate 与 keep in touch 为同义替换，online games 为原文重现。A 选项是本次活动要做的，但题干问及上次活动。C, E 均为被否定信息。

Section 3

场景介绍

学生 Russ 向个人导师询问做课题汇报的技巧和准备方面的建议。该学生担心纳米技术课题过于专业学术，无法解释清楚。后来在导师的建议下决定只关注于纳米技术对人们生活的实际影响。导师帮助 Russ 梳理了汇报的整体逻辑，并就 Russ 上一次课题汇报的表现给出修改建议，包括结构、肢体语言、眼神、表达和讲义准备。

本节必背词汇

consult	v. 咨询，商议	approach	v. 接近，靠近
presentation	n. 演讲，展示	chronological	adj. 编年的，按时间顺序的
nanotechnology	n. 纳米技术	display	n./v. 展示，展出
struggle	v. 奋斗，努力	repellent	adj. 防水的；阻止的
allocate	v. 分配，安排	additive	n. 添加剂，添加物
assume	v. 假定，认为	motorcycle	n. 摩托车
fascination	n. 着迷，迷恋	helmet	n. 头盔
overview	n. 概观，综述	exploration	n. 探测，勘探

essential	*adj.* 必要的，本质的	abruptly	*adv.* 突然地，唐突地
tailor	*v.* 调整，适应	odd	*n.* 奇特的事物，怪人
audience	*n.* 听众，观众	laptop	*n.* 笔记本电脑
initially	*adv.* 最初地，起始地	scratch	*v.* 挠，抓
modify	*v.* 修改，改变	specific	*adj.* 具体的，详细的
rubbish	*n.* 垃圾	handout	*n.* 讲义

词汇拓展

argument	*n.* 讨论，争论	seminar	*n.* 研讨会
assessment	*n.* 评估	supervise	*v.* 监督，监管
preparation	*n.* 准备	workshop	*n.* 学术专题讨论
qualified	*adj.* 有资格的		

文本及疑难解析

1. Should I assume the other students don't know much, and give them a kind of general introduction, or should I try and make them share my fascination with a particular aspect? 我应该假设其他人不怎么了解（纳米技术领域）而大致介绍一下，还是应该和大家分享一下我对某一个领域的迷恋呢？本句中 fascination 一词字面含义为"迷恋"，考生可理解为 Russ 对某一领域的喜爱。

2. While it can be good to include slides, you could end up spending too long looking for suitable ones. You might find it better to leave them out. 尽管有幻灯片挺好的，但你有可能花太多时间在寻找合适的内容上。你可能会发现还是不要的好。leave...out 指"排除"。

3. That would be fine if you had an hour or two for the presentation, but you might find that you can't do anything with the answers you get, and it simply eats into the short time that's available. 如果你的演讲有一两个小时还可以，但你可能会发现听众的回答没什么意义，而且会消耗本来就不多的时间。eat into 表示"消耗"，等同于 use up.

4. Let's say it was better in some respects than in others. With regard to the structure, I felt that you ended rather abruptly, without rounding it off. 一些方面肯定比另一些方面好。关于结构，我觉得结尾有点仓促，没有圆满结束。考生需掌握短语 round off.

5. And you kept scratching your head, so I found myself wondering when you were next going to do that, instead of listening to what you were saying! 你总是挠头，所以我发现我一直在关注你什么时候会再挠，而不是去听你的内容！本句中 when you were next going to do that 也可以表达为 when you were going to do that next，语义相同。

题目解析

本节由单选题 21~25 和搭配题 26~30 组成。难度稍高。

21. 本题需理解题干含义为"做课题汇报的主要困难是什么"。原文中由 struggling 一词引出答案。A，C

选项具有极强迷惑性。Russ 表示之前不了解该课题，但现在了解很多，与 A 选项内容相关，但并非题干所指的困难。Russ 又提及可以说很多，但是在有限的 20 分钟内讲不完，与 C 选项内容相关，但依然并非题干所指的困难。真正的困难是在大致讲解还是关注于某一个具体问题之间的纠结，因此答案为选项 B。

22. 本题可由题干词 approach 进行定位。三个选项原文均有涉及，但只有在 A 选项内容出现后，学生 Russ 给予了肯定答案 perhaps I should do that。

23. 本题可由题干词 slides 进行定位。考生需要掌握 omit 与 leave out 为同义替换。

24. 本题可由题干词 start 进行定位。选项 A 最先被提及，但立即被否定，导师认为没有足够的时间且可能收集到的答案毫无意义。选项 B 并未提及。选项 C 中的 example 与原文中 a particular way 相对应。

25. 本题可由题干词 next 进行定位。选项 B 中的 notes 原文有所提及，但也被明确指出要 ignore。选项 C 未提及。选项 A 中的 summarise 与原文 a single short sentence that ties together the whole presentation 相对应。

26~30. 本题可以用题干定位。搭配题大多考查选项与原文间的同义替换，考生需要掌握以下同义词才能解题：

题号	题干	选项	原文替换
26	structure	lacked a conclusion	without rounding it off
27	eye contact	not enough	...looking at the audience and only occasionally glancing at your notes.
28	body language	sometimes distracting	...I found myself wondering when you were next going to do it, instead of listening to what you were saying!
29	choice of words	not too technical	...explained what they meant...
30	handouts	useful in the future	...people would be able to refer to later on.

Section 4

场景介绍

本节介绍了两种长时记忆类型：情节记忆和语义记忆。情节记忆指体验，而语义记忆通常指客观事实（通过客观知识的累积获得）。情节记忆在心理学中包含三个步骤：铭记、保持、修复。有部分神经学病症对情节记忆会有影响，例如阿尔茨海默症、精神分裂症、孤独症。有些病症可以由药物控制，但有些会严重影响学习和工作。

本节必背词汇

series	n. 系列	factual	adj. 客观事实的
episodic	adj. 情节的；由片段组成的	previous	adj. 之前的，早先的
mentally	adv. 精神上，心理上	encode	v. 编码
distinct	adj. 差异的，区分的	consolidation	n. 巩固，加强
semantic	adj. 语义的	retrieval	n. 收回，挽回

initial	*adj.* 最初的，初始的	visual	*adj.* 视觉的
register	*v.* 登记，注册	prompt	*n.* 提示，催促
recollection	*n.* 回忆，追忆	neurological	*adj.* 神经学的
stabilise	*v.* 稳定，稳固	autism	*n.* 孤独症
facilitate	*v.* 帮助，促进	impairment	*n.* 损害，损伤
indefinitely	*adv.* 无限期地；不明确地	profound	*adj.* 深远的，严重的
frequency	*n.* 频率，频次	symptom	*n.* 症状
fade	*v.* 消退，逐渐褪去	reasonably	*adv.* 合理地，明智地
conscious	*adj.* 有意识的；自觉的	medication	*n.* 药物
olfactory	*adj.* 嗅觉的	intimate	*adj.* 亲密的，亲近的
auditory	*adj.* 听觉的	absence	*n.* 缺乏，缺少

词汇拓展

behave	*v.* 行为，行动	mental	*adj.* 精神的，内心的
behavioural	*adj.* 行为的	moral	*adj.* 道德的，道义的
conflict	*n.* 冲突，矛盾	optimism	*n.* 乐观，乐观主义
cure	*v.* 治疗，治愈	personality	*n.* 个性
diagnosis	*n.* 诊断，判断	psychological	*adj.* 心理上的，心理学的
frustration	*n.* 挫折，挫败	variation	*n.* 差异
gender	*n.* 性别	well-being	*n.* 幸福；福利

文本及疑难解析

1. Episodic memories include various details about these events, for example, when an event happened and other information such as the location. 情节记忆包括事件的各种细节，比如发生的时间以及地点等其他信息。

2. To build upon a previous example, remembering where you parked your car is an example of episodic memory, but your understanding of what a car is and how an engine works are examples of semantic memory. （情节记忆）建立于之前已有的经验，记得把车停在哪里是一种情节记忆，但知道什么是车以及引擎的工作原理是什么是语义记忆。

3. Unlike episodic memory, semantic memory isn't dependent on recalling personal experiences. 不像情节记忆，语义记忆不依赖于个人经历的回顾。

4. Consolidation is most effective when the information being stored can be linked to an existing network of information. 当存储的信息和已经存在的信息网络能够联系起来的时候，记忆的保持会非常有效。consolidation 一词字面含义为"增强"，在神经学领域对记忆步骤的定义中，将该概念译为"保持"。

5. These help episodic memory retrieval by acting as a prompt. For example, when recalling where you parked your car you may use the color of a sign close to where you parked. 这些（指代嗅觉的、听觉的、

视觉的因素）作为一种提示，可以帮助情节记忆修复。比如，在回忆你把车停在哪里时，你可能会用到停车位附近标识上的颜色。

6. There are a wide range of neurological diseases and conditions that can affect episodic memory. These range from Alzheimer's to schizophrenia to autism. An impairment of episodic memory can have a profound effect on individuals' lives. For example, the symptoms of schizophrenia can be reasonably well controlled by medication; however, patients' episodic memory may still be impaired and so they are often unable to return to university or work. 有许多神经学疾病和相关问题会影响情节记忆，包括阿尔茨海默症、精神分裂症、孤独症。情节记忆的损害会对个人生活造成巨大影响。比如，精神分裂症的症状可以由药物合理控制，但病人的情节记忆依然受损，往往导致他们无法上学和工作。

7. Episodic memories can help people connect with others, for instance by sharing intimate details about their past; something individuals with autism often have problems with. This may be caused by an absence of a sense of self. 情节记忆可以有效帮助人们与他人建立联系，比如和别人分享过去经历中的细节，这正是孤独症患者存在问题的方面。这可能是由自我感知的缺失造成的。sense of self 应理解为"自我感知"而非"自我认知"。

🔧 题目解析

本节为典型的学术报告填空。（连续填空，以句子或笔记形式呈现）。整体难度中上。

31. 题干词 details 原文重现。题干中 the time 与原文 when 呼应，考生需要定位与 time 并列且为名词的信息。location 一词符合含义及词性。

32. 本题可由题干词 semantic memory 进行定位。答案为直叙。

33. 本题稍难。在原文中距 32 题稍有距离，可以由题干词 recall 进行定位，原文中的 personal experience 可能会给考生带来与 ____ information 无法直接对应的错觉。由题干可判断该空填写名词或形容词。此处仅有 personal 一词符合。

34. 题干词 give to an event 原文重现。答案为直叙，难度较低。

35. 由题干语法可判断需要定位名词。题干词 encoding 原文重现，帮助定位。考生需充分理解原文含义才能解题。本题稍难。

36. 题干词 effective 原文重现，定位较容易。由题干语法预测需要定位名词，指"信息的 ____"。network 一词符合含义及语法。

37. 由题干词 retrieval 进行定位，考生需把握 strength 与 strong 相呼应。定位到答案句后寻找符合题干语法的名词。仅 frequency 一词匹配。

38. 题干词 prompt 原文重现，可以帮助定位。答案为直叙，本题难度不高。

39. 题干词 games 原文重现，可以帮助定位。题干中 stimulate 与原文中 keep...active 对应。根据题干语法可预测本题填写名词。brain 一词匹配含义及语法。.

40. 本题由题干词 absent, autism 进行有效定位。通过题干语法可判断需要填写名词。考生需要把握 concept 与 sense 此处含义及用法相通，self 为答案。

Reading Passage 1

📖 篇章结构

体裁	说明文
主题	肉桂贸易在欧洲的发展
结构	第一段：肉桂在古代欧洲的各种用途
	第二段：肉桂运往欧洲的传统方式
	第三段：葡萄牙人对肉桂的垄断
	第四段：荷兰人取代葡萄牙人
	第五段：荷兰人继续垄断肉桂贸易并增加了产量
	第六段：英国人取代荷兰人及肉桂贸易的衰落

🌐 解题地图

难度系数： ★★★

解题顺序： NOTES COMPLETION → TRUE/FALSE/NOT GIVEN

友情提示： 本文基本遵循历史事件发展的时间顺序，叙事线索非常清晰，是一篇对考生来说比较友好的简单说明文；且文后两个题型都是顺序出题的类型，作为第一篇文章非常适合使用平行阅读的方法：每大致略读一段文章或部分正文，就分别对比两个题型中的前两道，具体来说也就是第 1、2 题和第 10、11 题；根据题干进行初步判断：刚刚读过的正文内容是否包含问题中的相关信息。如有对应，则精读相关部分进行解题；如果没有，则继续回到刚才读到的正文处，继续向后略读文章。按照这个推进顺序，稳步进行略读和精读两个动作。尤其是，由于第二个题型的前两道题目里都包含了若干大写和数字，这对于定位格外有帮助，考生就更可以迅速判断已读过的文本里是否对应了解题相关信息，进而提升作答效率。

🔤 必背词汇

1. indicate v. 显示，指示

   A survey of retired people had *indicated* that most are independent and enjoying life.
   一项对退休人员的调查表明，他们中的大部分人生活自立而愉快。
   Dreams can help *indicate* your true feelings. 梦能代表你的真实情感。

2. scent n. 气味

   Flowers are chosen for their *scent* as well as their look. 选花不仅要观其形，还要闻其香。
   A police dog picked up the murderer's *scent*. 一条警犬搜出了凶手的气味。

3. treat *v.* 治疗；对待（名词形式为 treatment）

Doctors *treated* her with aspirin. 医生用阿司匹林给她治疗。

Many patients are not getting the medical *treatment* they need. 许多病人都没有得到他们需要的医疗。

4. quantity *n.* 数量

Cheap goods are available, but not in sufficient *quantities* to satisfy demand.

便宜的货物倒是有，但量不足，满足不了需求。

the less discerning drinker who prefers *quantity* to quality 重量不重质、不怎么识货的饮酒者

5. take over 接管；取代

I'm going to *take over* the company one day. 我总有一天会接管这家公司。

Cars gradually *took over* from horses. 汽车逐渐取代了马匹。

6. maintain *v.* 保持，保存

Such extrovert characters try to *maintain* relationships no matter how damaging these relationships may be.

这类外向的人设法保持住感情关系，不论这些关系多么有害。

The government was right to *maintain* interest rates at a high level. 政府维持高利率是正确的。

7. diminish *v.* 减少，消退

The threat of nuclear war has *diminished*. 核战的威胁变小了。

Universities are facing grave problems because of *diminishing* resources.

由于资源的减少，大学正面临着严重的问题。

认知词汇

cinnamon	*n.* 肉桂		consumption	*n.* 消耗，消费
fragrant	*adj.* 芳香的		merchant	*n.* 商人
spice	*n.* 香料；调料		rival	*n.* 竞争对手
inner	*adj.* 内部的		camel	*n.* 骆驼
bark	*n.* 树皮		via	*adv.* 通过，经由
sub-continent	*n.* 次大陆，亚大陆		sail	*v.* 航海，航行
biblical	*adj.* 圣经的		virtual	*adj.* 实际上的，事实上的
ingredient	*n.* 原料		monopoly	*n.* 垄断
anoint	*v.* 涂抹		exorbitantly	*adv.* 过高地，过于昂贵地
token	*n.* 标志，象征		couple	*v.* 由……所伴随
mourner	*n.* 哀悼者		spur	*v.* 刺激
funeral	*n.* 葬礼		cultivation	*n.* 培养，种植
primary	*adj.* 首要的，最初的		ethnic	*adj.* 人种的，民族的
additive	*n.* 添加剂		peel	*v.* 剥离，削
purchase	*n./v.* 购买		pliable	*adj.* 柔韧的，柔软的
condiment	*n.* 佐料，调味品		curl	*n./v.* 卷曲
exotic	*adj.* 异域风情的，异国的		tribute	*n.* 贡品
banquet	*n.* 宴会		enslave	*v.* 奴役
disposal	*n.* 掌控；支配		fort	*n.* 堡垒；要塞
ailment	*n.* 疾病		generate	*v.* 产生，创造
indigestion	*n.* 消化不良		tenfold	*adj.* 十倍的
elite	*n.* 精英		displace	*v.* 代替

ally	*v.* 结盟	appetite	*n.* 胃口
overrun	*v.* 侵占，推翻	alter	*v.* 改变
occupy	*v.* 占领	exhausted	*adj.* 耗尽的
permanently	*adv.* 永久地	strip	*v.* 剥离，剥掉
expel	*v.* 驱逐	cultivate	*v.* 耕种；开垦
lucrative	*adj.* 有利可图的	supplement	*v./n.* 补充，增补
inhabitant	*n.* 居民	available	*adj.* 可获得的，可用的
harshly	*adv.* 苛刻地	supersede	*v.* 超越
boost	*v.* 增加		

❀ 佳句赏析

1. It was known in biblical times, and is mentioned in several books of the Bible, both as an ingredient that was mixed with oils for anointing people's bodies, and also as a token indicating friendship among lovers and friends.

   - **参考译文**：早在圣经时期它就已为人们所知晓，在《圣经》的好几个章节中都有所提及，既是作为一种与油混合在一起用来涂抹人们身体的原料，也是作为一种展示爱人和朋友间情谊的象征。
   - **语言点**：本句的主干为 It was known..., and is mentioned... 这个句子主干本身并不难理解，读者需格外注意的是主干结束后的 both as...and as... 结构，这部分虽然很长，但却不是句子主干结构，而是介词短语成分，表明肉桂分别具有的、作为 ingredient "原料" 和 token "标志" 的两种身份。ingredient 后面由 that 引导的是一个常见的定语从句，而 token 后面由 indicating 所带领的则是由非谓语动词后置构成的修饰成分。

2. In the Middle Ages, Europeans who could afford the spice used it to flavour food, particularly meat, and to impress those around them with their ability to purchase an expensive condiment from the 'exotic' East.

   - **参考译文**：在中世纪，买得起这种香料的欧洲人用它来给食物，特别是肉类，进行调味，以及向周围的人炫耀自己有能力购买一种来自"异域"东方的昂贵佐料。
   - **语言点**：本句的主干为 Europeans...used it to..., and to... 由于在这个主干成分中插入了多种补充说明的修饰成分，所以可能会对读者造成一定干扰。一一来看这些修饰成分的话，Europeans 后面的 who could afford the spice 是常见定语从句成分，将欧洲人的范围进一步缩小到"能买得起这种香料"的群体；第一个 to 后面的 flavor food 补充说明肉桂的用途，又用 particularly meat 来进一步说明调味对象的细节是肉类；第二个 to 后面的动词词组用法为 impress sb. with sth. "用某事来给某人留下深刻印象"，对象是 those around them "周围的人"，用来震撼他人的方法是展示自己的能力，ability 后面的所有部分都是在补充说明具体做什么的能力。

3. These prices, coupled with the increasing demand, spurred the search for new routes to Asia by Europeans eager to take part in the spice trade.

   - **参考译文**：这样的价位，再加上不断上涨的需求，刺激了急于加入香料贸易的欧洲人去寻找通往亚洲的新路线。
   - **语言点**：本句的主干为 These prices,..., spurred the search... 主语与谓语动词之间用两个逗号分隔开来的部分是一个非谓语动词成分，表明与 prices "价格"伴随而来的还有 demand "需求"；search 后面分别跟着若干不同的短语成分来进行细节补充说明：for new routes to Asia 表示搜寻的是"通往亚洲的新路线"；by Europeans 表示是欧洲人在进行这种搜寻；eager to take part in the spice trade 表示是那些热切想要参与香料生意的欧洲人。

4. When the Portuguese arrived, they needed to increase production significantly, and so enslaved many other members of the Ceylonese native population, forcing them to work in cinnamon harvesting.

- 参考译文：葡萄牙人到达以后，他们需要大幅度增加产量，因此奴役了锡兰岛上许多其他的原住民人口，逼迫他们进行采集肉桂的劳动。
- 语言点：本句的主干为 they needed to..., and so enslaved... 也就是说，葡萄牙人发出了两个有因果关系的动作，原因是 needed to increase production significantly "需要大幅度增加产量"；结果则是 enslaved many other members of the Ceylonese native population "奴役了锡兰岛的本土居民"。句子最后一个逗号后面的部分，是一个常见的非谓语动词形式，表明葡萄牙人奴役锡兰人的方式是"强迫他们进行肉桂采集生产"。

5. Not only was a monopoly of cinnamon becoming impossible, but the spice trade overall was diminishing in economic potential, and was eventually superseded by the rise of trade in coffee, tea, chocolate, and sugar.

- 参考译文：不但对肉桂的垄断正在变得不再可能，而且这种香料贸易总体上的经济潜力也在缩减，最终被咖啡、茶叶、巧克力和糖的交易上升所超越。
- 语言点：在有 not only, hardly, seldom 等否定性副词出现在句首的句子里，后面的语序会发生倒装的情况，本句就是如此。如果对这种语序感到陌生，不妨先找准 not only...but (also)... 这个最主要结构，然后将倒装部分恢复为正常语序来理解，也完全可以看懂句意。如果按照这种方式，则 not only 倒装部分的正常语序句应为：a monopoly of cinnamon was becoming impossible，即"肉桂的垄断正在变得不可能"；but 后面的部分是正常语序，但此部分有两个并列的谓语动词结构，句子主干为 the spice trade...was diminishing..., and was eventually superseded... 表示这种香料生意一方面地位不断下滑，另一方面最终会被其他货物贸易所赶超。。

✿ 试题解析

Questions 1~9

- **题目类型**：NOTES COMPLETION
- **题目解析**：这几道笔记填空题难度都不高。小标题本身都是专有名称，可以直接在原文中找到一模一样的对应处；题干本身也几乎没有包含任何生僻的词汇，与原文对应句都形成了简单同义替换关系。考生只需平时认真积累基础词汇，做题时耐心扫描、找到相应句子，即有可能正确找到所有答案，全不失分。

题号	定位词	文中对应点	题目解析
1	Biblical times	第一段第二句： It was known in biblical times, and is mentioned in several books of the Bible, both as an ingredient that was mixed with oils for anointing people's bodies, and also as a token indicating friendship among lovers and friends.	本题定位简单，可以直接在原文中找到一模一样的定位词 biblical times 所在的句子，此句的详细解析可以参见前文"佳句赏析"的第一句。题干问"可以加在 ____ 里"，而题干中的 added to 也可直接在原文句中找到对应的 mixed with，由此锁定答案为 oils。

题号	定位词	文中对应点	题目解析
2	show	第一段第二句： It was known in biblical times, and is mentioned in several books of the Bible, both as an ingredient that was mixed with oils for anointing people's bodies, and also as a token indicating friendship among lovers and friends.	从笔记小标题的格式中其实不难看出：本题与上一题共用 Biblical times 这个定位线索，答案也出自同一句。题干问"用来显示人们之间的 ____"，考生只需掌握"动词 indicate 与 show 有着同义替换关系"这个基础词汇知识，便可轻松找到答案为 friendship。
3	Ancient Rome	第一段第三句： In ancient Rome, mourners attending funerals burnt cinnamon to create a pleasant scent.	本题的定位也非常容易：直接利用"古罗马"即可找到对应句。题干问"在 ____ 使用它的甜气味"，可知答案应当是某个场合或地点；考生只需具备题干中 smell 与原文中 scent 的同义替换词汇知识，即可确定答案为 funerals。
4	Middle Ages	第一段倒数第二句： At a banquet, a host would offer guests a plate with various spices piled upon it as a sign of the wealth at his or her disposal.	本题可用"中世纪"这个专有名称定位到原文处，但题干问"能显示出一个人的 ____"，包含"中世纪"的原文句本身却没有提及；本句的句式结构略复杂，详细解析可以参见前文"佳句赏析"的第二句。考生需耐心再向下阅读一句，才能通过题干中 indication 与原文中 sign 的同义替换关系，确定答案为 wealth。
5	treatment, health problems	第一段最后一句： Cinnamon was also reported to have health benefits, and was thought to cure various ailments, such as indigestion.	接下来的所有题目都与"中世纪"这个时间段有关，不过文章的第一和第二段里都有这个时期，因此还需借助其他关键词来帮助更精确定位。本题的题干问"已知它能治疗 ____ 和其他健康问题"，分析这个题干可知，空格内应该填某种具体健康问题的名称，因此即使考生不认识原文中 ailment 这个"健康问题"的同义替换，应该也可以通过 health problems"健康问题"、cure"治疗"和 such as 的举例功能，推理出答案应为 indigestion。
6	grown	第二段第四句： They took it from India, where it was grown, ...	题干问"生长在 ____"，很明显空格内需要填一个地点名称，而考生只需按题干里唯一的定位线索 grown 顺序阅读原文进行寻找，即可看到包含一模一样单词的对应句，分析可得答案为 India。
7	merchants, Mediterranean	第二段第四句： They took it from India, where it was grown, on camels via an overland route to the Mediterranean.	题干问"商人们使用 ____ 将肉桂带到地中海地区"，可知空格内需要填一个可以作为交通运输工具的名词。本题与上一道题共用同一个定位句，考生还是应当在利用关键词定位以后仔细阅读细节，找到答案为 camels。

题号	定位词	文中对应点	题目解析
8	Mediterranean, arrived	第二段第五句： Their journey ended when they reached Alexandria.	本题的定位紧跟上一题，虽然利用"地中海"这个关键词，找到的还是第二段第四句话，但阅读题干"到达地中海的 ____"，可知空格内需要填一个比地中海地区更为具体的地名，而定位句中并没有符合这个要求的信息，考生需继续向下再读一句，才能根据 reached "到达"这个信息锁定答案为 Alexandria。
9	traders, Europe	第二段第六句： European traders sailed there to purchase their supply of cinnamon, then brought it back to Venice.	题干问"商人们将它带到 ____ 并将它再卖到欧洲的各个目的地去"，可知答案仍然应当为某个地点，利用题干中的 traders 和 Europe 都可以定位到相关位置，进而确定答案为 Venice。

Questions 10~13

- **题目类型**：TRUE/FALSE/NOT GIVEN
- **题目解析**：这几道判断题难度比较适中：每道题干中均有数字或大写关键词，原本是非常容易的；但这些数字和大写却不够特殊，在文章的若干个自然段中都有出现，所以考生在定位之余还需耐下心来，多读几句原文并不忘对比题干，才能更准确地得出结论、顺利解题。

题号	解题关键词	文中对应点	题目解析
10	Portuguese, Ceylon, 16th century	第三段最后一句和第四段第一句： In the late 16th century, for example, they enjoyed a tenfold profit when shipping cinnamon over a journey of eight days from Ceylon to India. When the Dutch arrived off the coast of southern Asia at the very beginning of the 17th century, they set their sights on displacing the Portuguese as kings of cinnamon.	题干：The Portuguese had control over the cinnamon trade in Ceylon throughout the 16th century. 译文：葡萄牙人在整个16世纪里都控制着锡兰岛上的肉桂贸易。 本题出得相当巧妙。虽然题干里给出了诸如 Portuguese, Ceylon和16th century多个容易定位的信息，考生却无法单凭其中任何一个所对应的原文句确定答案，而是需要耐心读完包含这些关键词的每个句子，才能得出结论：葡萄牙人确实是在16世纪的大部分时间里、至少是直到16世纪末期都一直控制着锡兰岛的肉桂贸易；然而这是否意味着整个16世纪都是如此、没有任何例外呢？单凭第三段最后一句的相关信息似乎还不足以确定，需要继续看到下一段的首句，知道荷兰人是在17世纪初才取而代之的，从而确认答案为TRUE。

题号	解题关键词	文中对应点	题目解析
11	Dutch, Portuguese, Ceylon	第四段第一、四句：When the Dutch arrived off the coast of southern Asia at the very beginning of the 17th century, they set their sights on displacing the Portuguese as kings of cinnamon. ... By 1640, the Dutch broke the 150—year Portuguese monopoly when they overran and occupied their factories.	题干：The Dutch took over the cinnamon trade from the Portuguese as soon as they arrived in Ceylon. 译文：荷兰人一到达锡兰，立刻就从葡萄牙人手中接管了肉桂贸易。 本题虽然包含若干大写名称，但无论是荷兰人、葡萄牙人，还是锡兰岛，都不是独一无二的关键词，而是文章若干段落中都出现过的信息；不过考生可以借助判断题的"有序特征"，从上一道题的结束处向后文继续阅读，可知荷兰人是在17世纪初就到达了锡兰岛，却是直到1640年也就是约四十年后才真正取代了葡萄牙人的肉桂垄断地位，与题干信息中的as soon as形成矛盾抵触关系，因此答案为FALSE。
12	Dutch, larger quantities, wild trees	第五段最后一句：Eventually, the Dutch began cultivating their own cinnamon trees to supplement the diminishing number of wild trees available for use.	题干：The trees planted by the Dutch produced larger quantities of cinnamon than the wild trees. 译文：荷兰人所种植的肉桂树能比野生树出产更大量的肉桂。 本题仅凭"荷兰人"这个大写无法精确定位，因为文章的第四和第五段里都大量出现了这个名称，考生需加上"野生树"这个信息才能找到真正的出题句；然而本句只是说"荷兰人以自己种植的肉桂树来补充野生树产量的不足"，目的是增加肉桂总产量，并未将二者各自的产量进行比较，因此本题答案应为NOT GIVEN。
13	maintained, economic importance, 19th century	第六段最后一句：Not only was a monopoly of cinnamon becoming impossible, but the spice trade overall was diminishing in economic potential, and was eventually superseded by the rise of trade in coffee, tea, chocolate, and sugar.	题干：The spice trade maintained its economic importance during the 19th century. 译文：这种香料贸易在19世纪期间保持了其经济上的重要性。 本题可以借助"19世纪"这个数字快速定位到文章最后一段，但包含数字本身的句子并不能直接帮助解题，考生需耐心再向后多读两句，直到看懂本段最后一句才能找到明确的解题信息。本句的详细解析可以参见前文"佳句赏析"的第五句，它说到肉桂贸易的经济潜力在19世纪期间逐步减少，这与题干信息形成矛盾抵触，由此可得答案为FALSE。

带肉桂到欧洲

肉桂是一种甜味、芬芳的香料，产自樟脑属肉桂树的内层树皮，原产地是印度次大陆。早在圣经时期它就已为人们所知晓，在《圣经》的好几个章节中都有所提及，既是作为一种与油混合在一起用来涂抹人们身体的原料，也是作为一种展示爱人和朋友间情谊的象征。在古罗马，参加葬礼的哀悼者们会燃烧肉桂来制造一种令人心怡的气味。不过，这种香料最常见的用途，主要还是作为食品和饮料的一种添加剂。在中世纪，买得起这种香料的欧洲人用它来给食物，特别是肉类，进行调味，以及向周围的人炫耀自己有能力购买一种来自"异域"东方的昂贵佐料。在宴会上，主人会为客人们奉上一个盘子，里面摆放着各式各样的调味品，以此来昭示他或她拥有多少财富可供支配。肉桂还被记载为有益健康，被认为能治疗各种小病小痛，例如消化不良。

到了中世纪末期，欧洲的中产阶级开始渴慕精英阶层的生活方式，包括他们对各种香料的消费。这导致了对肉桂和其他调料的需求增长。当时，肉桂是由阿拉伯商人们进行运输的，他们严密地保守着这种香料的来源，不让其他潜在的竞争者知道。他们将它从生长之地印度取走，放在骆驼上经由一条陆上路线运到地中海地区。他们的旅途终点是亚历山大港，欧洲商人们会航行到那里去购买他们提供的肉桂，再把它带回到威尼斯。这种香料接下来再从这个大贸易城辗转到整个欧洲的各个市场。由于陆上贸易路线使得每次只能携带少量这种香料到达欧洲，也由于威尼斯对这项生意有着实际的垄断权，因此威尼斯人得以将肉桂的价格制定得高得离谱。这样的价位，再加上不断上涨的需求，刺激了急于加入香料贸易的欧洲人去寻找通往亚洲的新路线。

追逐着肉桂市场指日可待的高利润，葡萄牙商人们在接近15世纪末的时候来到了印度洋上的锡兰岛。在欧洲人来到岛上之前，当地统治者已经在有组织地进行肉桂采集了。被称为 Salagama 的少数民族会在雨季里将树皮从肉桂树的嫩枝上剥离下来，此时的潮湿树皮更为柔韧可塑。在剥皮的过程中，他们把树皮卷成了直到今天还与这种香料联系在一起的"棍"状（其实也就是说，这种香料直到今天还保持了这种形状）。然后 Salagama 人会将制好的成品作为一种形式的贡品献给国王。等葡萄牙人到达以后，他们需要大幅度增加产量，因此奴役了锡兰岛上许多其他的原住民人口，逼迫他们进行采集肉桂的劳动。在1518年，葡萄牙人在锡兰建起了一座堡垒，这令他们得以守护该岛，因此帮他们树立起了肉桂贸易中的垄断地位并产生了极高额的利润。例如，在16世纪晚期，他们通过八天的行程将肉桂从锡兰运往印度，从中能够享受到十倍的利润。

当荷兰人在17世纪之初来到南亚的海岸边时，他们将目光瞄准了代替葡萄牙人成为肉桂之王这个目标。荷兰人与锡兰境内的一个岛国 Kandy 建立了结盟关系。作为对方支付大象和肉桂的回报，他们保护了本土国王不受葡萄牙人的欺压。到1640年的时候，荷兰人打破了葡萄牙人150年来的垄断，推翻了后者并占领了其工厂。到1658年，他们已经永久性地将葡萄牙人从岛上驱逐了出去，由此赢得了对这门一本万利的肉桂买卖的控制。

为了保住自己对市场的掌控，荷兰人就像在他们之前的葡萄牙人那样，以非常严苛的方式对待岛上居民。出于不断提升产量的需要，也为了满足欧洲对肉桂不断攀升的胃口，荷兰人开始改变锡兰人的采集方法。随着时间的推移，岛上的肉桂树供应由于大规模的剥皮做法而逐渐几近耗尽。最终，荷兰人开始培植他们自己的肉桂树来补充野生树木数量的减少，以供继续生产使用。

接下来，在1796年，英国人来到了锡兰，就此取代了荷兰人对肉桂垄断的控制。到19世纪中叶的时候，一种品质较低的肉桂得到了欧洲人口味的认可，这种香料的生产随后达到了每年1000吨。此时，肉桂已经被遍植印度洋地区的其他许多地带，以及西印度群岛、巴西和圭亚那。不但对肉桂的垄断正在变得不再可能，而且这种香料贸易总体上的经济潜力也在缩减，最终被咖啡、茶叶、巧克力和糖的交易上升所超越。

Reading Passage 2

篇章结构

体裁	议论文
主题	催产素的作用
结构	A 段：对催产素的传统看法有待修改
	B 段：先前人们对催产素完全正面的看法
	C 段：一些研究发现催产素的作用因人而异
	D 段：另一些研究发现催产素的作用还因社交活动中的对方而有所不同
	E 段：之前被研究者忽视的现象
	F 段：催产素之所以作用复杂的原因

解题地图

难度系数： ★★★★

解题顺序： MATCHING INFORMATION → MATCHING FEATURES → SUMMARY COMPLETION → MATCHING INFORMATION

友情提示： 本文中包含一个许多考生都比较畏惧的题型："哪段包含如下细节信息"。这种题考查考生准确理解题干信息、迅速读懂每段每句意思并准确寻找到与题干相匹配信息的多方面能力，难度比较高。不过，由于本篇是一套试题中的第二篇文章，考生的答题时间仍相对比较充分，想要全面照顾所有题型的阅读策略仍然应是平行阅读：先大致浏览一段内容，对比"段落匹配"题的选项中是否有同义替换信息；再查看"人名匹配"题中作为选项出现的大写人名，如刚才读过的段落里提及了某个人名，就迅速回到刚才读过的段里、找到具体细节，对比做题，如果完全没有提及任何人名，则本段与解答此种匹配题无关；进而对比摘要填空题的第一道题干，按照"有相关信息解题、无相关信息不必回看"的原则，稳步向后文进行速读和精读的交替动作。按照这种顺序逐段推进，即可比较理想地达成"文章只看一遍而查看过所有题型中的所有题目"这个目标。

必背词汇

1. complex *adj.* 复杂的

   in-depth coverage of today's *complex* issues 对当今复杂问题的深入报道

   a *complex* system of voting 一套复杂的选举体制

2. perplex *v.* 使困惑，使忧虑（形容词形式为 perplexed 或 perplexing）

   It *perplexed* him because he was tackling it the wrong way. 这件事令他困惑和忧虑，因为他处理得不对。

She is *perplexed* about what to do for her daughter. 她很困惑，不知该为女儿做些什么。

3. lonesome *adj.* 孤独的，孤单的

In the beginning I felt very *lonesome* in London. 起初，我在伦敦觉得非常孤独。

The house she had always thought of as overcrowded was *lonesome* when her children grew up and went out on their own.

先前她认为这屋子过于拥挤，但当其子女长大成人出去独立生活后，这里又显得孤寂。

4. ignore *v.* 忽视，忽略

They had *ignored* the warning signs. 他们对警报信号置之不顾。

His article *ignores* the fact that the environment can exaggerate small genetic differences.

他的文章忽视了环境可能会放大基因的微小差异这一事实。

5. jealousy *n.* 嫉妒；猜忌

At first his *jealousy* only showed in small ways — he didn't mind me talking to other guys.

开始时，他的猜忌还表现得不是十分明显——他并不介意我和其他男孩子说话。

Her beauty causes envy and *jealousy*. 她的美丽招人妒羡。

6. envy *n./v.* 羡慕；嫉妒

Their economy is the *envy* of the developing world. 他们的经济令发展中国家羡慕。

I don't *envy* the young ones who've become TV superstars and know no other world.

我不羡慕那些成为电视明星而对其他一无所知的年轻人。

7. involve *v.* 涉及，牵扯

Nicky's job as a public relations director *involves* spending quite a lot of time with other people.

尼基的工作是公共关系主管，需要花相当多的时间与其他人打交道。

I seem to have *involved* myself in something I don't understand.

我似乎已经将自己卷入了一个不明事件。

8. release *v.* 分泌，释放；解除

Divorce *releases* both the husband and wife from all marital obligations to each other.

离婚解除了夫妻之间的所有婚姻义务。

The contraction of muscles uses energy and *releases* heat. 肌肉的收缩消耗能量并释放热量。

9. cooperative *adj.* 合作的（动词形式为 cooperate，名词形式为 cooperation）

I made every effort to be *cooperative*. 我尽力配合。

friendly and *cooperative* relations between the two countries 两国之间的友好合作关系

认知词汇

oxytocin	*n.* 催产素		prairie	*n.* 草原
positive	*adj.* 积极的		vole	*n.* 田鼠，野鼠
negative	*adj.* 消极的		mate	*v.* 交配
chemical	*n.* 化学物质		trigger	*v.* 触发，引发
hormone	*n.* 荷尔蒙		attachment	*n.* 情感联系；附件
gland	*n.* 腺体		reputation	*n.* 名誉
aware	*adj.* 意识到的		sniff	*n./v.* 吸，闻
reinforce	*v.* 加强		empathetic	*adj.* 感同身受的，有同理心的
bond	*n.* 联系，纽带		generous	*adj.* 慷慨的

revise	v. 修正，更新		promote	v. 提升，促进
wholly	adv. 完完全全地		previously	adv. 先前地
optimistic	adj. 乐观的		subtlety	n. 微妙性，微妙之处
circumstance	n. 场景，情况		individual	n. 个人 adj. 个人的
impact	n./v. 影响		nuanced	adj. 细致入微的
interaction	n. 互动，交互作用		propel	v. 推进，驱动
emerge	v. 出现		investigation	n. 调查
groundbreaking	adj. 突破性的，全新的		pinpoint	v. 确定，准确描述
colleague	n. 同事		core	n. 核心
volunteer	n. 志愿者		catalogue	v. 把……分类
anonymous	adj. 匿名的		hypothesis	n. 假说
guarantee	v. 确保		mutually	adv. 相互地
nasal	adj. 鼻腔的		exclusive	adj. 唯一的，排他的
spray	n./v. 喷		anxiety	n. 焦虑
placebo	n. 安慰剂		spotlight	n. 聚光灯；注意焦点
charitable	adj. 慈善的		clue	n. 线索
constructively	adv. 建设性地		posture	n. 姿态，立场
universally	adv. 普遍地		flicker	n. 闪烁，闪现
enhance	v. 增强		dip	n./v. 下沉，下降
contrasting	adj. 形成鲜明对比的		attuned	adj. 适应的，熟悉的
competitive	adj. 有竞争性的		identify	v. 确认，辨认
inhale	v. 吸入		overly	adv. 过度地，过分地
administer	v. 服药，用药；执行		prone to	倾向于
outcome	n. 结果		cue	n. 线索
disposition	n. 性情，倾向		octopus	n. 章鱼
emotion	n. 情绪		evolutionary	adj. 进化的
adept	adj. 内行的，熟练的		stretch	n./v. 拉伸；延伸
rejection	n. 抗拒，抑制		molecule	n. 分子
reveal	v. 揭示		co-opt	v. 指派，增选
dose	n. 一剂（药物等）		primitive	adj. 原始的；基本的
favouritism	n. 偏袒，偏爱		manifest	v. 显示，表明
bias	n. 偏见		context	n. 语境，上下文

佳句赏析

1. It was through various studies focusing on animals that scientists first became aware of the influence of oxytocin.

   - 参考译文：科学家们最初注意到催产素的影响力是通过各种各样在动物身上所进行的研究。
   - 语言点：本句采用了 It was...that... 的强调句型结构，读者只要看清楚这一点，便能明白：that 之前的部分是本句要强调的对象，即"通过各种各样的动物实验"，而 that 后面是这个句子的其他部分，也就是科学家们注意到了催产素的作用。

2. In a groundbreaking experiment, Markus Heinrichs and his colleagues at the University of Freiburg, Germany, asked volunteers to do an activity in which they could invest money with an anonymous person who was not guaranteed to be honest.

   - 参考译文：在一场突破性的实验中，德国弗赖堡大学的 Markus Heinrichs 及其团队要求志愿者们进行一项活动：他们可以把钱投资在一个匿名的人身上，而这个人并不能确保会是诚信的。

- 语言点：本句的主干是 Markus Heinrichs and his colleagues...asked volunteers to do an activity... 第一个逗号前的状语和人名之后的大写介绍对于读者来说应该都不困难，真正使句子显得不易理解的部分在于主干之后的修饰部分。其中，in which they could invest money with an anonymous person 修饰的是 activity，表明志愿者们到底进行的是何种活动，而 who was not guaranteed to be honest 则是修饰实验中这个匿名人士，进一步说明志愿者的投资对象的细节情况。

3. Simone Shamay-Tsoory at the University of Haifa, Israel, found that when volunteers played a competitive game, those who inhaled the hormone showed more pleasure when they beat other players, and felt more envy when others won.
    - 参考译文：以色列海法大学的 Simone Shamay-Tsoory 发现，当志愿者玩起一项竞争性游戏时，那些吸入这种荷尔蒙的人在战胜其他玩家时展示出了更多的愉悦，而在其他人赢了的时候则感受到更多嫉恨。
    - 语言点：本句的主干是 Simone Shamay-Tsoory...found that... 真正给出实际信息的是宾语从句中的内容。从句中带有三个由 when 引导的时间状语，第一个 when volunteers played a competitive game 表明实验进行的时候，另外两个 when 则分别描述了在两种不同的情况下实验对象的具体表现，宾语从句的主干结构根据后两个 when 的时间情况分别带有两个谓宾结构：those...showed more pleasure when..., and felt more envy when...，而跟在主语 those 后面的 who inhaled the hormone 则是进一步修饰说明 those 即实验对象的定语从句。

4. She believes that oxytocin acts as a chemical spotlight that shines on social clues — a shift in posture, a flicker of the eyes, a dip in the voice — making people more attuned to their social environment.
    - 参考译文：她相信催产素的作用就像某种化学聚光灯，照耀着种种社交线索——姿势的一个改变，眼睛的轻轻一眨，嗓音的突然压低——使得人们更加适应自己的社会环境。
    - 语言点：本句的主干非常简单：She believes that... 真正有意义的仍是 that 引导的宾语从句，这个从句自身的主谓宾结构也不复杂：oxytocin acts as a chemical spotlight... 造成句子长难的主要因素在于各种修饰成分，其中 that shines on social clues 是常见定语从句，修饰前面的 spotlight 一词，随后由两个破折号隔开来的部分是对 social clues 的进一步举例说明，再接下来是由 making 引导的非谓语动词结构，阐述催产素发生作用所产生的结果。

5. Oxytocin probably does some very basic things, but once you add our higher-order thinking and social situations, these basic processes could manifest in different ways depending on individual differences and context.
    - 参考译文：催产素大概会产生一些非常基础的功用，但是一旦你再加上我们的高阶思考能力和社交场合因素，这些基础过程就会根据个体差异和当时的语境而产生不同的呈现方式。
    - 语言点：本句由 but 转折词连接了两个句子结构，转折前的主谓宾结构非常简单好懂，理解难点主要集中在转折后的句子里。从 but 到下一个逗号之间的成分，是由 once 引导的条件句，表示"一旦如何如何"，逗号之后的部分是这个条件句的结果，也是句子的主干结构所在，主谓成分是：these basic processes could manifest，in different ways 和 depending on individual differences and context 分别是后置的介词短语和非谓语动词成分，进一步修饰说明"这些表现有不同的方式"和"要看具体个人和场合的不同"。

❄ 试题解析

Questions 14~17

- **题目类型**：MATCHING INFORMATION
- **题目解析**：这种"考查细节信息位于正文中哪一段"的搭配题型难度较高，但切记不可因为担心时间不足而匆匆略读题干就开始划定位词并回到原文开始定位。有时某个题干的整句意思表达并不是单独某一词可以承担的，需要读懂题干的真正意思（包括词组的固定搭配和特殊用法等）才有可能准确定位。由于答案就是段落字母，所以解析部分不再重复"答案是……"。

  考生还需特别留意一点：此部分题目要求中出现了 NB 的提示，这个拉丁文缩写提醒的内容是"会有某个字母选项被选用不止一次"。通常情况下，NB 的提示意味着"只会有一个字母被选中两次"，但少数情况下也会出现例外，例如本套试题第三篇中的情况就是这样，考生还需具体问题具体分析最为安全。

题号	定位词	文中对应点	题目解析
14	beneficial effects	B 段倒数第二句： These follow-up studies have shown that after a sniff of the hormone, people become more charitable, better at reading emotions on others' faces and at communicating constructively in arguments.	题目：reference to research showing the beneficial effects of oxytocin on people 译文：提到了一些显示催产素对人们产生有益影响的研究 在"段落匹配信息"这种类型的题目中，经常会有诸如reference, account, mention这类词汇出现，它们表达的意思都是"提到，说到"，考生切勿将此处的reference理解为该词的其他意义例如"参考"等，徒增理解难度。本题干意思清楚，也不包含任何艰深词汇，考生只需认真通读每段每句，即可最终对应到B段相应位置解题。
15	reasons, complex	F 段整段	题目：reasons why the effects of oxytocin are complex 译文：催产素的效果之所以复杂的原因 如果考生发现文章F段第一句里perplexing这个形容词与题干中complex形成了同义对应关系的话，此题就显得相当简单了，只要耐心看到此处，即可解题。如若不然，通过对本段后面几个句子的阅读，其实也能得到这个大致印象：催产素在每种生物身上都有，虽然自身成分原始而简单，但组合出的作用却多种多样。这样一来，也可对应题干作答。
16	period, little scientific attention	B 段第四、五句： The study was the start of research into the effects of oxytocin on human interactions. 'For eight years, it was quite a lonesome field,' Heinrichs recalls.	题目：mention of a period in which oxytocin attracted little scientific attention 译文：提到了某个时期里催产素并没有吸引到科学研究的兴趣 此题的解题关键之一在于考生需要认识lonesome"孤独的"，再结合本段上文中说这才开启了人们对催产素的各种研究，从而更加确定这里便是对应于题干意思的位置。

剑桥雅思真题精讲 *13* · 学术类

70

题号	定位词	文中对应点	题目解析
17	ignore, certain aspects	E 段第二、三句： Bartz has recently shown that in almost half of the existing research results, oxytocin influenced only certain individuals or in certain circumstances. Where once researchers took no notice of such findings, ...	题目：reference to people ignoring certain aspects of their research data 译文：提到人们忽视了他们研究数据中的某些方面 此题的难度仍然主要体现在词汇认知方面。题干里的ignore是雅思阅读文章中的常客，很多做过以往真题的考生对它并不陌生，由此对应到E段中的took no notice，即可比较轻松地解题了。

Questions 18~20

- **题目类型**：MATCHING FEATURES
- **题目解析**：这道匹配题的难度适中：选项一方都是人名大写，考生可先在文章中找到每个人名的位置，再阅读人名附近的文章内容解答；但人名给了六个，对应题干却只有三条，因此考生要阅读的内容可能会多一些，这提升了一些难度。不过有趣的是，本文的出题人倒是非常贴心地在文中依次出现的前三个人名里设置了对应的观点出题，也就是说，考生按照文章顺序每找到一个人名、耐心阅读此人名附近的文章内容，即可对应选出一道题目，后三个人名实际上与解题没有任何关系，无需再去细读其观点表达。

题号	定位词	文中对应点	题目解析
18	Markus Heinrichs	B 段第二、三句： In a groundbreaking experiment, Markus Heinrichs and his colleagues at the University of Freiburg, Germany, asked volunteers to do an activity in which they could invest money with an anonymous person who was not guaranteed to be honest. The team found that participants who had sniffed oxytocin via a nasal spray beforehand invested more money than those who received a placebo instead.	题目：People are more trusting when affected by oxytocin. 译文：人们在受到催产素影响时会更易于相信他人。 此题的难点，其一在于题干中的trusting一模一样地出现在了A段里，考生如果注意到了这一点可能会受到一定迷惑，A段中并未指明是谁的实验发现了这一点，因此无法据此答题；难点之二在于，考生定位到了相应人名以后，需真正看懂此处的两个句子（其中包含人名的一句结构略复杂，详细解析可以参见前文"佳句赏析"中的第二句），就会发现虽然句中并没有明确使用trusting一词，但所谓"吸入催产素的实验对象愿意将更多的钱投资在一个既不认识、也不能确定其是否诚信的人身上"，无疑表达的就是trusting这个意思，于是找到正确的对应答案。

题号	定位词	文中对应点	题目解析
19	Simone Shamay-Tsoory	C 段第二句： Simone Shamay-Tsoory at the University of Haifa, Israel, found that when volunteers played a competitive game, those who inhaled the hormone showed more pleasure when they beat other players, and felt more envy when others won.	题目：Oxytocin increases people's feelings of jealousy. 译文：催产素增加了人们的嫉妒感。 此题的难度主要来自于对考生词汇认知水平的考查：题干中的jealousy直接对应于原文定位句中的envy，考生只要认识这两个单词，就能比较轻松地完成匹配答题。此处的对应原文句结构略复杂，详细解析可以参见前文"佳句赏析"中的第三句。
20	Jennifer Bartz	C 段倒数两句： Jennifer Bartz from Mount Sinai School of Medicine, New York, found that it improves people's ability to read emotions, but only if they are not very socially adept to begin with. Her research also shows that oxytocin in fact reduces cooperation in subjects who are particularly anxious or sensitive to rejection.	题目：The effect of oxytocin varies from one type of person to another. 译文：催产素的作用会取决于不同类型的人而有所不同。 此题的难度比较高。一方面，它仍在考查考生对于vary这个动词的认知水平，而动词vary及其同根词various（形容词）、variety（名词）都是雅思阅读文章中的高频常客，对于考生来说不应是陌生词汇；另一方面，定位到的两句原文中并未直接出现vary或可以直接形成同义替换关系的词汇，考生还需真正读懂这两句，并提炼出"催产素在一些人身上产生的作用和在另一些人身上产生的作用有很大不同"这个意思，才能顺利匹配答案。 还需特别提醒的一点是，D段第一句中另一个人DeClerck的发现有着不小的迷惑作用，因为此句中包含一模一样的题干词vary，乍一看貌似也是在说"对人的影响不同"；然而耐心细读就会发现，这里说的"不同"，指的是"我们与之互动的对象"不同，与题干意思不符。

Questions 21~26

- **题目类型**：SUMMARY COMPLETION
- **题目解析**：此部分题目涉及的答案范畴跨度比较大，因此增加了考生定位的难度。由于填空题在绝大多数情况下都是顺序出题的，因此考生在解答此类题目时，不妨先尝试快速浏览一下题干部分，寻找是否有帮助定位的数字大写等信息。比如此处的前两道题，题干本身并没有什么太显眼的定位关键词；而向后阅读便可发现，第三题的题干中有 2005 这个更好寻找的定位信息，则可先回原文找到这个年份，由此确定前两道题的大致位置，在缩小的原文范围中更安心地寻找答案。后几道题的题干中都包含大写信息，因此虽然答案彼此相距略远，倒也不算太难寻找。

剑桥雅思真题精讲 *13* · 学术类

72

题号	解题关键词	文中对应点	题目解析
21	earliest findings, involving	A 段第二句： It was through various studies focusing on animals that scientists first became aware of the influence of oxytocin.	题干问"关于催产素与情感纽带的最早研究发现来自于涉及____的研究"，可知空格内需要的是作为研究对象的一个名词。依靠后文2005这个数字信息，考生不难确定本题与下一题的出处应当都是文章的第一段，进而也就不难通过earliest与first的对应关系找到出题句。关于本句的详细解析，考生可以参见前文"佳句赏析"中的第一句，利用involve与focus on的同义替换关系可知，答案为animals。
22	humans	A 段第四句： It is also released by women in childbirth, strengthening the attachment between mother and baby.	题干问"还发现人类在____过程中会分泌催产素"，考生只需从上一题向后顺序阅读，便能找到原文中的women与题干的humans对应。无论题干句还是对应原文句的结构都不复杂，考生只要认识release与produce的同义替换关系，即可确定答案为childbirth。
23	2005, either...or...	B 段第三句： The team found that participants who had sniffed oxytocin via a nasal spray beforehand invested more money than those who received a placebo instead.	本题虽然定位不难，但题干本身比较复杂，需要考生耐心分析读懂。题干问"在2005年的一场实验中，参与者要么被使用了催产素，要么被给了____，这场实验强化了人们认为这种荷尔蒙有着积极性影响的看法。"用2005这个数字信息定位并不难，但包含数字的句子里并没有相关信息，考生需耐心向下再读两句，才能看出在这场实验中，给一些人用了催产素，而另一些人则给了placebo；即使并不认识placebo是"安慰剂"的意思，根据原文这种排列关系也能将它确定为空格内应当填写的答案。
24	University of Haifa	C 段第二句： Simone Shamay-Tsoory at the University of Haifa, Israel, found that when volunteers played a competitive game, those who inhaled the hormone showed more pleasure when they beat other players, and felt more envy when others won.	本题可以凭借大写名称迅速定位，不过题干本身也略为复杂，需要考生耐心阅读。题干问"在海法大学的一项研究中，参与者进行了一项____，这表明催产素也有可能触发一些消极情绪。"可知空格内需要填写一个实验对象所参与进行的单数名词，此处无论是题干中的词组take part in，还是原文中的对应词play，都不构成任何难点，正确答案应为game。
25	University of Antwerp	D 段第二句： Studies conducted by Carolyn DeClerck of the University of Antwerp, Belgium, revealed that people who had received a dose of oxytocin actually became less cooperative when dealing with complete strangers.	本题虽然距离上一题答案比较远，但可以通过大写名称帮助快速定位。题干问"安特卫普大学的一项研究显示了在催产素的作用影响下，人们缺少去帮助____的意愿"，可知空格内应为一个表示"人们帮助对象"的名词，耐心对比定位句，可以通过原文less cooperative与题干中lack of willingness之间的对应，确定答案为strangers。

题号	解题关键词	文中对应点	题目解析
26	University of Amsterdam	D 段第三句：Meanwhile, Carsten De Dreu at the University of Amsterdam in the Netherlands discovered that volunteers given oxytocin showed favouritism: Dutch men became quicker to associate positive words with Dutch names than with foreign ones, for example.	本题与前两道题的情况类似，虽然可以借助大写名称进行比较快速的定位，但考生却需认真耐心地阅读分析本身就很复杂的题干句。本句问"与此同时，在阿姆斯特丹大学进行的研究表明，被用了催产素的人会认为自己国家中的、对他们来说很熟悉的_____比那些来自其他文化的有着更为积极的联系"；回到原文的定位句中，虽然句式结构也比较长难，却可以通过同样的比较结构以及原文中动词形式associate与题干中名词形式association的对应关系，确定答案应为names。

参考译文

— 催产素 —

被称为"爱情荷尔蒙"的化学物质的积极和消极影响

A　催产素是一种化学物质，一种由脑垂体分泌的荷尔蒙。科学家们最初注意到催产素的影响力是通过各种各样在动物身上所进行的研究。他们发现，它有助于加强草原鼠配偶之间的亲密度——这种动物一生只找一个交配对象，它也能在母羊身上激发其对待初生小羊羔的母性行为。女性在生产过程中也会释放出这种元素，它加强了母亲与婴儿之间的情感纽带。很少有什么化学物质能拥有像催产素那样的好名声，它有时候被称作"爱情荷尔蒙"。据称，只要吸进那么一小下，就能使一个人变得更愿意信任别人、更有同理心、更慷慨和更乐于合作。然而，是时候修正一下这个全盘乐观的看法了。新一波研究显示：它的效果会根据不同的人和场合而呈现出极大的不同，且它对我们社会交往行为所产生的影响不光可以是好的，也同样可能会是坏的。

B　催产素在人类行为中所扮演的角色第一次崭露头角是在 2005 年。在一场突破性的实验中，德国弗赖堡大学的 Markus Heinrichs 及其团队要求志愿者们进行一项活动：他们可以把钱投资在一个匿名的人身上，而这个人并不能确保会是诚信的。研究组发现，那些事先通过喷鼻剂吸入了催产素的参与者比那些只吸入安慰剂的人投资了更多的钱。这项研究开启了对催产素如何作用于人类相互之间行为的探索。"在八年的时间里，它一度是一个无人问津的领域"，Heinrichs 回忆道。"现在，每个人都深感兴趣。"这些后续研究显示，在吸入了这种荷尔蒙之后，人们会变得更加慈悲为怀，更善于读懂他人脸上的情绪，以及在意见不合的争论中进行建设性的沟通对话。综合来看，这些研究结果点燃了这样一种观念：催产素广泛提升了我们社交属性中的那些积极方面。

C　接下来，几年之后，与此相反的研究发现开始冒头。以色列海法大学的 Simone Shamay-Tsoory 发现，当志愿者玩起一项竞争性游戏时，那些吸入这种荷尔蒙的人在战胜其他玩家时展示出了更多的愉悦，而在其他人赢了的时候则感受到更多嫉恨。更有甚者，使用催产素还会根据一个人的性格特征而呈现出截然相反的效果。纽约西奈山医学院的 Jennifer Bartz 发现：它确实能增强人们解读情绪的能力，但这只是在那些人原本就并不擅长社交的情况下才成立。她的研究还显示，在那些尤为焦虑或对别人的拒绝排斥格外敏感的实验对象身上，催产素实际上降低了他们的合作性。

D　另一项发现是：催产素的效果取决于我们在跟谁互动而各有不同。比利时安特卫普大学的 Carolyn DeClerck 所开展的几项研究表明，吸收了催产素的人在与完完全全的陌生人打交道时实际上是变得更不合作了。与此同时，荷兰阿姆斯特丹大学的 Carsten De Dreu 也发现，用了催产素的志愿者们表现出了偏好倾向：比方说，荷兰人会更迅速地将荷兰语名字而不是一些外国名字与一些积极词汇联系起来。按照 De Dreu 的说法，催产素驱使人们去关爱处在自己社交圈中的人们并护卫他们不受外部危险的侵扰。这样看来，催产素似乎是强化了人们的偏见，而不是像先前以为的那样，在总体上提升了人们的善念。

E 其实从一开始，就存在着这些微妙之处的迹象。Bartz 最近指出，在几乎一半的现有研究结果中，催产素都只影响了某些个体或是在某些情况下才起作用。研究者们一度并未对这些发现引起重视，而现在，对催产素效用的更细致入微的理解正在推动着调查研究沿一些新的思路深入进行下去。在 Bartz 看来，理解这种荷尔蒙到底能做什么的关键在于锁定它的核心功能，而不是去对它那些看似无穷无尽的效用进行分类。存在着几种理论假说，它们彼此之间并不排斥。催产素有助于减少焦虑和畏惧。或者它就是能够驱使人们去找到各种社交纽带。她相信催产素的作用就像某种化学聚光灯，照耀着种种社交线索——姿势的一个改变，眼睛的轻轻一眨，嗓音的突然压低——使得人们更加适应自己的社会环境。这就能够解释为什么它能让我们更有可能去注视他人的眼睛并能提升我们辨别情绪的能力。但是，它也可能会令那些过度敏感或倾向于用最坏的方式解读社交线索的人们面临更糟的局面。

F 催产素的故事现在已经变得更加复杂了，也许我们并不应该对此感到吃惊。这种荷尔蒙在从章鱼到绵羊的每种生物身上都能找到，而它的进化根源能够向前追溯五亿年之久。"它是一种非常简单而古老的因子，被组合出了许多不同的功能"，美国芝加哥伊利诺伊大学的 Sue Carter 这样说。"它作用于大脑最原始的一些部分，例如杏仁体，因此它将会对几乎所有（脑活动）都产生许多影响。"Bartz 也赞同这个看法。"催产素大概会产生一些非常基础的功用，但是一旦你再加上我们的高阶思考能力和社交场合因素，这些基础过程就会根据个体差异和当时的语境而产生不同的呈现方式。"

Reading Passage 3

篇章结构

体裁	说明文
主题	潮流对商业策略的影响
结构	第一段：经理人往往忽视了潮流对消费者的影响
	第二段：本文的双重写作目的
	第三段："渗透与扩充"策略及蔻驰的案例
	第四段：Tesco 的案例对以上策略的运用
	第五段："融合与超越"策略及耐克的案例
	第六段："抵制与重申"策略及 ME2 的案例
	第七段：可以分别运用三种策略的情境
	第八段：潮流是产品创新的机遇

解题地图

难度系数： ★★★★★

解题顺序： MULTIPLE CHOICE → MATCHING FEATURES → MATCHING SENTENCE ENDINGS

友情提示： 本篇的难度相当高。一方面，文章的行文风格比较曲折，充斥着大量结构复杂的长难句，给考生顺利理解文章造成了不小的障碍；另一方面，虽然前两个题型中都包含了大量大写信息帮助定位，有两道选择题甚至直接指明了去哪一段找，但由于这个题型本身难度偏高，选项的混淆性也大，因此即使找到了相应段落，也要求考生能够比较精准地读懂内容。加之此时已做到了考试的最后一篇文章，一些考生难免剩余时间有限，无法顺利读完全文。因此，不妨按照文章题型的排列顺序，依次解答；同时灵活处理具体题目，既要耐心细读正在解答的题目，在没有读懂或没有把握的情况下也不必太过"执着"，可适当跳过一些感觉格外困难的题目，争取最大化地利用考试时间，做出更多题目，从而争取获得更加理想的成绩。

必背词汇

1. spot *v.* 找准，锁定 *n.* 斑点，地点

   Vicenzo failed to *spot* the error. 维森佐没能发现这个错误。

   They stayed at several of the island's top tourist *spots*. 他们在岛上最著名的几处旅游景点做了停留。

2. misinterpret *v.* 错误地解读（前缀 mis- 表示"错误"，动词 interpret 意为"解读"或"翻译"）

   He was amazed that he'd *misinterpreted* the situation so completely.

   他对自己完全误解了形势感到很吃惊。

   The prince's words had been *misinterpreted*. 王子的话被误解了。

3. unaware *adj.* 没注意到的，无意识的（与 aware 互为反义词）

   Many people are *unaware* of just how much food and drink they consume.

   许多人不知道自己到底消耗掉多少食物和饮料。

   Smokers are well *aware* of the dangers to their own health. 吸烟者们都很清楚吸烟对其健康的危害。

4. recognize *v.* 认出；承认

   The receptionist *recognized* him at once. 那位接待员马上认出了他。

   It was *recognized* that this solution could only be temporary. 人们认识到，这种解决方式只能是暂时的。

5. maintain *v.* 保持，维持

   Such extrovert characters try to *maintain* relationships no matter how damaging these relationships may be.

   这类外向的人设法维持感情关系，不论这些关系多么有害。

   The government was right to *maintain* interest rates at a high level. 政府维持高利率是正确的。

6. modify *v.* 修改，调整

   The club members did agree to *modify* their recruitment policy. 俱乐部成员确已同意修改他们的入会政策。

   The plane was a *modified* version of the C-130. 这架飞机是 C-130 的改进机型。

7. implement *v.* 实施，执行

   The government promised to *implement* a new system to control financial loan institutions.

   政府承诺要实施新的制度来控制金融贷款机构。

   The report sets out strict inspection procedures to ensure that the recommendations are properly *implemented*. 报告列出了严格的检查程序，确保正确地实施这些建议。

8. original *adj.* 原始的；有创意的

The inhabitants have voted overwhelmingly to restore the city's *original* name of Chemnitz.

居民以压倒性的投票数决定恢复该市原来的名字"开姆尼兹"。

It is one of the most *original* works of imagination in the language.

这是用这种语言创作的最具想象力的原创作品之一。

9. appeal *n.* 吸引力 *v.* 呼吁；申诉

On the other hand, the idea *appealed* to him. 另一方面，这个主意对他有吸引力。

He said they would *appeal* against the decision. 他说他们将对这项决议提出申诉。

10. address *v.* 应对，处理

Mr. King sought to *address* those fears when he spoke at the meeting.

金先生在会上讲话时试图消除那些恐惧。

US policy has failed to adequately *address* this problem. 美国的政策没能充分地解决这个问题。

11. extend *v.* 扩大，延伸

A table *extended* from the front of her desk to create a T-shaped seating arrangement.

一张桌子从她的办公室前端伸出，形成 T 型的座位排列。

This year they have introduced three new products to *extend* their range.

今年他们已引入了三种新产品以扩大产品范围。

12. collaborate *v.* 合作

Much later he *collaborated* with his son Michael on the English translation of a text on food production.

后来他和儿子迈克尔合作，把一篇有关食品生产的文本翻译成英语。

He turned his country house into a place where professionals and amateurs *collaborated* in the making of music. 他把他的乡间小屋变成了业内外人士合作制作音乐的场所。

13. incentive *n.* 鼓励

There is little or no *incentive* to adopt such measures. 几乎没有什么激励政策来促使人们采取这样的措施。

Many companies in Britain are keen on the idea of tax *incentives* for R&D.

英国的许多公司都欢迎对研发采取税收鼓励的提议。

14. scheme *n.* 计划；方案

schemes to help combat unemployment 有助于解决失业问题的方案

They would first have to work out some *scheme* for getting the treasure out.

他们首先得想出某种计划把珍宝取出来。

15. charge *v.* 收费；充电

Some banks *charge* if you access your account to determine your balance.

如果你查看账户余额，有些银行要收费。

There was nothing in the brochure about having to drive it every day to *charge* up the battery.

手册里没有提到每天都要驾驶它，以给电池充电。

16. highlight *v.* 突出，强调 *n.* 最精彩的部分

Last year Collins wrote a moving ballad which *highlighted* the plight of the homeless.

去年柯林斯写了一首感人的叙事诗，突出描写了无家可归者的苦境。

This incident *highlights* the care needed when disposing of unwanted plants.

这一事件突显了处理废弃植物时所需的慎重。

认知词汇

profound	adj. 巨大的，深远的
aspiration	n. 渴望；抱负
peripheral	adj. 外围的，边缘的
core	n. 核心
innovation	n. 创新
adopt	v. 采用；收养
minimum	n. 最小量，最小值
response	n. 反应
jeopardize	v. 危及，使危险
cede	v. 转让，让给
rival	n. 竞争对手
spur	v. 激发
expansively	adv. 宽广地，开阔地
engender	v. 产生，造成
proposition	n. 命题，主张
personnel	n. 职员；人事部门
adept	adj. 内行的，熟练的
exploit	v. 开发，利用
infuse	v. 浸泡，灌输
augment	v. 增加，增强
retain	v. 保留，持有
attribute	n. 属性，象征 v. 归因于
unleash	v. 发泄，爆发
downturn	n. 下滑，衰退
opulence	n. 富饶，大量
luxury	n. 奢侈，奢侈品
initiate	v. 开创；提出
tough	adj. 严苛的；坚硬的；坎坷的
launch	v. 启动；发射
vibrant	adj. 充满生机的，生气勃勃的
conventional	adj. 传统的
avert	v. 防止，避免
recession	n. 衰退
mindset	n. 观念模式
renewal	n. 更新，复兴
retailer	n. 零销商
demonstrate	v. 证明
commitment	n. 承诺，投入
tangible	adj. 有形的，真实的

accumulate	v. 积累
printer	n. 打印机
cartridge	n. 墨盒
insulation	n. 绝缘
redeem	v. 挽回，补偿；救赎
streak	n. 条纹；特征
radical	adj. 激进的，非传统的
transcend	v. 超越
entail	v. 牵扯，涉及
novel	adj. 新奇的
incorporate	v. 吸收，包含
irrelevant	adj. 无关的
integrate	v. 整合，使成为一体
digital	adj. 数字的，数码的
reputation	n. 声望，名声
performance	n. 表现；表演
athletic	adj. 体育的
kit	n. 装备
comprise	v. 包括，由……构成
sensor	n. 传感器
attach	v. 附加，附属
amateur	adj. 业余的
apparel	n. 服装，衣饰
temporarily	adv. 暂时地
accomplish	v. 建立；取得
device	n. 设备
graphic	adj. 图表的
component	n. 成分，元件
skateboard	n. 滑板
enhance	v. 增加
virtual	adj. 虚拟的
cater to	迎合
counter	v. 反驳，对立，抵消
obesity	n. 肥胖症
perspective	n. 观点，视角
reinvigorate	n. 振兴，使再振作
disparity	n. 差异，不一致
clash	v. 冲突，交锋
perceive	v. 接收，感知

佳句赏析

1. But in the course of conducting research in a number of industries and working directly with companies, we have discovered that managers often fail to recognize the less obvious but profound ways these trends are influencing consumers' aspirations, attitudes, and behaviors.
   - 参考译文：但是在一系列行业中进行研究和直接与各种公司合作的过程中，我们发现经理们往往没能意识到这些潮流正在以并不显著但却意义深远的方式影响着消费者的渴望、态度和行为。
   - 语言点：本句的主干结构其实特别简单：we have discovered that... 然而仅仅看出这个带宾语从句的主干结构对理解此句的帮助还不够大，因为无论是第一个逗号前面的状语部分，还是宾语从句自身的结构，都为考生制造了理解难点。状语从句的主体结构是：in the course of conducting...and working...，也就是在完成 conduct 和 work 这两个动作的过程中；宾语从句的主干结构是：managers often fail to recognize the...ways...，ways 前面的 less obvious but profound 是由转折词 but 连接的两个修饰形容部分，ways 后面的所有内容则是进一步修饰 ways 的定语从句部分。

2. The purpose of this article is twofold: to spur managers to think more expansively about how trends could engender new value propositions in their core markets, and to provide some high-level advice on how to make market research and product development personnel more adept at analyzing and exploiting trends.
   - 参考译文：本文的目的有两个：驱动经理人更广泛发散地思考潮流如何在他们的核心市场内创造新的价值主题，并针对如何使市场调查与产品研发人员更加娴熟地分析和利用潮流提供一些高水平的建议。
   - 语言点：本句主干结构为 The purpose of this article is twofold: to spur..., and to provide... 冒号后面的细节说明是两个不定式结构，进一步给出文章的两个写作目的。第一个不定式的主干结构为：to spur managers to think more expansively about...，之后由 how 引导的宾语从句是具体思考的内容，从句的主干为 trends could engender new value propositions；第二个不定式的主干结构为 to provide some high-level advice on...，之后又是一个宾语从句给出建议的内容，从句的主干为 how to make...personnel more adept at analyzing and exploiting...

3. One strategy, known as 'infuse and augment', is to design a product or service that retains most of the attributes and functions of existing products in the category but adds others that address the needs and desires unleashed by a major trend.
   - 参考译文：有一条策略，称为"浸透与扩充"，是设计一项产品或服务，保留了同类现有产品的大部分特质和功能但又添加了一些能照顾到一场主要潮流所释放的需求和欲望的新特点。
   - 语言点：本句主干为 One strategy, ..., is to design a product or service... 位于主语和系动词之间、用两个逗号隔开的插入部分是对 strategy 的进一步说明，不难理解；难点在于 that 后面所引导的非常复杂的定语从句。这个从句的主干结构是：that retains most of the attributes and functions...but adds...，也就是既保留了某些内容，又增加了其他内容。attributes and functions 后面的 of existing products in the category 是对这两个名词的进一步修饰限定，说明它们的来源是现有的产品；others 后面的 that address the needs and desires 是修饰 others 的定语从句，unleashed by a major trend 又是修饰 needs and desires 的非谓语成分。

4. With that in mind, Tesco, one of the world's top five retailers, introduced its Greener Living program, which demonstrates the company's commitment to protecting the environment by involving consumers in ways that produce tangible results.

- 参考译文：了解到这种情况后，Tesco，这个世界最大的五家零售商之一，推出了它的"更环保生活项目"，以此昭示这家公司对保护环境的承诺，通过一些能产生明显效果的方式让消费者也参与其中。
- 语言点：本句的主干是 Tesco, ..., introduced its Greener Living program... 在这个主干之前或之间出现的修饰成分，无论是句首的伴随状语 With that in mind，还是两个逗号隔开的插入语 one of the world's top five retailers，对考生来说应该都不算困难。真正使句子复杂难解的部分全部来自于 which 后面引导的各种补充说明成分。一一来看：which demonstrates the company's commitment to protecting the environment 是定语从句的主干部分，by involving consumers 说明的是公司证明自己致力于环保的方式，即"让顾客参与进来"，in ways that produce tangible results 则是具体让顾客参与的方式，其中 that 后面引导的又是修饰 ways 的定语从句。

5. This entails combining aspects of the product's existing value proposition with attributes addressing changes arising from a trend, to create a novel experience — one that may land the company in an entirely new market space.
   - 参考译文：这涉及将产品的现有价值定位与能顾及一场潮流中所产生变化的新特征结合起来，共同创造出一种新奇的体验——这种体验也许能将公司带入一个全新的市场空间。
   - 语言点：本句的主干是 This entails combining...with... 考生需重点注意学习 combine A with B 结构，表示将两方内容融合在一起。在这个句子里，combine 后面的对象是介词结构 aspects of the product's existing value proposition，虽然略长却不难理解；with 后面的对象则是由非谓语动词成分 addressing changes arising from a trend 修饰的 attributes 这个单词。细分一下，这个成分里的 addressing changes 才是直接修饰 attributes 的内容，arising from a trend 则是直接修饰 changes、间接修饰 attributes 的。接下来，to create a novel experience 是进行 combine 这种行为所要达成的目的，破折号后面的部分则是一个带定语从句的同位语结构，解释说明这场新奇体验（novel experience）也许可以达到的功效。

6. A third approach, known as 'counteract and reaffirm', involves developing products or services that stress the values traditionally associated with the category in ways that allow consumers to oppose — or at least temporarily escape from — the aspects of trends they view as undesirable.
   - 参考译文：第三种策略，称为"抵制与重申"，涉及到开发这样一些产品或服务，强调的是传统上就与产品序列联系在一起的价值体系，所采用的方式则能允许消费者去否定——或者至少是暂时地逃离——这场潮流中在他们看来不那么吸引人的方面。
   - 语言点：本句的主干结构为 A third approach, ..., involves developing products or services... 这个主干结构之间用两个逗号隔开的插入成分是修饰 approach 的定语部分，非常容易理解；难点是 products or services 之后由 that 所引导的定语从句，由于定语从句带着极多修饰成分，所以显得极其复杂。这个从句的主干结构是 that stress the values...in ways...，如果加上其修饰的对象一起看，就是"以某些方式强调了某些价值的"产品或服务。在这个从句里，values 后面的 traditionally associated with the category 是修饰限定"价值"的非谓语动词成分，表明这些价值是"传统上就与品牌系列联系在一起的"。至于用什么方式去强调这些价值，这就要看 ways 后面由 that 所引导的定语从句。如果觉得这个定语从句还是太长，影响一次性理解的话，考生不妨将两个破折号隔开的部分忽略掉，先抓住定语从句的主干 that allow consumers to oppose...the aspects of trends，辨认出 they view as undesirable 是省略了 that 或 which 连接词的、修饰 trends 的又一个定语从句，再回过头来看破折号内的补充说明成分，就能有效降低理解的难度。

⚙ 试题解析

Questions 27~31

- **题目类型**：MULTIPLE CHOICE
- **题目解析**：本部分选择题的难度相当高。虽然题干问题要么明确指点答案出自哪一段，要么有大写数字等帮助迅速定位的关键词，但考生却无法只靠阅读包含关键词的单独一句话来确定答案，而是需要比较准确地通读全段或一段的大部分内容才能解答。本文长难句众多，而选择题的选项又很长，在这种问题和原文都比较复杂的情况下，考生尤其要有耐心，本着"宁可不完全做完，也要每看一道题都力争看懂、做对"的原则，反复对比原文信息，注意选项表述细节，稳步寻找正确答案。

题号	定位词	文中对应点	题目解析
27	first paragraph	第一段第二句： But in the course of conducting research in a number of industries and working directly with companies, we have discovered that managers often fail to recognize the less obvious but profound ways these trends are influencing consumers' aspirations, attitudes, and behaviors.	题干：In the first paragraph, the writer says that most managers 译文：在第一段里，作者认为大多数经理人 题干直接提示了答案位于第一段中。本段虽然篇幅不长，只有三句话，但直接对应正确答案的第二句话结构比较复杂，详细解析可以参见前文"佳句赏析"中的第一句，读懂此句即可顺利锁定正确答案为选项D：没有意识到潮流对消费者生活所可能具有的重要影响。 A项说"没能找准当下的主要消费者潮流"，这与原文中第一段第一句"大多数经理能辨认出时下主要潮流"的信息相矛盾；B项说"犯了只专注于主要的消费者潮流的错误"，然而原文中根本没有提及他们是否"专注于"潮流；C项说"错误解读了与当前消费者潮流相关的市场调查数据"，更是完全没有出现的内容。
28	third paragraph	第三段第三、四句： The Coach brand had been a symbol of opulence and luxury for nearly 70 years, and the most obvious reaction to the downturn would have been to lower prices. However, that would have risked cheapening the brand's image.	题干：According to the third paragraph, Coach was anxious to 译文：按照第三段的说法，蔻驰非常渴望去 本题不但从题干可知去第三段寻找，而且还可以进一步根据Coach这个大写名称跳过第一句，从第二句开始阅读；不过考生需拿出耐心多看几句，才能比较清楚地整体了解。特别需要格外留意第三和第四句中都使用了would have done的虚拟语气，表示"原本"最明显的办法是降价，但"如果这样做"就会自降品牌身价。言下之意，实际情况其实与此相反。如果继续阅读，还能从下一句的Instead进一步确认，对比可知正确答案为选项C：守护其作为奢侈品生产商的声望。 A项说"照搬一些其竞争者的做法"，这与第三段最后一句话中提到的"与其他很多公司的降价行为相反"矛盾；B项说"维持了所有产品的价格"，这与文中"推出了价格更为亲民的新系列"不相符；D项说"修改了其品牌的整体外观以适应当时的经济气候"，属于故意曲解原文中的表述，因为文中说的是"新产品系列采用了更浓烈亮丽的色彩来迎合人们当时的心境"，至于原本的产品序列是否也有更改，并未被提及。

题号	定位词	文中对应点	题目解析
29	Tesco, Greener Living	第四段最后一句：Tesco has not abandoned its traditional retail offerings but augmented its business with these innovations, thereby infusing its value proposition with a green streak.	题干：What point is made about Tesco's Greener Living programme? 译文：文中关于Tesco的"更环保生活项目"说了什么？ 本题的难度极高，首先是因为考生无法只凭包含关键词的一两句就确定答案，而是需要基本通读一整段才能明白段落的中心思想；其次本段大量出现了"环保"相关的词汇和细节内容，因此提及"环保"内容的B选项对解答构成了极大的干扰。其实，本段首句就点明了中心思想：引用Tesco的案例是为了进一步证明先前所说过的策略，即"渗透和扩充"，换言之，是在不改变自身核心产品的基础上增加新的条线，于是接下来就只是用一个环保主题的例证来进行具体说明，而非把中心思想放在"环保"本身上面，本段最后一句的收尾总结也进一步证明了这一点，由此对应正确答案选项A：它不需要Tesco非得调整自己的核心商业运作活动。 B项说"它成功地吸引到了一群更有环保意识的客户"，此项颇有迷惑性，因为原文确实多次提及"环保"相关的细节内容，但Tesco这么做的目标是为了迎合顾客对环保的关注，重点在"目的"本身，而没有明确提及"结果是否真的吸引到了更多重视环保的顾客"，考生需格外留意区分；C项说"它的主要目标是提升消费者对环境问题的意识"，本项虽然也在说"环保"，但比较好辨别，因为文中意思是说消费者已经开始重视环境问题了，无需Tesco再去提醒；D项说"这并非是Tesco第一次推出这类举措"，这是原文完全不曾提及的内容。
30	Nike	第五段第三句：At first glance, spending resources to incorporate elements of a seemingly irrelevant trend into one's core offerings sounds like it's hardly worthwhile.	题干：What does the writer suggest about Nike's strategy? 译文：作者关于耐克的策略提出了什么看法？ 本题正确答案的对应信息虽然可以在段落里找到具体一句，但考生却无法仅凭这一句就确定无误地作答，还要对比其他选项进行依次排除，才能最终锁定的正确答案应为选项D：这种策略也许看起来并没有什么显著的利润。 A项说"它在当时是一项风险极高的策略"，文中只是提到"看似不太值得"，说"风险极高"未免有些过度引申了；B项说"这项策略只有一个大型公司才能负担得起去执行"；C项说"这类策略如果放在过去是完全不可能的"，这两项内容都是原文完全没有提及的信息。

剑桥雅思真题精讲 13 · 学术类

题号	定位词	文中对应点	题目解析
31	ME2	第六段最后三句：What set it apart was that it incorporated the traditional physical component of children's play...The ME2, introduced in mid-2008, catered to kids' huge desire to play video games while countering the negatives, such as associations with lack of exercise and obesity.	题干：What was original about the ME2? 译文：ME2的创新之处在哪里？ 本题仍延续了前面几题的特点：看似容易定位，却无法只看某句作答，而是要耐心准确阅读所定位到段落的每一句，综合理解才能找到正确答案D项：这款手持游戏解决了人们对不健康生活方式的担忧。 A项说"它包含一些为体育行业发展出来的技术"；B项说"它吸引到了那些热切想要提升自身健康状态的年轻人"；C项说"它利用了当下电子游戏有着多彩立体画面的潮流"；虽然这三个选项中都包含出现在原文中的若干词汇，然而仔细对比全句却会发现，它们都不是原文中表达的意思。

Questions 32~37

- **题目类型**：MATCHING FEATURES
- **题目解析**：本部分搭配题的难度适中，一方面因为作为选项的四个公司名称均为大写，比较容易定位；另一方面由于在第一个题型的解答过程中也都涉及了这四家公司的相关信息，考生对文章内容已经有了一定的了解。但此部分题目要求中出现了 NB 的提示。如前文的解释，这个拉丁文缩写提醒的内容是"会有某个字母选项被选用不止一次"。通常情况下，有 NB 提示的题目部分都意味着"只会有一个字母被选中两次"，但本文就是一个少数的例外：共有六道题目而只有四个选项，如果只有一个字母选项重复使用的话，显然是不够用的。

题号	定位词	文中对应点	题目解析
32	iToys	第六段最后一句：The ME2, introduced in mid-2008, catered to kids' huge desire to play video games while countering the negatives, such as associations with lack of exercise and obesity.	题干：It turned the notion that its products could have harmful effects to its own advantage. 译文：它将"认为其产品可能会产生有害影响"的理念扭转成了反而对其自身有利。 本题干对应的原文内容在解答第31题时就有所涉及，由于两题在文章中位置紧邻，考生应当还有印象，因此解答难度并不算高，答案为选项D。
33	Nike	第五段第五句：In 2006, they teamed up with technology company Apple to launch Nike+, ...	题干：It extended its offering by collaborating with another manufacturer. 译文：它通过与另一家制造商合作而拓展了自己的产品。 本题的主要考查点在于词汇认知，考生需认识extend，collaborate和manufacturer这几个在雅思阅读文章中出镜率都很高的单词，看懂题干意思，再回原文寻找到正确答案C就不是难事了。

题号	定位词	文中对应点	题目解析
34	Tesco	第四段第二句： With that in mind, Tesco, one of the world's top five retailers, introduced its Greener Living program, which demonstrates the company's commitment to protecting the environment by involving consumers in ways that produce tangible results.	题干：It implemented an incentive scheme to demonstrate its corporate social responsibility. 译文：它执行了一项鼓励性政策来展示自己的企业社会责任感。 本题与上一题的考查方式比较类似，也要求考生能准确认知implement, incentive, scheme和demonstrate这几个词，理解题干本身的意思，再回到原文寻找正确答案就是顺理成章的事情了。最直接与题目对应的原文句子结构比较复杂，详细解析可以参见"佳句赏析"中的第四句。此外，由于之前解答选择题第29题时，考生已经出于理解需要读过本段中的大部分内容，因此在这里找到对应正确选项为B应该并不困难。
35	Coach	第三段第五句： Instead, they initiated a consumer-research project which revealed that customers were eager to lift themselves and the country out of tough times.	题干：It discovered that customers had a positive attitude towards dealing with difficult circumstances. 译文：它发现顾客对处理困难处境有着积极的态度。 本题的对应句与选择题第28题的定位处前后相连，考生在之前的作答过程中其实也需阅读此句才能更安心地锁定该题答案。因此，在做到本题时难度已经降低了不少，可以比较轻松地找到正确答案应为A。
36	Nike	第五段第三句： At first glance, spending resources to incorporate elements of a seemingly irrelevant trend into one's core offerings sounds like it's hardly worthwhile.	题干：It responded to a growing lifestyle trend in an unrelated product sector. 译文：它对一项原本不相干产品领域中的不断增长的生活方式潮流做出了回应。 本题的定位处和内容考查与选择题第30题几乎没有什么差别，因此考生虽然在解答选择题时费了一些周折，多读了几句文章，但在此处又得到了耐心读懂的回报，可以准确快速地匹配到正确答案为C。
37	Coach	第三段第三、四句： The Coach brand had been a symbol of opulence and luxury for nearly 70 years, and the most obvious reaction to the downturn would have been to lower prices. However, that would have risked cheapening the brand's image.	题干：It successfully avoided having to charge its customers less for its core products. 译文：它成功地避免了在其核心产品上降低对顾客的收费。 题干本身的意思表达得很直白：避免少收顾客的钱，其实也就是"给自家商品降价"的另一种说法。前文与"产品减价"有关的唯一一家公司就是Coach，正确答案当然应该为A。

- 题目类型：MATCHING SENTENCE ENDINGS
- 题目解析：此种类型的长句子配对题比较特殊，混合了乱序搭配题和顺序填空题的特征。从名称（Complete each sentence）来看，应属填空题这个大类，所以题目大体符合行文顺序；但是将题干与选项进行匹配的做法又类似于搭配题型，不时会有某道题目出现乱序的情况。所以总体来看，并不容易定位和解答。比较好的应对策略是先按照顺序题型处理，一次利用两道题目回文章定位，将符合顺序原则的题目解答完毕后再寻找乱序题目。本篇中的三道题虽然在第39题和第40题之间出现了小小的乱序情况，但答案比较集中，并不太难寻找；只是每道题的题干都比较长，语法结构也相对复杂，因此考生需要耐心先真正读懂问题本身，再看清楚四个选项的句意，才能更准确地进行定位和匹配。

题号	定位词	文中对应点	题目解析
38	changes, impacting	第七段第一句：Once you have gained perspective on how trend-related changes in consumer opinions and behaviors impact on your category, you can determine which of our three innovation strategies to pursue.	题干：If there are any trend-related changes impacting on your category, you should 译文：如果有任何与潮流有关的变化正在影响你的产品，你应当 本题没有像前两个题型那样包含具体公司品牌，考生不妨以此为线索，绕过前面有各种大写名称作为具体案例说明的段落，向后寻找，即可更加顺利地定位到相应出题位置；再耐心对比题干和定位句，可知正确答案应为选项B：找到最合适的创新策略来运用。
39	negative	第七段最后一句：Finally, if aspects of the category clash with undesired outcomes of a trend, such as associations with unhealthy lifestyles, there is an opportunity to counteract those changes by reaffirming the core values of your category.	题干：If a current trend highlights a negative aspect of your category, you should 译文：如果当下的潮流突出了你的产品的消极不良方面，你应当 考生在完成了第31题选择题和第32题搭配题后，几乎可以直接从题干出发，跳过回原文定位的动作直接匹配答案。因为读到这个阶段，很明显文中提到"产品有不良方面"的唯一一家品牌，正是出现在第六段里、用来说明"抵制与重申"策略的玩具公司ME2产品，对应正确答案C项：利用"抵制与重申"策略来强调品牌的传统价值。
40	new focus, increasing lack of connection	第七段第三句：If analysis reveals an increasing disparity between your category and consumers' new focus, your innovations need to transcend the category to integrate the two worlds.	题干：If the consumers' new focus has an increasing lack of connection with your offering, you should 译文：如果消费者的新关注点与你的产品之间越来越缺乏关联度，你应当 本题主要考查的其实是考生的词汇认知水平：题干中的increasing lack of connection直接对应原文中的increasing disparity，只要能准确定位到此处，考生即使不认识后半句里的transcend和integrate，也能正确匹配到答案D：运用"融合与超越"策略来整合两个产品世界。

最大化地利用潮流

哈佛商学院的专家给经理人的建议

大多数经理都能分辨出当下的主要潮流。但是在一系列行业中进行研究和直接与各种公司合作的过程中，我们发现经理们往往没能意识到这些潮流正在以并不显著但却意义深远的方式影响着消费者的渴望、态度和行为。对于那些被经理们视为对他们的核心市场来说无甚关系、不怎么沾边的潮流，情况尤其如此。

许多人在他们的创新战略中会忽视潮流因素，或者采取一种"先等等看"的方式，结果被竞争者领了先。往最轻里说，这样的反应意味着损失赢利机会。最严重的情况下，这种态度会导致把行业更新迭代的机会拱手让给竞争对手而危及一家公司。本文的目的有两个：驱动经理人去更广泛发散性地思考潮流可以如何在他们的核心市场内创造新的价值主题，并针对如何使市场调查与产品研发人员更加娴熟地分析和利用潮流提供一些高水平的建议。

有一条策略，称为"浸透与扩充"，是设计一项产品或服务，保留了同类现有产品的大部分特质和功能但又添加了一些能照顾到一场主要潮流所释放的需求和欲望的新特点。可以作为佐证的一个案例是手袋中的"玻琵"（Poppy）系列，由蔻驰（Coach）公司为了应对 2008 年的经济衰退而创立。蔻驰品牌作为华丽和奢侈的象征已有近 70 年了，原本要应对这场衰退，最显而易见的反应会是降价。然而，那样做将冒着品牌形象贬值的风险。于是他们没有这样去做，而是启动了一项消费者调查项目，发现顾客都热切渴望将自己和整个国家带出这段低迷时期。利用这样的发现，蔻驰公司推出了价位较低的"玻琵手袋"系列，它们有着浓烈明亮的色彩，比传统的蔻驰产品看起来更为年轻和俏皮。创造这个子品牌使得蔻驰得以避免了全线降价行为。与许多用减价来应对经济衰退的公司不同，蔻驰将这种新的消费者心态视为了一个创新和自我更新的机遇。

这种策略的另一个例证是超市 Tesco 在面临消费者们越来越关注环境问题时所做出的反应。了解到这种情况后，Tesco，这个世界最大的五家零售商之一，推出了它的"更环保生活项目"，以此昭示这家公司对保护环境的承诺，通过一些能产生明显效果的方式让消费者参与其中。比如，Tesco 的顾客可以通过这样一些活动获得积分：反复使用购物袋，回收罐头盒和打印机墨盒，以及购买家居绝缘材料。就像其他常规购物所获得的积分那样，这些环保积分也可以兑换现金。Tesco 并没有摒弃其传统的零售供应，而是利用这些创新扩充了自己的业务，就此为它的价值定位注入了一抹环保色彩。

一项更为激进的策略是"融合与超越"。这涉及将产品的现有价值定位与能顾及一场潮流中所产生变化的新特征结合起来，共同创造出一种新奇的体验——这种体验也许能将公司带入一个全新的市场空间。乍看起来，耗费资源去将一场看似毫不相关潮流的元素融入自身的核心产品之中，好像并不值得。但是不妨参考一下耐克公司的行动：将数码革命融入了其自身的高性能运动鞋履概念之中。在 2006 年，他们与科技公司苹果联合推出了"Nike+"，一套数码运动装备，包括一个附加在跑鞋上的传感器和一部连接到用户 iPod 播放器上的无线接收装置。通过将耐克面向业余运动爱好者的原始价值定位与针对数码产品消费者的服务结合起来，"Nike+"运动装备和网络界面将这家公司从专注于运动服饰的着眼点带向了一个新的吸引其顾客的领域。

第三种策略，称为"抵制与重申"，涉及开发这样一些产品或服务，强调的是传统上就与产品序列联系在一起的价值体系，所采用的方式则能允许消费者去否定——或者至少是暂时地逃离——这场潮流中在他们看来不那么吸引人的方面。达成了这一目标的一个产品是 ME2，一款由加拿大 iToy 公司所生产的电子游戏。通过重申这款玩具产品与体育锻炼之间的关联，ME2 得以抵制掉数码游戏设备的一些被大众普遍视为消极因素的不利影响。就像其他手持游戏一样，这款设备呈现了一系列激动人心的互动式游戏，配备全色彩液晶显示屏和先进的立体画面。它的与众不同之处在于它还吸收了儿童游戏的传统运动因素：它内置了一台计步器，可以记录并用积分奖励体育运动（散步、跑步、骑自行车、滑滑板、爬楼梯）。孩子可以使用这些积分来提升玩游戏所需的各种虚拟技能。ME2 在 2008 年中面世，既迎合了儿童想玩电子游戏的极大渴望，又打消了一些负面看法，例如游戏与缺乏运动和肥胖之间的联系。

一旦你能获得这样的视角，了解到消费者理念和行为中与时尚潮流有关的那些变化会如何影响到你的产品序列，你就能确定该采用我们这三条创新策略中的哪一条了。当你产品的基本价值定位对于受到潮流影响的消费者来说仍然是有意义的，"浸透与扩充"策略将能令你复兴产品系列。如果分析显示出在你的产品与消费者的新关注点之间有了越来越大的差别，那么你的创新行为就需要超越原有的产品类型来融合两个不同的世界。最后，如果你产品的某些方面正好撞上了一场潮流中那些不令人悦纳之处，例如与不健康的生活方式之间发生了关联，也就有了一场机遇，通过重申你产品序列的核心价值来对抗这些变化。

那些影响了人们如何看待周遭世界并塑造了他们对产品和服务有何期待的潮流——无论是技术的、经济的、环境的、社会的，还是政治的——为所有公司提供了成长发展的独特机遇。

Writing

Task 1

📔 题目要求

（见《剑桥雅思官方真题集13：学术类》P51）

🖊 审题

题目翻译：下面的图表显示了1918年和2011年之间英格兰和威尔士的自有住房家庭与租赁住房家庭的比例。选取并汇报主要特征，总结信息，并在相关处进行对比。

☕ 考生作文

（见《剑桥雅思官方真题集13：学术类》P128）

🐚 参考译文

提供的柱状图描述了1918年至2011年英格兰和威尔士买房或租房的比较情况。

1918年租房家庭高达78%，然后1939年到1953年间趋向平稳。从1961年到1981年，租房家庭急剧下降到35%，然后一直保持到2001年。2011年租房家庭比例稍有增加，为38%。

在相同的年份里，自有住房家庭在1918年到1953年间从21%增长到32%。1939年至1953年比例上逐渐增长。然后在1991年攀升到69%。2001年到2011年期间，自有住房下降了，为62%。

大体上，1918年至2011年期间，租赁住房家庭和自有住房家庭都有增有减。有一年两者百分比相同，1971年均为50%。

☕ 考官点评

（见《剑桥雅思官方真题集13：学术类》P128）

🐚 参考译文

考生呈现了所有的主要内容和趋势，包括1971年自有住房家庭和租赁住房家庭的数量相同这一事实。相关论述有日期和百分比的支持，文章结尾有简短概述。组织清晰，作者依次描述了每个类别。词汇量合乎要求，但经常有拼写错误（comprssion 应为 comparison，dramaticly droped 应为 dramatically dropped，stated 应为 stayed，yeas 应为 year，leveled 应为 levelled，Genarally 应为 Generally，prectarge 应为 percentage）。不过这些错误没有明显阻碍交流。综合使用了各种语法结构，也有一些复杂句式，虽然这些复杂句并不总是正确，不过意思还是清晰的。

🌸 分析

本文得分 6.0 分，在 task achievement, coherence and cohesion, lexical resource, grammatical range and accuracy 四个方面的得分都是 6 分。具体分析如下。

写作任务完成情况

本文在内容方面为比较典型的 6 分水平。柱状图的主要内容和趋势都得到了描述：第二段涉及租房家庭在起点年份的比例，然后是变化情况：平稳、下降和略有增加，最后指出终点年份的比例。第三段描述了自有住房家庭从起点年份到最高点的变化情形，然后是最后十年的下降。最后一段为概述（overview），指出两种家庭的比例都有升有降，而且在 1971 年自有住房家庭和租赁住房家庭的数量相同。6 分作文在内容方面与 5 分作文的最大区别就在于 6 分作文有清晰的概述，并得到数据的支持。但和 7 分相比的话，概述的描述不够到位，细节的选择和描述也不够充分和精确。

概述部分可提高的地方

本文的结尾概述基本符合要求，但我们可以这样改进：From 1918 to 2001, the considerable decrease in the percentage of households renting to live was accompanied by a corresponding rise in the percentage of households in owned accommodation, while in 1971 the number of households in owned and rented accomodation was the same. After 2001, the trend was reversed. （从 1918 年到 2001 年，自有住房家庭的比例显著增加，在此期间租赁住房家庭比例相应减少，而在 1971 年两者数量相同。2001 年之后，趋势反过来了。）

细节描述不够准确的地方

第二段第三、四句，作者说"从 1961 年到 1981 年，租房家庭急剧下降到 35%，然后一直保持到 2001 年。"事实上，1981 年租房家庭比例为 40%，1991 年才是 32% 左右。

连贯与衔接

得分 6 分。文章的组织架构比较清晰，作者按照先租房家庭后自住家庭的顺序进行安排。

文章组织

事实上，描述这种横轴为年份的柱状图的时候，如果我们把租赁住房家庭和自有住房家庭每个年份的顶端连在一起的话，就相当于是两条曲线。最简单的描述方式是在主体段落分别描述租赁住房家庭和自有住房家庭各自的变化趋势，然后在结尾段对这两者进行比较。描写变化的时候，通常需要描述起点值，然后是上升或下降的趋势，有特别的地方也需要指出来，比如发生转折或保持不变的情形。结尾的比较，可以有动态的对比，例如都是上升或下降的幅度，或是两者相反的趋势，也可以有静态的对比，例如起点年份和终点年份两者数值的比较，以及两者相交的情形（即数值相同的年份）。

使用得当的衔接手段

文章除了通过年份来体现时间先后顺序之外，还使用了以下关联词和指示代词：

第二段第二句：then
第二段第四句：this
第三段第一句：the same years
第三段第三句：then
第四段第一句：generally

词汇丰富程度

本文使用的词汇量合乎任务的要求，也有尝试使用不常用词汇（less common lexical items），但拼写错误较多，虽然没有影响到交流。

使用较好的词汇表达

depict, comparison, level, dramatically, slight, decline, drop

改写的努力

第一段第一句：可以看出考生试图改写题目原文。shows 替换成 depicts，owned and rented accommodation 改写为 buying or renting houses，between...and... 改用了 from...to...，但 comprssion 拼写错误，应为 comparison。

拼写错误

第一段：comprssion 应为 comparison（比较）

第二段：leveled of 应为 levelled off（保持平稳），dramaticly droped 应为 dramatically dropped（急剧下降），stated 应为 stayed（保持）

第三段：yeas 应为 year（年），graduate 应为 gradual（逐渐）

第四段：Genarally 应为 Generally（总之），throug 应为 throughout（自始至终），prectarge 应为 percentage（百分比）

用词错误

第二段：between...to... 应为 between...and...（从……到……）

第三段的 has raise 和第四段的 has raised 应为 rose。此处不应该用及物动词 raise，而应该用不及物动词 rise。

语法多样性及准确性

语法方面，本文为 6 分。文章使用了一些复杂句式，基本传达了应有的意思，不过有一些不至于影响交流的语法错误。

句式使用方面，用得较好的复杂句式除了第一句之外，比较典型的就是 there be 结构的运用。

第四段第二句：The was a year that the were the same prectarge and it was 1971 which 50%（有一年两者百分比相同，1971 年均为 50%。）本句尝试使用了 there be 结构以及定语从句，但语法和拼写错误明显。可改为 There was a year (1971) in which the percentage of households in owned and rented accomodation was the same (50%).

Task 2

题目要求

（见《剑桥雅思官方真题集 13：学术类》P52）

审题

题目翻译：一些人认为如今我们的选择太多了。你在何等程度上同意还是不同意这一说法？

考生作文

（见《剑桥雅思官方真题集 13：学术类》P129）

参考译文

答案很复杂，因为我们生活中有很多选择，而且所有这些选择都是不同种类的。在某些情况下，我会说能够从各种各样的选择中挑选是件好事。以美食为例。每个人自己的收藏夹列表里都有不同的膳食。事实上如果你生活在大家庭里，那么要想做出每个人都喜欢的饭菜几乎是不可能的。因此我觉得能到购物中心从许多不同的食物类型里挑选真的不错。我总能找到看上去美味的东西。

当然，也有人说这有悖于进化论。他们声称以前我们每个人都务农的时候，生活很完美。我个人不同意这一点。我很高兴我能够选择最符合自己能力的工作。我的意思是没有人是一样的，我们为什么要做一样的事呢？不同种类的大学给我们机会，让我们成为我们想要成为的人。我们有选择的权利。

不过我认为有个方面我们的选择太多。这个具体领域是电视。频道有好几百个，因此你总能找到值得看的。你真的能整天坐在沙发上看电影。我觉得人们户外活动做得少了就是电视频道众多的结果。从这一点上我同意我们的选择太多了。

总之，我认为我们不能笼统地谈论选择，因为选择有不同种类。有的时候选择众多是好事，而另外的时候选择太多会有负面影响。

考官点评

（见《剑桥雅思官方真题集 13：学术类》P129）

参考译文

考生解释了他 / 她为什么既同意又不同意题目的说法，满足了"你在何等程度上同意或不同意这一说法？"的要求。他 / 她选出两个不同意的领域（食物和工作），并提供清晰的例子来支持观点，然后指出同意的一个领域（电视频道），再次提供了支持，并进行了论证。组织符合逻辑，清晰的行文推进贯穿全文。恰当地使用了一系列衔接手段（Take for example, Actually, Therefore, Naturally, However, This specific area, From this point of view, In conclusion）。词汇量足够，体现出一定的灵活性和准确性，使用不常见词汇，对语体及搭配有一定认识（Complex, list of favourites, fits...my abilities, specific area, many available channels）。只有一个拼写错误（beome），可能是笔误。语法和拼写掌握较好，使用了不同的复杂结构，大部分句子没有任何错误。

分析

本文得分 7.0 分，具体分析如下：

写作任务回应情况

本文在内容方面得分为 7 分。6 分作文的特点是文章涉及题目中的所有内容，不像 5 分作文经常会部分跑题。7 分作文和 6 分作文相比，不仅观点更加切题和明确，而且论证更加充分合理。

同意 / 不同意（agree/disagree）类型的文章一般有三种写法。这三种写法只要能针对写作任务中的问题进行回应，并展开充分论证，都可以拿高分。

写法一：Agree 并支持

第一种是同意题目观点（agree）。文章开头段明确表示同意，两到三段主体段落从不同角度论证同意的理由，结尾再次表明态度。范文参见"剑 9"的 Test 2。

写法二：Disagree 并反驳

另一种是不同意题目观点（disagree），文章主体段落可以从不同角度论证为什么不同意，也可以采用让步反驳（concession and refutation）的方法，先分析为什么持同意观点的人有一定的道理，然后提出自己的理由进行反驳。当题目中包含绝对化的表达时，这种反驳式的写法更便于展开论证。例如"剑5"的 Test 1 题目中的 every，"剑8"的 Test 3 题目中的 best，还有实考中出现过的 only 等等。

写法三：部分同意部分不同意

第三种写法是对同意与不同意两方面的观点都进行考查，提出并论证在什么条件下持同意观点，在另外什么情况下持不同意观点。这种写法如果论证充分的话会是个亮点，但对考生的能力要求较高。范文可参见"剑6"的 Test 1。该篇考生作文得分为 7.5 分，但在写作任务回应情况方面得分为 8 分。

本文采用的是第三种写法。第一段指出这个问题很难得出简单的答案，因为存在很多不同种类的选择。通过美食为例指出有时候选择多是件好事，因为更多的选择更有可能满足更多人不同的喜好。第二段以工作为例继续论证选择多的益处，可以让我们发挥自己的能力，从事自己喜爱的工作。第三段论证由于电视频道选择太多，导致人们花太多时间看电视，减少了户外活动。文章结尾总结自己的立场，指出选择多既是好事又是坏事。

连贯与衔接

本文在连贯与衔接方面得分为 7 分。文章组织符合逻辑，行文清晰。主要亮点在于各种衔接手段的使用。

连接性词组的使用

第一段第三句：Take for example（表示举例）

第四段第一句：In conclusion（表示总结）

指示代词的使用

第三段第二句：This specific area，其中 this 指代上一句话 ...there is one topic where...we have too many choices

第三段第六句：From this point of view，其中 this 指代上一句话 ...people doing less outdoor activities...

句子副词的使用

不像普通的副词通常修饰动词、形容词或其他副词，句子副词修饰整句话或句子里的分句，起到上下文承接的作用。

第一段第五句：actually 的确，事实上（口语常用，用于补充说明、强调事实或表达观点）

第一段第六句和第三段第三句：therefore 因此（比较正式，由于前一句话或前一个分句导致的结果）

第二段第一句：naturally 自然（表示正常发生，预料之中的）

第三段第一句：however 但是（表示转折，与先前不同的）

除了本文中出现的 actually, therefore, naturally, however 之外，apparently, basically, briefly, certainly, clearly, evidently, fortunately, hopefully, ideally, indeed, interestingly, ironically, predictably, presumably, regrettably, seriously, similarly, strangely, surprisingly, thankfully, theoretically, truthfully, ultimately 等都是比较常见的句子副词。

词汇丰富程度

本文在词汇方面得分为 7 分。词汇的使用体现出一定的灵活性和准确性，对语体和搭配有认知。

文中使用的不常见词汇（less common lexical items）

complex（复杂的）gastronomy（美食学）list of favourites（收藏夹列表）evolution（进化）claim（声称）back in the old days（从前，想当年）technically（严格按照事实地）fit to（适合）be meant to（有意要，打算）specific（具体的，特定的）channel（频道）literally（真正地，确实地）available（可获得的）

文中的个别拼写错误
第二段倒数第二句：beome 应为 become

语法多样性及准确性

本文在语法方面得分 7 分。语法掌握较好，使用了不同的复杂结构。复杂句式既有多样性，又有准确度。

从句（subordinate clauses）

第一段第一句：since 引导的原因状语从句

第一段第五句：if 引导的条件状语从句，that 引导的定语从句

第一段第六句：that 引导的宾语从句

第一段第七句：that 引导的定语从句

第二段第一句：who 引导的定语从句，that 引导的宾语从句

第二段第二句：that 引导的宾语从句，when 引导的时间状语从句

第二段第四句：that 引导的宾语从句，that 引导的定语从句

第二段第六句：who 引导的宾语从句

第三段第一句：where 引导的状语从句

第三段第三句：that 引导的定语从句

第三段第六句：that 引导的宾语从句

第四段第二句：while 引导的比较状语从句

形式主语（formal subject）

第一段第二句、第五句、第六句：it 引导的形式主语

第四段第二句：it 引导的形式主语

There be 句型

第二段第一句；第三段第一句

情态动词

第一段第二句和第六句，第二段第五句，第三段第六句，第四段第一句：would，委婉表达观点。

第二段第四句，第三段第四句：could，表示可能性。

分词结构（gerunds）

第三段第五句：ing 分词结构

Part 1

在第一部分，考官会介绍自己并确认考生身份，然后打开录音机/笔，报出考试名称、时间、地点等考试信息。考官接下来会围绕考生的学习、工作、住宿或其他相关话题展开提问。

🔍话题举例

Age

1. **Are you happy to be the age you are now? [Why?/Why not?]**

   Well, I'd say so. I think I used to be a lot more *awkward* when I was a teenager, but now I've *matured* a lot and I think now I have a clearer picture of the *direction* I want my life to *take*.

awkward 尴尬的，懵懂的	mature 成熟
take...direction 走向……方向	

2. **When you were a child, did you think a lot about your future? [Why?/Why not?]**

   I don't think so. I mean when you're young, you tend to *live in the present*. I think I was a happy child so I was just *blissfully oblivious of* what was *ahead*.

live in the present 活在当下	blissfully oblivious of 对……幸运地无知
ahead 在将来	

3. **Do you think you have changed as you have got older? [Why?/Why not?]**

   Well, I think we all have, haven't we? Don't we all get more *down-to-earth* and *practical* as we get older? But for me, I think I'm still *as foolish as ever*. "Stay hungry, stay foolish" — that's my *motto*!

down-to-earth [习语] 脚踏实地的	practical 现实的
as...as ever 一如既往地……	motto 座右铭

4. **What will be different about your life in the future? [Why?]**

   What will be different? Hmm... I think studying abroad would definitely *make a difference* in my life. I'll have to learn to be more independent and open-minded to survive living alone in a different culture. And of course I hope a master's degree from a *prestigious university* will help me *get ahead* in the future.

make a difference 带来（通常是积极的）改变	prestigious university 名牌大学
get ahead [习语]（在职场或生活中）占取先机	

Part 2

考官给考生一张话题卡（Cue card），考生有1分钟准备时间，并可以做笔记（考官会给考生笔和纸）。之后考生要作1~2分钟的陈述。考生讲完后，考官会就考生阐述的内容提一两个相关问题，由考生作简要回答。

> Describe a time when you started using a new technological device
> (e.g. a new computer or phone).
> You should say:
>   what device you started using
>   why you started using this device
>   how easy or difficult it was to use
> and explain how helpful this device was to you.

➡ 话题卡说明

科技是雅思口语中的常考话题，本题也体现了雅思的与时俱进，强调使用"新"科技的体验，而不是单纯描述一个科技产品。使用以下策略可以有意识地增加语法结构的丰富度。

开篇介绍	I'm not really *obsessed with electronics* so I'm not always *upgrading* my phone *to the latest model* or *trying out new gadgets*. But anyway I think I can talk about the time when I first *switched from* PC to Mac last year.
选择要点	First, I think I'll tell you about why I made this decision. Well, actually I'd been using PC for years and it was not that I didn't have anything to complain but it's just a habit. But after my old laptop *crashed* the third time my friend convinced me to try the latest MacBook.
比较对比	Now Apple has long *had a reputation for* brilliant product design, but this didn't make my first encounter with a MacBook any less exciting. I hope this doesn't sound too much like a *product placement*, but it really felt great to hold the laptop in your hands. The surface was *cool to the touch*, but it was slightly rounded so it had an organic feeling. It opened and closed all so elegantly and of course the *much-coveted* keyboard *lived up to its reputation* — it's smooth and *crisp*.
让步	Although the design really *had me at first glance*, it took me another month or so to finally get used to the *operating system* which is vastly different from Windows.
举例	For example, I still find it hard to *wrap my head around* how iTunes works. "Synchronization" is *a concept very difficult to grasp* when you have been copying and pasting files for all your life.
使用否定	But of course I wouldn't say my MacBook is not user-friendly. On the contrary, it is all very *intuitive*. Once you *get the hang of* it, you'll *feel right at home* with its use.
使用否定	I find it especially helpful because I'm also using an iPhone and and iPad. It would have been *a total pain in the neck* to transfer files across different systems. I should have bought a MacBook years ago!

重点词句

be obsessed with electronics 痴迷于电子产品
upgrade to the latest model 换到最新型号
try out new gadget 试用新的电子设备
switch from...to... 从……换到……
crash （电脑）崩溃
have a reputation for 以……闻名
product placement 植入广告
cool to the touch 触感凉凉的
much-coveted 众人艳羡的
live up to one's reputation 名副其实

crisp 手感清脆的
...had me at first glance 第一眼就吸引了我
operating system 操作系统
wrap one's head around... [习语] 理解……
grasp a concept 理解一个概念
intuitive （操作）符合直觉的
get the hang of... [习语] 熟悉，弄明白
feel right at home 感觉非常放松自信
a pain in the neck [习语] 烦人的事情

Part 3

　　第三部分：双向讨论（4~5 分钟）。考官与考生围绕由第二部分引申出来的一些比较抽象的话题进行讨论。第三部分的话题是对第二部分话题卡内容的深化和拓展。

话题举例

Technology and education

1.　**What is the best age for children to start computer lessons?**

Best age to start computer lessons... Haven't the children today already taught themselves how to use the smart phones and tablet computers? I know many parents are worried about the negative effects of all the electronics, but in my opinion, it's better to *go with the flow*. After all, technology is increasingly *an integral part of* our modern life and there are now a great number of educational apps that are great for children. Some of them are designed for *toddlers*! As far as I know, there're also apps and courses that are intended to help children become little computer programmers and they are hugely popular among *children of all ages*. So I guess my answer to this question is "*it's never too early and it's never too late!*"

go with the flow 顺应时势
toddler 蹒跚学步的孩童
It's never too early and it's never too late. 什么时候开始都可以。

an integral part of ……的重要部分
children of all ages 各年龄段的儿童

2.　**Do you think schools should use more technology to help children learn?**

That's a big yes for me. I think it's safe to say that *computer and internet literacy* has become ever so vital in our modern society. Needless to say, computer-based or even better, *tablet-based* learning activities *have a natural appeal to* children. There're other advantages, too. For example, by using a computer system, the students' learning data could be recorded and later analyzed to *provide valuable feedback* to teaching and learning. Students of different levels could also be assigned different online practice to help them learn *at their own pace*.

computer and internet literacy 对电脑和网络的了解	tablet-based 基于平板电脑的
have a natural appeal to 对……有天然的吸引力	provide valuable feedback 提供有价值的反馈
at one's own pace 根据某人自己的节奏	

3. **Do you agree or disagree that computers will replace teachers one day?**

Now this I'd say no. Although I do believe some of the teacher's responsibilities *are bound to* be replaced by computers, such as giving lectures or presentations. I mean why do you still have to *sit through* one lecture after another in class when all the great lessons on any topics are freely available online and can be watched anytime anywhere? However, I think it's highly unlikely that teachers will be gone from the classroom and every student will be looking at a screen. One reason is teaching is never one way and students *thrive on timely and constructive feedback* from the teacher and their peers. What's more, as long as we're still humans not *cyborgs*, we still crave *social interaction* and human relationships so I'd say teachers are *here to stay*.

be bound to ……一定会发生	sit through 坐着熬过
thrive on 因为……而成长，变强大	timely and constructive feedback 及时而有建设性的反馈
cyborg 半机械人	social interaction 社交
here to stay 不会消失	

Technology and society

1. **How much has technology improved how we communicate with each other?**

Well, as always, technology *cuts two ways*. Long distance communication has certainly been made easier by mobile phones and video chats, and *social networking sites* have made it possible for almost any two people in the world to connect with each other. However, people are also complaining about the *detrimental effects* of technology on their real-life relationships as family and friends now spend more time looking at their phones than looking at each other. And some say the *personalization algorithms* used by Facebook, Twitter and other News apps are creating this '*echo chamber*' where people no longer hear the opinions that are different from their own.

cut two ways 有利有弊	social networking sites 社交网站
detrimental effects 不利的影响	personalization algorithm 个性化推送
echo chamber 回音室现象（人们只听到跟自己相同的观点）	

2. **Do you agree that there are still many more major technological innovations to be made?**

That's a difficult question since I'm not really following the news in the science world closely. However, I think human beings *have a natural tendency to explore the unknown* and there're still a lot of "*new frontiers*" to explore, such as *the outer space*, *artificial intelligence* and *genetic engineering*. So I think *there's every opportunity that* more major technological innovations will be made in these fields. But I have to admit it seems *we've reached the point now where* the next big breakthrough will inevitably *pose certain ethical challenges*, like what has been described in the sci-fi series 'Black Mirror', where almost every seemingly *innocuous* innovation ends up in a terrible tragedy.

have a natural tendency to 有一种自然的倾向去……	explore the unknown 探索未知
new frontier 新的前沿	the outer space 外太空
artificial intelligence 人工智能	genetic engineering 基因工程
there's every opportunity that 非常有可能	we've reached the point where 我们发展到了这样
pose ethical challenges 带来伦理的挑战	的阶段
innocuous 无害的	

3. **Could you suggest some reasons why some people are deciding to reduce their use of technology?**
Well, this is hardly surprising *given* the widespread internet addiction and all sorts of health conditions related to our *dependency on technology*. The Hollywood director Christopher Nolan famously doesn't own a mobile phone, which hasn't been stopping him from making some of the greatest movies of all time. He believes this is good for his creativity and *time management*. I just wish I could do the same! But *then again*, there're so many technologies that we cannot simply *do away with* and I think it's *irrational* to *blame* all our problems in life *on* the development of technology. *Technophobia* will not lead us anywhere!

given... 考虑到……	dependency on technology 对科技的依赖
time management 时间管理	then again [习语] 表转折
do away with 抛弃	irrational 不理性的
blame something on 把某事怪罪到……上	technophobia 对科技的恐惧

Listening

Section 1

📖 场景介绍

一位打算搬去 Banford（地名）居住的男士，电话询问一位当地居民关于该地生活的相关事宜。这些事宜包括当地租金、交通及周边环境等。

📖 本节必背词汇

suburb	*n.* 郊区，城郊	rush hour	交通高峰期
flat	*n.* 公寓	engineering	*n.* 工程；工程学
reasonable	*adj.* 合理的；公平的	brand new	全新的，崭新的
typically	*adv.* 通常，一般	aspect	*n.* 方面
bill	*n.* 账单	dentist	*n.* 牙科医生
definitely	*adv.* 肯定地；确定地	appointment	*n.* 预约
cycle	*v.* 骑自行车	estate agent	房地产经纪人
nightmare	*n.* 噩梦	appreciate	*v.* 感谢，感激
hardly	*adv.* 几乎不，几乎没有	preferable	*adj.* 更好的，更可取的

📖 词汇拓展

art gallery	美术馆	in advance	提前
bedsit	*n.* 起居室兼卧室	opera house	歌剧院
cab	*n.* 出租车	outskirt	*n.* 郊区，市郊
dormitory	*n.* 学生宿舍	reserve	*v.* 预订，预约
downtown	*n.* 市中心	rural area	农村地区
expense	*n.* 费用，花费	studio	*n.* 单间公寓
fare	*n.* 车费；船费	underground	*n.* 地铁
hall of residence	学生宿舍	urban area	城市地区

⚙ 文本及疑难解析

1. That doesn't include bills or anything. 那个价格不包括账单和其他费用。bills 通常指：water bill（水费账单）、electricity bill（电费账单）、gas bill（燃气账单）以及 phone bill（电话账单）。

2. Are the transport links easy from where you live? 你住的地方交通便利吗?

3. Is it safe to cycle around the city? 在市里骑自行车安全吗? 本句中的 cycle 用作动词,表示"骑自行车"。

4. They're always doing engineering work and you have to take a bus to Hadham and pick up the train there, which is really slow. 他们总是(在周末)实施工程作业,你得乘坐公交车去 Hadham,然后在那儿坐火车,这个过程相当漫长。pick up 在这里意为"乘坐"。

5. Sounds like Banford's got it all. 听起来 Banford 这个地方什么都有。

⚙️ 题目解析

第 1~10 题是 Section 1 典型的笔记填空题。

1. 用 £ 符号判断答案信息为数字,原文提到的"850 英镑"即为答案。之后出现的"900 英镑"为干扰信息,需要考生适当理解原文。

2. 用 transport 定位,之后听到的交通方式 bike 即为答案。

3. 用 city centre 定位,用 limited 判断空格处所填词性为名词,之后文中出现的名词 parking 即为答案。注意原文中的 hardly(几乎没有)同义替换题干中的 limited(有限的)。

4. 用 London 和 train 联合定位,接下来听到的"30 分钟"即为答案。之后提及的"45 分钟"是指坐火车从 Banford 到 London 的时间。

5. 用 train service 来定位,题干中的 poor 在此意为"差的,不好的",对应原文中的 It's weekends that are a problem,此处 weekends 为复数,表示每一个周末。

6. 用 new 来定位,紧接着出现的 cinema 即为答案。原文中的 has only been open a couple of months 替换题干中的 opened recently。

7. 本题难度较大,原文出现的 arts centre 和 school 均为干扰信息,答案是 hospital,原文中的 one of the best in the country 对应题干中的 excellent reputation。

8. 本题有一定难度,出现了答案前置。可利用 Bridge Street 来定位,借助瞬时记忆填出答案 dentist。

9. 考生可利用介词 on 判断空格处所填信息为日期,meet 和 after 5.30pm 原文重现,可初步判断答案为 Tuesday 或 Thursday,结合原文中随后出现的 Thursday's preferable,确定答案为 Thursday。

10. 本题有一定难度,出现了答案前置,利用 opposite the station 来定位,借助瞬时记忆填出答案 café。

Section 2

🗂️ 场景介绍

一个关于如何选择适合自己的体育活动的介绍,主讲人介绍了跑步、游泳、骑自行车和瑜伽这些运动的优点,分析了人们花钱注册会员却不能坚持运动的原因。

🔤 本节必背词汇

| physical activity | 体育活动 | crowded | adj. 人多的,拥挤的 |
| put off | 推迟,拖延 | regular | adj. 定期的,有规律的 |

relatively	*adv.* 相对地	qualification	*n.* 资格，资历
incredibly	*adv.* 极端地，极其地	permanent	*adj.* 永久的
accessible	*adj.* 可接近的，可达到的	sign up	报名，注册
invest	*v.* 投资	membership	*n.* 会员，成员
attract	*v.* 吸引	determination	*n.* 决心
solitary	*adj.* 孤独的，单独的	commitment	*n.* 投入，奉献
fanatic	*n.* 入迷者，痴狂者	realistic	*adj.* 现实的，实际的
flexible	*adj.* 灵活的	treat	*n.* 款待
trainer	*n.* 教练	setback	*n.* 挫折，阻碍

📖 词汇拓展

aerobic	*adj.* 有氧的	kick-boxing	*n.* 有氧搏击操
assessment	*n.* 评估	scheme	*n.* 方案
badminton	*n.* 羽毛球	stadium	*n.* 体育馆
bowling alley	保龄球馆	stretch exercise	拉伸运动
fitness center	健身中心	subscription fee	（俱乐部）会员费
golf course	高尔夫球场	tennis court	网球场
instruction	*n.* 指示	treadmill	*n.* 跑步机
judo	*n.* 柔道	trial	*n.* 试用

⚙ 文本及疑难解析

1. Many people are put off by the idea of having to fit a visit to the gym into their busy day — you often have to go very early or late as some gyms can get very crowded. 很多人一想到要在他们繁忙的一天里安排去健身房的时间，他们就感到非常困扰，因为你需要去得非常早或者非常晚，其他时间段的健身房都非常拥挤。be put off by 意为"因……而感到烦扰、困惑或挫败"。

2. But make sure you get the right shoes — it's worth investing in a high quality pair and they don't come cheap. 但要确保有双合适的鞋，买一双高品质的鞋还是值得的，尽管这样的鞋都不便宜。

3. But don't expect to find it easy — it can be surprisingly challenging, especially for people who aren't very flexible. 但也别指望它会很容易，尤其对于那些身体不是很灵活的人来说，这有可能非常具有挑战性。surprisingly 本意为"出人意料地"，在此修饰 challenging，意为"非常"。

4. Make sure you get someone with a recognised qualification, though, or you could do yourself permanent damage. 但是要确保找一个有认证资质的人，否则你可能受到永久性的伤害。though 在这里引导让步状语从句，意为"但是"。

5. So many people waste lots of money by signing up for membership and then hardly ever go. 很多人因为注册（健身房）会员而浪费了很多钱，然后又几乎不去（健身）。hardly 是一个否定副词，意为"几乎不"。

✿ 题目解析

第 11~16 题为配对题。

11. 题干定位，but 后面引导答案，原文中的 short space of time 和 big difference 分别对应 F 选项中的 fast 和 results。

12. 题干定位，原文中提到任何人都能跑步，哪怕一开始你只能跑几米，对应 D 选项中的 fitness level unimportant（健康水平不重要）。

13. 题干定位，原文中的 at any time of year（一年中的任何时间）对应 A 选项 not dependent on season（不受季节影响）。

14. 题干定位，原文中的 fun 同义替换 B 选项 enjoyable。

15. 题干定位，原文中提到伤到自己的可能性较小，对应 C 选项 low risk of injury（受伤的风险低）。

16. 题干定位，but 后面引导答案，原文中的 encourage 替换 G 选项 motivating。

第 17~20 题为多选题。

17~18. give up 原文重现，用来定位。原文提到他们不再相信自己可以达成目标，也就是他们失去了信心，与 B 选项 loss of confidence 表达相符。also 表示并列，引导另外一个原因：需要 determination 和 hard work，也就是需要 effort，与 C 选项表达相符。

19~20. set goals 原文重现，用来定位。be realistic（现实一些）对应 B 选项中的 achievable aims（可实现的目标）。紧接着出现的 some people advise writing goals down 为干扰信息，因为后文提到采用灵活的方法会更好，比如 give yourself a really nice treat every time you reach one of your goals，这句话中的 treat 是一个名词，意为"款待，好处"，对应 D 选项中的 rewards。

Section 3

🗒 场景介绍

导师和学生 Jim 讨论一个作业设计项目。该作业项目是关于织物染色过程中各类染色剂的获取途径、使用规范以及部分染色剂的特性说明。

📖 本节必背词汇

textile	n. 纺织品；织物	fibre	n. 纤维
dye	n. 染料	nylon	n. 尼龙
fabric	n. 布料	teaspoon	n. 一茶匙（的量）；茶匙
exhibition	n. 展览会；展出	chop up	切碎，剁碎
carpet	n. 地毯	artificial	adj. 人造的，非自然形成的
botanic garden	植物园	rinse	v. 冲洗，漂洗
specialise	v. 专门研究（或从事）	wash away	冲掉
investigation	n. 调查，研究	allergic	adj. 过敏的
variable	n. 变量，可变因素	reaction	n. 反应

permanent	*adj.* 永久的，长久的	fortune	*n.* 财富，财产
shade	*n.*（色彩的）浓淡，色度	quantity	*n.* 数量，数目
shellfish	*n.* 贝类动物	precisely	*adv.* 精确地
ingest	*v.* 摄取，食入	oxide	*n.* 氧化物
presumably	*adv.* 很可能，大概	rust	*v.* 生锈
crush up	捣碎	subtle	*adj.* 不明显的；微妙的

📖 词汇拓展

cashmere	*n.* 羊绒	polyester	*n.* 涤纶，聚酯
dioxide	*n.* 二氧化物	silk	*n.* 丝绸，丝织物
elastic	*adj.* 有弹性的，有弹力的	substance	*n.* 物质，东西
fade	*v.* 使暗淡；使褪色	temporary	*adj.* 暂时的，短暂的
genuine	*adj.* 真的	texture	*n.* 质地；手感
linen	*n.* 亚麻织物	tone	*n.* 色调，明暗
pigment	*n.* 色素；颜料	toxic	*adj.* 有毒的

⚙ 文本及疑难解析

1. I've been looking at how a range of natural dyes can be used to colour fabrics like cotton and wool. 我一直在研究如何用各种不同的天然染料来给布料染色，比如棉布和毛料。

2. Yes, I'd thought it'd just be a matter of teaspoon or so of dye, and actually that wasn't the case at all. 是的，我本以为这也就是一茶匙左右染料的事，但情况根本就不是这样的。that wasn't the case 为固定表达，通常意为"情况并非如此"。

3. I'd been going to try it out on nylon, but I abandoned that idea. 我之前一直打算在尼龙上试试看，但后来放弃了这个想法。try it out 意为"尝试做某事"，结合上下文可理解为"试着用 tartrazine（酒石黄）给尼龙染色"。

4. Yes. I didn't actually make that, I didn't have time to start crushing up insects to get the red colour and anyway they're not available here, but I managed to get the dye quite easily from a website. 是。事实上我没有制作那种染料，因为我不想浪费时间去磨碎昆虫来获得这种红色染料，而且我们这儿也没有这种昆虫，但我很容易地就从一个网站上弄到了这种染料。crush up 意为"捣碎"。

5. Apparently you can allow iron to rust while it's in contact with the fabric, and that colours it. 显然，你可以通过让铁在和布料接触的时候生锈这样的方式来给布料染色。colour 在句中作动词，意为"给……染色"。

⚙ 题目解析

第 21~24 题是单选题。

21. 本题难度较大，需要考生充分理解题干中的 first inspired，即最初是什么启发了 Jim。用题干原词 choose 进行定位。文中先提到 at that exhibition of textiles，此处容易误选 A 选项，但紧接着 Jim 解释说自己一直都对和颜色有关的东西感兴趣，没有涉及 first inspired 的概念。之后文中提到 years ago，Jim 和他父母在 Turkey 度假时去了一家地毯商店，他现在还记得那些让人惊艳的颜色。这里的 years ago 对应题干中的 first，故 C 选项为正确答案。而 B 选项则为 Jim 决定继续这个项目之后做的事情，与此题无关。

22. 用 practical investigation 进行定位。Jim 开始打算只用 one type of fibre，然后决定加入其他类型的 fibre，不是仅用 one type of dye 而是使用 various types。综合以上信息，答案为 A。

23. 用题干中的 experiments 进行定位。文中虽有提到 Jim 从网站上得到了一些现成的天然染料，但并没有 dyes were widely available on the internet 的信息，故 B 选项为干扰选项。紧接着 Jim 说 I had to chop up a whole pile of it "我不得不剁了一整堆的甜菜根"，可见要制作这种染料需要大量的天然材料，对应 A 选项。

24. tartrazine 原文重现，很好定位，但由于答案句中涉及生词，会影响部分考生判断答案。答案句 It came out a great colour, but when I rinsed the material, the colour just washed away 中 rinse 的意思为 "用清水冲洗"，wash away 的意思为 "冲走"。此句可译为 "它呈现出一个很好的颜色，但当我用水清洗它的时候，颜色就被冲掉了"。这跟 B 选项表达的 "染色不够持久" 相吻合。此题也可采用排除法，C 选项提到的 "该染料在尼龙上使用时没有效果" 跟原文表达的 "我本想在尼龙上试一试，但我放弃了这个想法" 不符，故 C 不是答案。A 选项 "该染料会引起轻微的过敏反应" 并不是 Jim 的观点而是 tutor 提出的，故 A 也不是答案。

第 25~30 题是配对题。

25. 题干定位，原文中的 not permanent 替换 C 选项中的 not long-lasting。

26. 题干定位，但要选出正确答案，需要考生在一定程度上理解原文。原文提到 Jim 切 beetroot 时手上染上亮红色，给毛料染色时却是稀奶油色，结果让他非常失望，对应 F 选项 "颜色和预期不符"。

27. 题干定位，原文中的 rare（稀有的）替换 H 选项中的 not generally available（一般不常见）。

28. 题干定位，原文中的 extremely dangerous if it's ingested（如果食入会很危险）对应 D 选项中的 poisonous（有毒的）。

29. 题干定位，原文中的 it cost a fortune 是一个固定表达，意思是 "这花了很多钱"，替换 A 选项 it is expensive（这很贵）。

30. 本题有一定难度，需要考生理解原文。题干定位，原文提到事实上金属会影响布料，但并不能仅凭此句得出答案，需结合后文提到的 you can't expect to get a lot of wear out of fabrics treated in this way，这句话中的 wear 为名词，意思是 "使用量；耐用性"，整句话意为 "用金属氧化物来染色的方法会影响布料，所以你别指望用这种方法处理过的布料能用很久"，对应 E 选项 it can damage the fabric（此方法会损毁布料）。

Section 4

📖 场景介绍

一段关于 tiliqua rugosa（一种名为 "松果蜥" 的蜥蜴）的独白。该独白讲述了这种蜥蜴的形态特征、生活习性以及食性等相关信息，并介绍了科学家针对这种蜥蜴所做的追踪实验。

reptile	*n.* 爬行动物	navigation	*n.* 导航
crocodile	*n.* 鳄鱼	territory	*n.* 领土，领地
lizard	*n.* 蜥蜴	landmark	*n.* 地标
doze	*v.* 打盹儿，小睡	observation	*n.* 观察，观测
description	*n.* 描述	reveal	*v.* 揭示
distinctive	*adj.* 有特色的	mate	*v.* 交配
lining	*n.* （器官内壁的）膜	monogamous	*adj.* 一夫一妻的
jaw	*n.* 下巴，颌	hatch	*v.* 孵出
beetle	*n.* 甲壳虫	track	*v.* 追踪
snail	*n.* 蜗牛	hypothesis	*n.* 假设
predator	*n.* 猎食者	avoidance	*n.* 避免，逃避
investigate	*v.* 调查	self-preservation	*n.* 自我保护

词汇拓展

ancestor	*n.* 祖先	mammal	*n.* 哺乳动物
bait	*n.* 诱饵	mane	*n.* 鬃毛
herbivorous	*adj.* 食草的	marine	*adj.* 海洋的
carnivorous	*adj.* 食肉的	migration	*n.* 迁徙
claw	*n.* 爪子；钳子	offspring	*n.* 后代
endanger	*v.* 使遭受危险	ostrich	*n.* 鸵鸟
extinction	*n.* 灭绝，绝种	parasite	*n.* 寄生虫
fin	*n.* 鱼鳍	penguin	*n.* 企鹅
genetic	*adj.* 基因的，遗传的	prey	*v.* 捕食
hoof	*n.* 蹄	scale	*n.* 鳞
intact	*adj.* 完整的	vegetation	*n.* 植被

文本及疑难解析

1. Today, I'd like us to have a look at another reptile — the lizard — and in particular, at some studies that have been done on a particular type of lizard whose Latin name is tiliqua rugosa. 今天，让我们来了解一下另一种爬行动物——蜥蜴，特别是来了解一下关于一种拉丁名为 tiliqua rugosa（松果蜥）的特殊类型蜥蜴的研究。

2. Actually, another threat to their survival isn't a predator at all, but is man-made — quite a large number of sleepy lizards are killed by cars when they're trying to cross highways. 事实上，对他们的生存来说，另

一种威胁根本不是猎食者，而是人为的：相当多的松果蜥在横穿高速公路时被车撞死。

3. It could be that it's to do with protecting their young — you'd expect them to have a much better chance of survival if they have both parents around. But in fact... 这可能是为了保护他们的幼体，你可能会以为，如果父母都在身边，这些幼体会有更好的生存机会。但事实上……

4. Another suggestion's based on the observation that male lizards in monogamous relationships tend to be bigger and stronger than other males. 另一个推测是基于一项观察：在一夫一妻制关系中的雄性蜥蜴往往比其他的雄性蜥蜴更大更强壮。

5. One surprising thing we discovered from this is that there were far fewer meetings between lizards than we expected — it seems that they were actually trying to avoid one another. 我们发现了一件令人惊奇的事：蜥蜴之间的碰面次数远比我们想象的要少得多，看起来他们是在试图回避对方。

✿ 题目解析

31~40 题为提纲填空题。

31. 利用副标题 description 和题干中的 Western and South Australia 以及 brown 联合定位，本题考点为答案前置，需要考生提前通过 blue 预测空格所填词性为名词，结合原文 the colour of their tongue, which is dark blue，得出本题答案为 tongue。

32. 原文中的 much bigger 替换题干中的 relatively large，题干中的 diet 原文重现，以此定位，此题容易误填 insects 和 animals，需注意题干中的 mainly 表示"大部分"，对应原文中的 mostly，故答案为 plants。

33. 利用题干中的原词 predators 和 large birds 进行定位，借助 birds 和空格的并列关系判断答案为名词，结合原文 but nowadays they're more likely to be caught and killed by snakes，snakes 是唯一符合要求的名词。

34. 此题较难，因定位词 navigation study 与答案相距较远且题目改写力度较大，考生需适当理解原文才能正确作答，原文说只要能看到天空，它们就能找到回家的路，也就是说它们用天空导航。后文的 landmarks 为干扰信息。

35. 副标题 observations in the wild 原文重现，用来定位，原文中的 reveal 替换题干中的 show，same 原词重现，直接引导答案 partner。

36. 用 possible reasons, survival 和 noted 联合定位，注意空格前的 little 在此意为"很少的"，对应原文中的 hardly，hardly 之后的 contact 即为答案。

37. 题干中的 provide 在原文中被替换为 give，答案 protection 随之出现。

38. 用副标题中的 tracking 和题干中的 GPS systems 进行定位，考生需要理解原文中的 fixed（固定）和题干中的 attached to（把……固定，把……附在）表达相同含义才能填出正确答案 tails。

39. 本题用 location 定位，原文中 how many 表达的含义即为题干中的 number，之后的 steps 为答案。

40. 题干中 trying to avoid one another 原文重现，用来定位，但题目改写力度较大，需要考生适当理解原文。原文说它们试图回避对方，可能是因为如果不回避的话，会造成严重的伤害，所以回避其实就是为了减少这种伤害的可能性，对应题目中的 reduce chances of injuries。

Reading

Reading Passage 1

📖 篇章结构

体裁	说明文
主题	椰子树的特点、作用及起源
结构	第一段：椰子在西方世界已经非常常见
	第二段：介绍椰子树各个部分的用途
	第三段：椰子果实的结构和作用
	第四段：椰汁的生物特性和作用
	第五段：椰子能在海中漂浮并在沿岸生长
	第六段：关于椰子起源的讨论持续了很久

🌐 解题地图

难度系数： ★★★

解题顺序： TABLE COMPLETION (1~8) → TRUE/FALSE/NOT GIVEN (9~13)

友情提示： 本文针对椰子树的生物学特性和起源等内容进行描述，全文以事实信息为主，在最后一部分，探讨了关于椰子发源地的不同说法，以及各自存在的问题。题型方面前 8 道题是 TABLE COMPLETION，主要针对椰子不同部分的特征和作用进行出题，后 5 道题为 TRUE/FALSE/NOT GIVEN，出题针对的段落相对比较靠后，解题时按照顺序进行定位即可。

🔤 必背词汇

1. endangered *adj.* 濒临灭绝的

   14 per cent of primate species are highly *endangered*. 14% 的灵长类物种处于高度濒危状态。

   This island is maintained as a sanctuary for *endangered* species. 那个岛继续作为濒危物种的保护区。

2. numerous *adj.* 许多的，很多的

   He has been late on *numerous* occasions. 他已经迟到过无数次了。

   The advantages of this system are too *numerous* to mention. 这套系统的好处不胜枚举。

3. initially *adv.* 最初，首先

   Forecasters say the gales may not be as bad as they *initially* predicted.
   预报员说大风也许不像他们起初预报的那么猛烈。

   Feathers *initially* developed from insect scales. 羽毛最初由昆虫的翅瓣演化而来。

4. solidify *v.* 巩固，凝固

   They *solidified* their position as Britain's top band. 他们巩固了自己作为英国顶尖乐队的地位。

   Opinion on this question began to *solidify*. 对这个问题的意见开始具体化了。

5. tolerate *v.* 忍受

   Few plants will *tolerate* sudden changes in temperature. 很少植物经受得住气温的突然变化。

   She can no longer *tolerate* the position that she's in. 她再也受不了自己的处境了。

6. origin *n.* 起源，开端

   There are some areas of wetland which are of ancient *origin*. 有一些湿地在古代就形成了。

   The *origin* of the word remains obscure. 该词的来源尚不清楚。

7. diversity *n.* 多样性，差异

   There is a need for greater *diversity* and choice in education.

   教育方面需要更加多元化和更大的选择性。

   Few countries have as rich a *diversity* of habitat as South Africa.

   几乎没有哪个国家像南非那样拥有如此多样化的动植物栖息地。

8. disperse *v.* 分散，传播

   The seeds are *dispersed* by the wind. 这些种子由风传播。

   The fog began to *disperse*. 雾开始散了。

🆎 认知词汇

coconut	*n.* 椰子	prominent	*adj.* 突出的
exotic	*adj.* 异国的；外来的	nutrient	*n.* 营养物，滋养物
merchant	*n.* 商人	cosmetics	*n.* 化妆品，装饰品
tropical	*adj.* 热带的	derivative	*n.* 衍生物，派生物
clichés	*n.* 陈词滥调	colonizer	*n.* 殖民者
envisage	*v.* 想象；面对	viable	*adj.* 能存活的，能生存的
slender	*adj.* 细长的，苗条的	indefinitely	*adv.* 不确定地，无限期地
timber	*n.* 木材，木料	germinate	*v.* 发芽，生长
replacement	*n.* 更换，代替	embryo	*n.* 胚胎，胚芽；初期
surmount	*v.* 越过；攀登	moisture	*n.* 水分；湿度
rosette	*n.* 莲座丛；玫瑰形饰物	dramatically	*adv.* 显著地，引人注目地
vein	*n.* 叶脉；血管	indigenous	*adj.* 本土的；国产的
waterproof	*adj.* 防水的，不透水的	intriguing	*adj.* 有趣的，迷人的
fibrous	*adj.* 纤维的，纤维状的	coral	*n.* 珊瑚 *adj.* 珊瑚的
manufacture	*v.* 制造，加工		

🌸 佳句赏析

1. Initially, the endosperm is a sweetish liquid, coconut water, which is enjoyed as a drink, but also provides the hormones which encourage other plants to grow more rapidly and produce higher yields.

   - 参考译文：起初，胚乳是甜味的液体——椰汁，经常被作为一种饮品，并且提供促进其他植物更快生长并带来更高产量的激素。

   - 语言点：本句中主句为 the endosperm is a sweetish liquid，之后 coconut water 作为同位语出现，与 a sweetish liquid 是同一个事物，定语从句 which is enjoyed as a drink 对其进行修饰，之后出现

并列结构 but also provides the hormones，此处省略了主语，并在后面的定语从句 which encourage other plants to grow more rapidly and produce higher yields 中继续进行解释。虽然修饰内容较长，但由于本身不存在被修饰部分的太多变化，因此阅读时认清句子结构，顺序阅读即可。

2. Literally cast onto desert island shores, with little more than sand to grow in and exposed to the full glare of the tropical sun, coconut seeds are able to germinate and root.
   - 参考译文：被顺利播撒到荒岛沿岸后，仅仅有沙地可以生长，并且暴露在热带阳光的完全照射下，椰树的种子依然可以生根发芽。
   - 语言点：本句首先出现三个并列的修饰成分，首先是 Literally cast onto desert island shores，之后是 with little more than sand to grow in，以及 exposed to the full glare of the tropical sun，然后出现主句 coconut seeds are able to germinate and root。本句主语为 coconut seeds，阅读时需要注意类似的、主语出现前有大量修饰结构的情况，并习惯在中文正常语序和英文的不同描述结构间转换。

3. 16th century trade and human migration patterns reveal that Arab traders and European sailors are likely to have moved coconuts from South and Southeast Asia to Africa and then across the Atlantic to the east coast of America.
   - 参考译文：16 世纪的贸易和人口迁移模式表明阿拉伯商人和欧洲水手们可能将椰子从亚洲南部或东南部带往非洲，之后穿过大西洋到达美洲东岸。
   - 语言点：本句主语为 16th century trade and human migration patterns，谓语动词为 reveal，之后的内容都是宾语从句部分，由两个分句组成，第一个是 Arab traders and European sailors are likely to have moved coconuts from South and Southeast Asia to Africa，第二个是 then across the Atlantic to the east coast of America，这一结构可以很好地帮助考生理解椰子在不同地方出现的过程，类似较长的描述性语言，进行拆分后，分别理解即可。

❀ 试题解析

Questions 1~8

- 题目类型：TABLE COMPLETION
- 题目解析：本部分题目针对椰子树各个部分的功能进行提问，可以通过表格第一列中的 trunk, leaves, flowers, fruits，结合对它们的描述，在原文中找到对应位置。

题号	定位词	文中对应点	题目解析
1	trunk, up to 30 metres	第二段第三、四句：The coconut palm has a smooth, slender, grey trunk, up to 30 metres tall. This is an important source of timber for building houses, and is increasingly being used as a replacement for endangered hardwoods in the furniture construction industry.	本题针对椰子树树干的作用提问，文中第二段第三句提到 a smooth, slender, grey trunk, up to 30 metres tall，这一描述与题目信息一致，而下一句开头的 This 指代 trunk，本句是由 and 连接的并列句，前半句对应题目中的 timber for houses，而后半句说到作为家具建造行业中木头的替代品，因此本题答案为 furniture。此外，由于本句中出现了 furniture construction industry 这一名词结构，在选择答案的时候需要注意理解句子含义。

题号	定位词	文中对应点	题目解析
2	flower, sap, drink	第二段最后一句： The flower stems may be tapped for their sap to produce a drink, and the sap can also be reduced by boiling to produce a type of sugar used for cooking.	本题针对椰子树的 flower 进行提问，首先在文中第二段最后一句找到这个单词，而 sap 和 drink 也出现在本句中。由于句中出现了 and 和 also，因此可以将句子与题目中的并列句进行对应，可以看到本题考查的是文中 be reduced by boiling to produce a type of sugar 这一部分，因此将句子与题目对应后，本题答案为 sugar。
3	middle layer	第三段第三句： The thick fibrous middle layer produces coconut fibre, 'coir', which has numerous uses and is particularly important in manufacturing ropes.	文中第三段说到果实的外壁分为三层，而本题是对中间层 middle layer 的考查，这一描述出现在文章第三段第三句，此处 which 引导的定语从句说明了其在 manufacturing ropes 方面非常重要，考虑到字数要求及空格前的 for 为介词，本题答案为 ropes。
4	inner layer	第三段第五句： An important product obtained from the shell is charcoal, which is widely used in various industries as well as in the home as a cooking fuel.	文章提到 inner layer 是在第三段第四句，也就是 the woody innermost layer, the shell，而本段四、五、六三句话都是针对 inner layer 的描述，其中第五句说到 an important product obtained from the shell is charcoal，可见 charcoal 是由 inner layer 获得，含义与题目中的 a source of 一致，因此本题答案为 charcoal。
5	inner layer, when halved	第三段第六句： When broken in half, the shells are also used as bowls in many parts of Asia.	题目中的 when halved 与第三段第六句开头的 when broken in half 一致，而本句中说到 the shells are also used as bowls in many parts of Asia，通过将本句与题目对应，结合词性判断，本题答案为 bowls。
6	coconut water, other plants	第四段第二句： Initially, the endosperm is a sweetish liquid, coconut water, which is enjoyed as a drink, but also provides the hormones which encourage other plants to grow more rapidly and produce higher yields.	关于 fruit 中的 coconut water 部分出现在文中第四段第二句，本句中 which is enjoyed as a drink 与题目中 a drink 一致，因此将本句中 provides the hormones which encourage other plants to grow more rapidly and produce higher yields 与题目中 for other plants 对应，同时在原文定位处选择适合的名词，因此本题答案为 hormones。
7	coconut flesh, oil and milk for cooking	第四段第四句： Dried coconut flesh, 'copra', is made into coconut oil and coconut milk, which are widely used in cooking in different parts of the world, as well as in cosmetics.	本题针对 coconut flesh 提问，首先在原文第四段中找到 brilliant white, fat-rich, edible flesh or meat，之后在其用途中，可以看到 coconut oil 和 coconut milk，这与题目中的表述是一致的，之后通过本段第四句的并列结构 as well as 进行定位查找，因此本题答案为 cosmetics。

题号	定位词	文中对应点	题目解析
8	glycerine	第四段第五句： A derivative of coconut fat, glycerine, acquired strategic importance in a quite different sphere, as Alfred Nobel introduced the world to his nitroglycerine-based invention: dynamite.	本题依然是针对 coconut flesh 的提问，定位词 glycerine 出现在文中第四段第五句，题目中问这是什么东西的 ingredient，而本句中说到了其衍生物获得了重要的地位，根据本句含义结合题目要求填写名词进行判断，本题答案为 dynamite。

Questions 9~13

- 题目类型：TRUE/FALSE/NOT GIVEN
- 题目解析：

9. Coconut seeds need shade in order to germinate.

参考译文	椰树种子需要树荫以生根发芽。
定位词	coconut seeds, germinate
解题关键点	needs shade
文中对应点	第五段第三句：Literally cast onto desert island shores, with little more than sand to grow in and exposed to the full glare of the tropical sun, coconut seeds are able to germinate and root. 本题说到关于椰子种子的问题，这一内容出现在文中第五段，本段开头说到叶子是 great maritime voyagers and costal colonizers of the plant world，之后开始说明其生物学方面的特点。第三句说到当 coconut seed 暴露在 the full glare of the tropical sun 的情况下，依然能够 germinate and root，说明并不需要树荫，这与题目中的表述是相反的。因此本题答案为 FALSE。

10. Coconuts were probably transported to Asia from America in the 16th century.

参考译文	椰子或许是在 16 世纪从美洲到达亚洲的。
定位词	coconuts, the 16th century
解题关键点	transported to Asia from America
文中对应点	第六段第二、三句：There were no coconut palms in West Africa, the Caribbean or the east coast of the Americas before the voyages of the European explorers Vasco da Gama and Columbus in the late 15th and early 16th centuries. 16th century trade and human migration patterns reveal that Arab traders and European sailors are likely to have moved coconuts from South and Southeast Asia to Africa and then across the Atlantic to the east coast of America. 本题涉及椰子的起源和生长地点的变化情况，文中第六段对这一话题进行了集中讨论，其中第二句说到在达伽马和哥伦布的航行之前，there were no coconut palms in West Africa, the Caribbean or the east coast of the Americas，也就是说在这个时间点上，美洲东岸是没有椰子树的，而之后一句又说到椰子是 from South and Southeast Asia to Africa and then across the Atlantic to the east coast of America，也就是从亚洲带往美洲，而题目中 transported to Asia from America 的表述与这一内容恰恰相反。因此本题答案为 FALSE。

11. Coconuts found on the west coast of America were a different type from those found on the east coast.

参考译文	美洲西岸发现的椰子与东岸发现的椰子属于不同种类。
定位词	coconuts found on the west coast of America
解题关键点	a different type, those found on the east coast
文中对应点	第六段第四至八句：But the origin of coconuts discovered along the west coast of America by 16th century sailors has been the subject of centuries of discussion. Two diametrically opposed origins have been proposed: that they came from Asia, or that they were native to America. Both suggestions have problems. In Asia, there is a large degree of coconut diversity and evidence of millennia of human use — but there are no relatives growing in the wild. In America, there are close coconut relatives, but no evidence that coconuts are indigenous. 本题说到美洲西岸的椰子，而这也是第六段第四句说到的 the subject of centuries of discussion，并在之后提出了两种不同的猜想，但是通读之后的几句话，对于美洲西岸的椰子与东岸的椰子是否属于不同品种，并没有提及。因此本题答案为 NOT GIVEN。

12. All the coconuts found in Asia are cultivated varieties.

参考译文	所有亚洲发现的椰子都是种植的变种。
定位词	the coconuts found in Asia
解题关键点	cultivated varieties
文中对应点	第六段第七句：In Asia, there is a large degree of coconut diversity and evidence of millennia of human use — but there are no relatives growing in the wild. 本题问到 the coconuts found in Asia，关于其描述出现在文中第六段第七句，文中提到 a large degree of coconut diversity and evidence of millennia of human use，同时 no relatives growing in the wild，也就是说这里的椰子没有野生的亲缘品种，题目中的 cultivated varieties 与本句信息一致。因此本题答案为 TRUE。

13. Coconuts are cultivated in different ways in America and the Pacific.

参考译文	椰子在美洲和太平洋地区以不同的方式被种植。
定位词	in America and the Pacific
解题关键点	cultivated in different ways
文中对应点	第六段第八、九句：In America, there are close coconut relatives, but no evidence that coconuts are indigenous. These problems have led to the intriguing suggestion that coconuts originated on coral islands in the Pacific and were dispersed from there. 第六段后半部分对亚洲和美洲两个起源地进行了讨论，但是在整个讨论中，对于 America 和 the Pacific 的椰子是否属于同一种类，并没有进行比较。因此本题答案为 NOT GIVEN。

参考译文

——— 椰子树 ———

一千年来，对生活在波利尼西亚和亚洲的人们来说，椰子扮演着极为重要的角色。但在西方世界，椰子一直属于非同一般的外来物种，有时会非常稀缺。13 世纪晚期，意大利商人旅行家马可波罗似乎在南亚看到了椰子，在约翰·曼德维尔 14 世纪中叶的旅行作品中也提到了"印度的巨大坚果"。如今，棕桐遮蔽的热带海滩形象在西方已成为常用的手法，用以推销度假、巧克力棒、起泡饮料，甚至爱情故事。

通常，我们会把椰子想象成棕色的炮弹形状，打开之后，会有甜味的白色果肉。但我们只看到了这种水果的一部分，并没有看到生长它们的那株植物。椰子树有光滑细长的灰色树干，它们可以长到 30 米高。这是一种用来建造房屋的重要木材来源，并且越来越多地被用于替换家具建造领域中濒临灭绝的硬木。树干被莲座状的树叶围绕，每一片最长可以长到六米。这些叶子中心有坚硬的叶脉，在世界上很多地方，在去除叶子的绿色部分后，它们被用作刷子。未成熟的椰花紧密地聚集在树干顶端的叶子中。敲打花梗得到的汁液可以用来生产饮品，也可以通过煮沸汁液进行浓缩来生产用于烹饪的食糖。

椰子树每年可以产生多达七十多枚果实，每个重达一公斤以上。椰果的外壁分为三层：不透水的外层、纤维状的中层、坚硬的内层。厚实的纤维中层产生"椰壳纤维"，它具有许多用途，在制造绳索方面尤为重要。木质的最内层椰壳，和其三个突出的"眼睛"围绕着种子。以椰壳为原料的重要产物是木炭，它被广泛用于各种产业中，也被作为家用的烹饪燃料。在亚洲的很多地方，椰壳切成两半后也被当作碗使用。

椰壳内是发育中的种子需要的营养物质（胚乳）。起初，胚乳是甜味的液体——椰汁，经常被作为一种饮品，并且提供促进其他植物更快生长并带来更高产量的激素。随着果实成熟，椰汁逐渐凝固以形成亮白的、富含脂肪的、可食用的果肉。干椰子果肉可以用来制作椰子油或椰奶，并在世界上不同地方被广泛用于烹饪和制作化妆品。随着阿尔弗雷德·诺贝尔为世界带来了基于硝化甘油的发明：炸药，椰子脂的衍生物——丙三醇——在一个截然不同的领域获得了战略性的重要地位。

椰子的生物特性使其成为植物世界伟大的航海者以及沿海的殖民者。巨大且富含能量的果实可以在水中漂浮并克服盐的影响，但并不是可以无限存活的；研究表明在海上漂浮大约 110 天之后，它们不再能够生长。被顺利播撒到荒岛沿岸后，仅仅有沙地可以生长，并且暴露在热带阳光的完全照射下，椰树的种子依然可以生根发芽。种子中随胚乳凝固产生的气穴可以保护胚芽。此外，帮助椰子在航行中漂浮的纤维果实壁贮存了水分，这些水分可以在椰子的幼苗开始生长时用来滋养根系。

关于椰子起源地的学术讨论已经进行了几个世纪。在欧洲探险者达·伽马和哥伦布 15 世纪末和 16 世纪初的航行之前，非洲西部、加勒比海或者美洲东岸都没有椰子树。16 世纪的贸易和人口迁移模式表明阿拉伯商人和欧洲水手们可能将椰子从亚洲南部或东南部带往非洲，之后穿过大西洋到达美洲东岸。但是 16 世纪水手们沿着美洲西岸发现的椰子源自何处成为了几个世纪以来讨论的主题。关于发源地，人们提出了两个截然不同的说法：它们来自亚洲，以及它们来自美洲本土。两种说法都存在问题。在亚洲，椰子的多样性程度很高，并且有千年来人类使用的证据——但并不存在野生的亲缘植物。在美洲，有很相近的椰子亲缘植物，但没有证据表明椰子来本土。这些问题导致了有趣的推断，即椰子发源自太平洋中的珊瑚岛并从那里散播到世界各地。

Reading Passage 2

📖 篇章结构

体裁	论说文
主题	儿语在婴儿大脑发展中的作用
结构	A 段：人们认为儿语对儿童大脑发展有帮助
	B 段：较早接触语言有利于儿童大脑发展
	C 段：父亲和母亲对儿童的说话方式不同
	D 段：儿语和一对一沟通都能够促进儿童学习语言
	E 段：儿语更能够吸引儿童的关注
	F 段：儿语可以有效促进婴儿的大脑激活

🌐 解题地图

难度系数： ★★★★

解题顺序： MATCHING (14~17) → SUMMARY (18~23) → MATCHING (24~26)

友情提示： 本文主要探讨儿语对儿童大脑发展的作用，文中出现较多与实验有关的描述，需要在阅读时清楚读懂每个实验的目的、过程、结果，以及之后对实验结果进行的解释和推断。解题时，尽管第一组题目是 MATCHING 的乱序题，但在这类 MATCHING FEATURES 的题目中，人名本身就是可以帮助定位的顺序出题内容，因此可以通过从选项入手的方式在原文中进行查找，而最后一组 MATCHING INFORMATION 是乱序题，在最后完成即可。

🔖 必背词汇

1. boost *v./n.* 推动，促进；增加

   The movie helped *boost* her screen career. 那部电影有助于她的银幕生涯的发展。

   It did give me a *boost* to win such a big event. 赢得如此重大的比赛确实使我信心倍增。

2. impact *n.* 影响，效果 *v.* 影响

   Her speech made a profound *impact* on everyone. 她的讲话对每个人都有深远的影响。

   All colour fades — especially under the *impact* of direct sunlight.

   所有颜色都会褪色——尤其是在阳光直射的影响下。

3. hypothesis *n.* 假设

   It would be pointless to engage in *hypothesis* before we have the facts.

   在我们还没掌握事实的情况下暗猜是毫无意义的。

   Her study is based on the *hypothesis* that language simplification is possible.

   她的研究基于语言可以简化这样一个假说。

4. standard *n.* 标准；水准 *adj.* 标准的

The *standard* of his living today is on the edge of subsistence. 他现在几乎快要无法维持生计。

We aim to maintain high *standards* of customer care. 我们的宗旨是始终以高标准为顾客服务。

5. auditory *adj.* 听觉的

Finally he overcame the *auditory* difficulties by three years' efforts.

通过三年的努力，他最终克服了听觉上的困难。

It's an artificial device which stimulates the *auditory* areas of the brain.

这是刺激大脑中听觉区域的人造装置。

6. property *n.* 性质，特性；财产

Be careful not to damage other people's *property*. 小心不要损坏别人的财物。

A radio signal has both electrical and magnetic *properties*. 无线电信号具有电、磁双重属性。

7. speculate *v.* 推测，推断

We all *speculated* about the reasons for her resignation. 我们大家都推测过她辞职的原因。

People *speculate* about virtuality systems, but we're already working on it.

人们才开始构思虚拟系统，我们已经在进行开发了。

8. uncover *v.* 发现；揭开

We ought to look below the surface of things and then *uncover* the essence of them.

我们应该透过事物的表面进行观察，然后揭示其本质。

Auditors said they had *uncovered* evidence of fraud. 审计人员说他们已经发现了欺诈的证据。

认知词汇

high-pitched	*adj.* 声调高的，声音尖锐的
exaggerated	*adj.* 夸张的
repetitious	*adj.* 重复的
fascination	*n.* 魅力，吸引力
pregnant	*adj.* 怀孕的
infant	*n./adj.* 婴儿（的）；幼儿（的）
gather	*v.* 收集，聚集
bilingual	*adj.* 双语的
prioritize	*v.* 区分优先次序
absurd	*adj.* 荒谬的，夸张的
speech-recognition	语音识别，语言识别
frequency	*n.* 频率
repertoire	*n.* 全部技能；全部节目
conversation	*n.* 交谈，对话
audio-recording	录音

babble	*v.* 呀呀学语，含糊不清地说
frequent	*adj.* 频繁的，时常发生的
socioeconomic	*adj.* 社会经济学的
context	*n.* 语境；上下文
universal	*adj.* 普遍的；通用的
synthesize	*v.* 合成；综合
induce	*v.* 诱导，引起
reaction	*n.* 反应
approximate	*v.* 近似，接近
theorize	*v.* 建立理论，推断
launch	*v.* 开始，发起；发射
syllable	*n.* 音节
activation	*n.* 激活
prompt	*v.* 促进；激发
recognize	*v.* 认出，识别

✿佳句赏析

1. Mark VanDam of Washington State University at Spokane and colleagues equipped parents with recording devices and speech-recognition software to study the way they interacted with their youngsters during a normal day.

   - 参考译文：斯波坎华盛顿州立大学的 Mark Vandam 和他的同事们给家长们配备了录音设备和语音识别软件，以研究他们在日常一天中与孩子们的交流方式。

   - 语言点：类似的实验内容描述，需要关注实验的目的、过程、结果，以及对结果的解释和推断。本句中主语 Mark VanDam of Washington State University at Spokane and colleagues 是进行实验的人，实验的基本操作是 equipped parents with recording devices and speech-recognition software，其中 recording devices 和 speech-recognition software 都属于比较常见的实验设备，之后的实验目的是 to study the way they interacted with their youngsters during a normal day，研究家长在日常一天中与孩子们的交流方式。

2. 'Finding activation in motor areas of the brain when infants are simply listening is significant, because it means the baby brain is engaged in trying to talk back right from the start, and suggests that seven-month-olds' brains are already trying to figure out how to make the right movements that will produce words,' says co-author Patricia Kuhl.

   - 参考译文："当婴儿确实是在听些什么的时候，在大脑的运动区发现激活非常重要，因为这意味着婴儿的大脑从一开始就参与交流，并表明 7 个月儿童的大脑已经在试图弄清如何做出可以产生话语的正确活动"，共同研究的 Patricia Kuhl 说。

   - 语言点：本句主句为 Finding activation in motor areas of the brain when infants are simply listening is significant，其中主语部分相对较长，并且有 when 引导的状语从句，阅读时需要首先认清这一主系表结构，之后 because 引导的分句由两个部分构成，一部分是 it means 之后的结论，另一部分是 and suggests that 之后的结论。雅思考试中长句不会特别多，如果出现了类似情况，按照句子结构进行拆分，找到每个分句进行阅读，并认清它们之间的关系就可以。

3. Another interesting finding was that while the seven-month-olds responded to all speech sounds regardless of language, the brains of the older infants worked harder at the motor activations of non-native sounds compared to native sounds.

   - 参考译文：另一项有趣的发现是，无论何种语言，7 个月大的儿童对所有声音都能作出反应，然而相比母语声音，年龄较大的婴儿的大脑在试图做出非母语声音的运动激活时需要更加努力。

   - 语言点：本句是针对研究发现进行的描述，由 Another interesting finding was that 可以判断此处为典型的表语从句，其中主句为 the brains of the older infants worked harder at the motor activation of non-native sounds compared to native sounds，前面的部分是 while 引导的让步状语从句：while the seven-month-olds responded to all speech sounds regardless of language。

✿试题解析

Questions 14~17

   - **题目类型**：MATCHING

- 题目解析：

题号	解题关键词	题目解析
14	individual attention	题目：the importance of adults giving babies individual attention when talking to them 译文：成年人与儿童谈话时给予他们个体关注的重要性 关于给予儿童个体关注的问题，在文中D段有所涉及，本段倒数第二句说到We also found that it really matters whether you use baby talk in a one-on-one context，之后在本段最后一句中，也说到了这样做的重要性：The more parents use baby talk one-on-one, the more babies babble, and the more they babble, the more words they produce later in life，根据这一观点，对应相关的人名即可。本题答案为B。
15	what babies hear, their own efforts to create speech	题目：the connection between what babies hear and their own efforts to create speech 译文：儿童听到的声音与他们努力试图主动说话之间的联系 关于儿童听到的声音与他们自身试图说话的话题出现在文章最后一段，本段主要通过记录大脑激活的情况，来判断儿童语言能力的发展，其中第三句的结论性语言说到The results suggest that listening to baby talk prompts infant brains to start practicing their language skills，也就是说听到baby talk会促进儿童主动练习说话，而之后的试验情况也是对这一结论的说明，因此这部分信息与题目表述一致，找到对应的人名Patricia Kuhl即可确定答案。本题答案为C。
16	two parents, speaking in a different way	题目：the advantage for the baby of having two parents each speaking in a different way 译文：父母二人以不同的方式讲话对婴儿的好处 关于父母二人以不同方式说话的内容出现在文中C段，针对父母亲说话方式的不同，以及这两种说话方式在儿童成长中所扮演的不同角色进行了描述，而这种情况是为了让儿童获得a wider repertoire of kinds of speech to practice，在内容确定后，在原文中找到本段主要的研究者Mark VanDam，然后对应选项即可。本题答案为A。
17	baby talk, vocalising	题目：the connection between the amount of baby talk babies hear and how much vocalising they do themselves 译文：婴儿听到的儿语的数量与他们自身发声的数量之间的联系 关于婴儿听到儿语的数量与发声的数量之间的关系出现在文章D段，其中第二句说到The study found that the more baby talk parents used, the more their youngsters began to babble，并在之后进一步解释到they found that frequent baby talk had dramatically boosted vocabulary，该表述与题目信息一致，之后寻找作出这一表达的研究者名字即可。本题答案为B。

Questions 18~23

- 题目类型：SUMMARY
- 题目解析：

题号	定位词	文中对应点	题目解析
18	Washington State University	C 段第二句： Mark VanDam of Washington State University at Spokane and colleagues equipped parents with recording devices and speech-recognition software to study the way they interacted with their youngsters during a normal day.	根据题目中的Washington State University可以定位至原文C段第二句。题目中的并列结构，对应原文中recording devices和speech-recognition software，题目中specialised computer programs是原文中speech-recognition software的同义替换，而之后的研究目的是一致的，因此本空与recording devices对应。本题答案为recording devices。
19	tended not to modify their ordinary speech patterns	C 段第三、四、五句： 'We found that moms do exactly what you'd expect and what's been described many times over,' VanDam explains. 'But we found that dads aren't doing the same thing. Dads didn't raise their pitch or fundamental frequency when they talked to kids.'	本题问到关于 speech patterns 的问题，原文C 段对这一问题进行了非常清楚的论述，其中母亲 do exactly what you'd expect and what's been described many times over，而父亲则是 didn't raise their pitch or fundamental frequency，也就是说父亲并没有改变自己的说话方式，这与题目中 tended not to modify their ordinary speech patterns 一致。本题答案为 fathers/dads。
20	a more adult type of speech, prepare infants for the language they will hear outside the family home	C 段第六、七句： Their role may be rooted in what is called the bridge hypothesis, which dates back to 1975. It suggests that fathers use less familial language to provide their children with a bridge to the kind of speech they'll hear in public.	本题问的是 an idea known as，之后出现了对这个 idea 具体内容的描述，而上一题中刚刚说明了父母在与儿童的沟通中使用不同的说话方式。在文中按顺序阅读不难发现第六句中提到了 bridge hypothesis，而本句中 what is called 与 an idea known as 表述一致，之后第七句中 It suggests... 是对 bridge hypothesis 的具体解释，与题目中的解释也能够对应。本题答案为 bridge hypothesis。
21	expands, types of speech which they can practise	C 段第八句： 'The idea is that a kid gets to practice a certain kind of speech with mom and another kind of speech with dad, so the kid then has a wider repertoire of kinds of speech to practice,' says VanDam.	本题针对儿童在家中听到不同类型语言所能够带来的好处进行提问，原文中这一信息出现在 C 段第八句，其中 so the kid then has a wider repertoire of kinds of speech to practice 与题目的表述一致，其中 a wider 与 expand 对应，types of speech 与 kinds of speech 同义替换。本题答案为 repertoire。
22	the University of Connecticut	D 段第一句： Scientists from the University of Washington and the University of Connecticut collected thousands of 30-second conversations between parents and their babies, fitting 26 children with audio-recording vests that captured language and sound during a typical eight-hour day.	根据题目中出现的大写字母，可以在D段第一句找到对应的内容。根据that the babies were equipped with判断空格处是实验中使用的设备，而原文对应句子中提到fitting 26 children with audio-recording vests，与该信息一致。本题答案为(audio-recording) vests。

题号	定位词	文中对应点	题目解析
23	heard a lot of baby talk, much larger	D 段第二、三句: The study found that the more baby talk parents used, the more their youngsters began to babble. And when researchers saw the same babies at age two, they found that frequent baby talk had dramatically boosted vocabulary, regardless of socioeconomic status.	关于研究发现的描述出现在 D 段第二、三句,其中第二句提到 the more baby talk parents used, the more their youngsters began to babble,第三句提到 frequent baby talk had dramatically boosted vocabulary,也就是说更多儿语能够帮助儿童促进词汇量增加。本题答案为 vocabulary。

Questions 24~26

- 题目类型:MATCHING
- 题目解析:

24. a reference to a change which occurs in babies' brain activity before the end of their first year

参考译文	提到婴儿接近一岁前大脑活动的变化
定位词	brain activity, before the end of the first year
文中对应点	F 段前四句:In a study published in *Proceedings of the National Academy of Sciences*, a total of 57 babies from two slightly different age groups — seven months and eleven and a half months — were played... The infants were placed in a brain-activation scanner... produce speech. The results suggest that listening to baby talk prompts infant brains to start practicing their language skills. 'Finding activation...how to make the right movements that will produce words,' says co-author Patricia Kuhl. 关于 babies' brain activity 以及 the end of their first year 的内容都出现在 F 段,其中首句介绍被试人员的时候提到了 seven months and eleven and a half months,而之后关于实验过程和结果的描述,也都体现了题目中 a change which occurs in babies' brain activity。因此本题答案为 F。

25. an example of what some parents do for their baby's benefit before birth

参考译文	家长在婴儿出生之前所做的对其有益活动的例子
定位词	parents, for their baby's benefit, before birth
文中对应点	A 段第二句:Most babies start developing their hearing while still in the womb, prompting some hopeful parents to play classical music to their pregnant bellies. 文章首段提到很多语言学家研究儿语对学习的影响,而很多儿童在胚胎中已经开始了听力能力的发展,之后举例说明家长为此所做的事情,也就是 play classical music to their pregnant bellies。因此本题答案为 A。

26. a mention of babies' preference for the sounds that other babies make

参考译文	提到婴儿更喜欢其他婴儿发出的声音
定位词	preference, the sound that other babies make

⑥⑤参考译文

儿语如何促进婴儿大脑成长

A 对儿童说话的典型方式——高音调、夸张、重复——对那些希望理解"儿语"如何影响学习的语言学家而言是充满吸引力的。多数婴儿在母亲的子宫中就开始发展听力了，这促使一些满怀希望的家长为自己未出生的孩子播放古典音乐。一些研究甚至表明婴儿早在出生前 10 周就能听到成人说话，并获得所在家庭中母语的基本元素。

B 较早接触语言或许对大脑有些好处——例如，研究表明在双语家庭中成长的儿童可以更好地学习如何处理信息。所以针对儿童的悦耳并有时较为夸张的语言是如何影响婴儿成长的？以下是最近一些探索儿语背后科学的研究。

C 根据一项新研究，父亲并不像母亲那样经常使用儿语，方式也不一样——这是完全没问题的。斯波坎华盛顿州立大学的 Mark VanDam 和他的同事们给家长们配备了录音设备和语音识别软件，以研究他们在日常一天中与孩子们的交流方式。"我们发现母亲在做的确实是你们所期望并多次描述的"，VanDam 解释道。"但是我们发现父亲并没有在做同样的事情。父亲们在同孩子们说话时并没有提高音调或基本频率。"他们的角色或许基于所谓的"桥梁假说"，这一说法可以追溯到 1975 年。该假说认为父亲使用比较少的家庭化语言以提供给孩子们一个桥梁，从而过渡到他们在公开场合听到的语言。"这一观点认为儿童同母亲练习一种特定的说话方式并与父亲练习另外一种，这就使儿童得以对各种说话方式进行更广泛的练习"，VanDam 说。

D 华盛顿大学和康涅狄格大学的科学家们收集了数千条家长与孩子之间时长为 30 秒的对话，给 26 位儿童配备了可以在一天 8 小时中获取语言和声音的录音背心。研究发现家长使用的儿语越多，他们的孩子越会试图跟着说话。当研究者观察两岁儿童时，他们发现频繁出现的儿语显著促进了词汇量的增加，不论社会经济地位如何。"那些听了大量儿语的儿童相比那些听成年人语言或者标准语言的孩子说话更多"，康涅狄格大学的 Nairán Ramírez-Esparza 说。"我们同样发现是否在一对一的情景下使用儿语也会有很大影响"，她补充道。"家长在一对一沟通的时候使用儿语越多，儿童就越会试图学着说话，儿童越学着说话，他们在以后的生活中使用的词汇就会越多。"

E 另一项研究表明家长或许希望与自己的孩子们一起，这样他们可以试着说更多自己的语言。麦吉尔大学和魁北克蒙特利尔大学的研究者们发现儿童或许喜欢听互相之间的话语而非成年人的——这或许解释了为什么儿语是家长普遍使用的工具。他们播放由一种特殊的合成设备制作的重复元音，这一设备模仿一位成年女性或一个儿童的声音。通过这种方式，只有听觉线索的影响被观测。该团队随后测量每种声音能够让婴儿保持关注多久。他们发现"婴儿的"声音能够让孩子保持关注多出接近 40% 的时间。婴儿的声音同样引起正在倾听的孩子们的更多反应，比如微笑或唇动，这都近似于发声的动作。该团队推断这种被其他婴儿的声音吸引会有助于促进发展说话能力的学习过程。"或许声音中的某些特性正在吸引他们的注意力，"研究的合著者 Linda Polka 说。"或者也有可能他们对那种特定的声音非常感兴趣是因为他们开始关注自身发声的能力。我们只是推断，但是这种声音可以引起他们的注意或许是因为他们将其作为自己或许可以发出的声音。"

F 在《美国科学院论文集》中发表的一项研究中，研究者给来自两个不同年龄组的（7个月以及11个半月）总共57名婴儿播放其母语（英语）和非母语（西班牙语）的音节。这些婴儿佩戴了大脑激活扫描仪，这一设备可以记录指导运动机能的脑区的活动，这种运动会产生语言。结果表明听儿语会促进婴儿大脑开始练习语言技能。"当婴儿确实是在听些什么的时候，在大脑的运动区发现激活非常重要，因为这意味着婴儿的大脑从一开始就参与交流，并表明7个月儿童的大脑已经在试图弄清如何做出可以产生话语的正确活动"，共同研究的 Patricia Kuhl 说。另一项有趣的发现是，无论何种语言，7个月大的儿童对所有声音都能作出反应，然而相比母语声音，年龄较大的婴儿的大脑在试图做出非母语声音的运动激活时需要更加努力。这一研究或许同样揭示了婴儿识别母语和其他语言的不同的过程。

Reading Passage 3

篇章结构

体裁	论说文
主题	关于哈拉帕文明衰落的研究
结构	A 段：哈拉帕文明曾非常繁荣，但并未留下关于自身的描述
	B 段：关于哈拉帕城市繁荣和衰退时的描述
	C 段：关于哈拉帕文明衰退原因的猜想
	D 段：研究发现过去的位置信息存在偏差
	E 段：研究发现了证明气候因素影响当地环境的证据
	F 段：研究者关注气候事件更广泛的影响
	G 段：研究者对当时哈拉帕文明的生活方式进行研究
	H 段：过往研究对当前社会的意义

解题地图

难度系数：　★★★★

解题顺序：　SUMMARY (32~36) → MATCHING (37~40) → MATCHING (27~31)

友情提示：　本文针对哈拉帕文明的兴旺和衰退进行描述，探讨哈拉帕文明衰退的原因，并提出对现代社会管理的启示。解题时首先完成 SUMMARY 部分的题目，之后完成 37~40 部分的 MATCHING FEATURES，这部分题目可以通过根据人名寻找观点的方式来解题，最后完成乱序出题的 MATCHING INFORMATION 题目即可。

必背词汇

1. **ancient** *adj.* 古代的，古老的
   They believed *ancient* Greece and Rome were vital sources of learning.
   他们认为古希腊和古罗马是知识的重要发源地。
   Ancient civilisations believed in the curative powers of fresh air and sunlight.
   远古文明相信新鲜的空气和阳光有治病的功效。

2. **flourish** *v.* 繁荣，兴旺
   These plants *flourish* in a damp climate. 这些植物在潮湿的气候下长势茂盛。
   The plant *flourishes* particularly well in slightly harsher climes.
   这种植物在气候条件稍差一点的地区长势尤其好。

3. **sophisticated** *adj.* 复杂的；精致的
   Honeybees use the most *sophisticated* communication system of any insect.
   蜜蜂之间所用的交流方式是昆虫中最为复杂的。
   Medical techniques are becoming more *sophisticated* all the time. 医疗技术日益复杂精妙。

4. **mystery** *n.* 秘密，谜，谜题
   It is one of the great unsolved *mysteries* of this century. 这是本世纪尚未解开的大奥秘之一。
   It's a complete *mystery* to me why they chose him. 我真无法理解他们为什么会选他。

5. **arrange** *v.* 安排；排列
   We've still got to *arrange* how to get to the airport. 我们还得安排如何到达机场。
   The books are *arranged* alphabetically by author. 这些书是按作者姓名字母顺序排列的。

6. **investigation** *n.* 调查，研究
   She is still under *investigation*. 她仍在接受调查。
   The police have completed their *investigations* into the accident. 警察已完成对这次事故的调查。

7. **recover** *v.* 恢复；找回
   The police eventually *recovered* the stolen paintings. 警方最终追回了失窃的油画。
   She is now fully *recovered* from her injuries. 她现在已经完全从伤痛中恢复过来了。

8. **heritage** *n.* 遗产，继承物
   The historic building is as much part of our *heritage* as the paintings.
   这座历史建筑和这些画一样，都是我们的文化遗产的一部分。
   Manchester has a rich cultural, economic and sporting *heritage*.
   曼彻斯特有丰富的文化、经济和体育遗产。

认知词汇

civilisation	*n.* 文明	transformation	*n.* 转换，改变，变形
shed light on	阐明，说明	ritual	*n.* 仪式，惯例 *adj.* 仪式的
luxury	*n.* 奢侈，奢华 *adj.* 奢侈的	demise	*n.* 死亡，终止
carve	*v.* 雕刻；切开	glacier	*n.* 冰河，冰川
representation	*n.* 代表；表现	succumb	*v.* 屈服，被压垮
archaeological	*adj.* 考古学的	speculation	*n.* 推测；思索
distinct	*adj.* 独特的，不同的	inaccuracy	*n.* 错误，不精确
alleyway	*n.* 胡同，小巷	geographic	*adj.* 地理的，地理学的
drainage	*n.* 排水，排水系统	flaw	*n.* 缺点，缺陷

fieldwork	*n.* 野外考察，现场考察	indicative	*adj.* 预示的；象征的
situate	*v.* 位于	drought	*n.* 干旱；缺乏
sediment	*n.* 沉积；沉淀物	variable	*adj.* 变量的；多变的
region	*n.* 地区；范围	cultivate	*v.* 培养；耕作
monsoon	*n.* 季风	combination	*n.* 结合，组合
evaporation	*n.* 蒸发	distinctive	*adj.* 有特色的，与众不同的

❀ 佳句赏析

1. Some have claimed that major glacier-fed rivers changed their course, dramatically affecting the water supply and agriculture; or that the cities could not cope with an increasing population, they exhausted their resource base, the trading economy broke down or they succumbed to invasion and conflict; and yet others that climate change caused an environmental change that affected food and water provision.

   • 参考译文：一些人认为巨大的冰川河流改变了线路，对供水和农业产生了显著影响；或者城市无法应对增长的人口，资源被消耗殆尽，贸易经济体系受到破坏，或者它们毁于侵略和冲突；而有些人认为气候变化导致了环境变化，这种变化影响了食物和水资源供应。

   • 语言点：本句 Some have claimed that 之后出现了宾语从句，主要对当时哈拉帕文明衰落的原因进行了可能性的分析，例如 major glacier-fed rivers changed their course，之后出现了 or that 这一并列结构，实际上省略了谓语 claimed，之后继续描述可能的原因，最后出现了 and yet others that，这一结构中也是省略了 claimed，之后的 climate change caused an environmental change that affected food and water provision 是对另一种可能的原因进行描述。

2. While it is possible that these local-scale processes were linked, the real archaeological interest lies in understanding the impact of these larger-scale events on different environments and different populations.

   • 参考译文：尽管这些地区规模的事件或许存在联系，真正的考古兴趣在于理解这些全球范围的事件对不同环境和不同人群的影响。

   • 语言点：本句首先出现了 while 引导的让步状语从句，内容为 While it is possible that these local-scale processes were linked，之后主句部分是典型的主谓宾结构，主语为 the real archaeological interest，谓语为 lies in，宾语为 understanding the impact of these larger-scale events on different environments and different populations。

3. By investigating responses to environmental pressures and threats, we can learn from the past to engage with the public, and the relevant governmental and administrative bodies, to be more proactive in issues such as the management and administration of water supply, the balance of urban and rural development, and the importance of preserving cultural heritage in the future.

   • 参考译文：通过调查对环境压力和威胁的应对方式，我们可以向过去的人们学习，从而与公众和相关的政府及行政机关进行沟通，使他们将来在一些问题的处理上更有前瞻性，比如水资源的管理，城乡发展的平衡，以及文化遗产保护的重要性。

   • 语言点：本句首先出现方式状语 By investigating responses to environmental pressures and threats，之后的句子中出现了并列结构 the public 和 the relevant governmental and administrative bodies，句子后半部分对 issues 的修饰中，也是通过三个并列的成分来进行描述，分别是 the management and administration of water supply，the balance of urban and rural development，以及 the importance of preserving cultural heritage in the future。

🌸试题解析

Questions 27~31

- 题目类型：MATCHING
- 题目解析：

27. proposed explanations for the decline of the Harappan Civilisation

参考译文	提出有关哈拉帕文明衰落的解释
定位词	explanations, the decline of the Harappan Civilisation
文中对应点	C段第一句：Some have claimed that major glacier-fed rivers changed their course, dramatically affecting the water supply and agriculture; or that the cities could not cope with an increasing population, they exhausted their resource base, the trading economy broke down or they succumbed to invasion and conflict; and yet others that climate change caused an environmental change that affected food and water provision. 有关哈拉帕文明衰落的解释出现在 C 段第一句，该句提到了人们的一些设想，例如 major glacier-fed rivers changed their course，cities could not cope with an increasing population，climate change caused an environmental change 等，这些都与题目中 proposed explanations 的表达一致。因此本题答案为 C。

28. reference to a present-day application of some archaeological research findings

参考译文	提到当前对于一些考古学研究发现的应用
定位词	a present-day application, archaeological research findings
文中对应点	H 段第二句：'By investigating responses to environmental pressures and threats, we can learn from the past to engage with..., to be more proactive in issues such as...' H 段主要描述了 Petrie 的观点，他认为考古学家通过对过去社会如何应对环境和气候变化的分析，可以从独特的角度为现代社会提出建议，并指出可以让有关部门和公众 be more proactive in issues such as the management and administration of the water supply, the balance of urban and rural development, and the importance of preserving cultural heritage in the future，而这里提到的就是题目中的 present-day application。因此本题答案为 H。

29. a difference between the Harappan Civilisation and another culture of the same period

参考译文	哈拉帕文明和另一个同时期文化的差异
定位词	difference, another culture of the same period
文中对应点	A段第三句：But their lack of self-imagery — at a time when the Egyptians were carving and painting representations of themselves all over their temples — is only part of the mystery. A 段对哈拉帕文明进行了基本的介绍，指出哈拉帕文明曾是发展兴旺的社会，但是关于他们自身的描述都没有留下，之后在本段第三句提到 at a time when the Egyptians were carving and painting representations of themselves all over their temples，这里埃及人在庙宇中雕刻和绘制自身形象是哈拉帕文明没有做过的，因此与题目中 a difference 一致，而题目中提到的 another culture 即 Egyptians。因此本题答案为 A。

30. a description of some features of Harappan urban design

参考译文	描述一些哈拉帕城市设计的特征
定位词	Harappan urban design
文中对应点	B 段第二、三句：As populations increased, cities were built that had great baths, ... Houses were arranged in blocks, with wide main streets and... B 段对哈拉帕文明的城市特征进行了描写，其中第二句写到 cities were built that had great baths, craft workshops, palaces and halls laid out in distinct sectors，之后在第三句中，进一步描写到 Houses were arranged in blocks, with wide main streets and narrow alleyways, and many had their own wells and drainage system，这都属于对哈拉帕城市设计方面的描述。因此本题答案为 B。

31. reference to the discovery of errors made by previous archaeologists

参考译文	提到发现一些之前考古学家出现的错误
定位词	errors, previous archaeologists
文中对应点	D 段第一、二句：A research team led by Petrie, ...this region was inhabited in the past. When they carried out a survey of how the larger area was settled in relation to sources of water, they found... ranging from several hundred metres to many kilometres. D 段提到之前考古学家在对地点判断上出现的一些错误，并指出了出现这种情况的原因，本段第一句就提到 many of the archaeological sites were not where they were supposed to be，而之后第二句中也写到 they found inaccuracies in the published geographic location of ancient settlements ranging from several hundred metres to many kilometres。因此本题答案为 D。

Questions 32~36

- 题目类型：SUMMARY
- 题目解析：

题号	定位词	文中对应点	题目解析
32	Yama Dixit, David Hodell, snails	E 段第一、二句： Now, research published by Dr Yama Dixit and Professor David Hodell, ..., has provided the first definitive evidence for climate change affecting the plains of north-western India, where... The researchers gathered shells of Melanoides tuberculata snails from the... lake and used geochemical analysis...	题目部分首先出现了人名 Yama Dixit 和 David Hodell，并在第一句中写到 the first definitive evidence of climate change，因此可以通过这一信息将题目定位在文中 E 段。本段首句的内容与题目部分一致，题目中的 collecting 与原文 E 段第二句 gathered 同义替换，snails 原词重现，因此可以在此处找到答案词 shells。
33	water levels	E 段第三句： 'As today, the major source of water into the lake is likely to have been the summer monsoon,' says Dixit.	E 段第三句提到 the major source of water into the lake，而题目中的结构为 water levels in a ____，因此不难判断此处空格对应原文中 lake 一词。本题答案为 lake。

题号	定位词	文中对应点	题目解析
34	evaporation, drought	E 段第四句： 'But we have observed that..., when the amount of evaporation from the lake exceeded the rainfall — indicative of a drought.' Hodell adds: 'We estimate that the weakening of the Indian summer monsoon climate lasted about 200 years...'	本题说到 less ____ than evaporation，这与原文中 E 段第四句的内容一致，原文中写到 the amount of evaporation from the lake exceeded the rainfall，比较的双方是 evaporation 和 rainfall，而之后的 indicative of a drought 与题目中 suggests that there was an extended period of drought 一致。本题答案为 rainfall。
35	Petrie and Singh's team, archaeological records	G 段第一、二句： Petrie and Singh's team is now examining archaeological records and trying to understand details of how people led their lives in the region five millennia ago. They are analysing grains cultivated at the time, and trying to work out...	题目中的 Petrie and Singh's team 以及 archaeological records 都出现在原文 G 段一句。题目中的 to look at 对应原文 G 段二句 They are analysing，因此本句的宾语 grains 与题目对应。本题答案为 grains。
36	They are also examining, links between	G 段第三句： They are also looking at whether the types of pottery used, and other aspects of their material culture, were distinctive to specific regions or were more similar across larger areas.	题目中 They are also examining 与原文中 They are also looking at 是同义替换关系，同时也都是带有 also 的并列结构，因此本题可以定位在 G 段第三句。本段中提到将 pottery 作为研究对象，因此题目中 objects including ____ 可以直接填写 pottery。本题答案为 pottery。

Questions 37~40

- 题目类型：MATCHING
- 题目解析：

题号	解题关键词	题目解析
37	changes to environmental conditions	题目：Finding further information about changes to environmental conditions in the region is vital. 译文：找到关于一个地区环境变化的更多信息至关重要。 F段说到：...it is essential that we obtain more climate data from areas close to the two great cities at Mohenjodaro and Harappan and also from the Indian Punjab，此处的几个地点与题目中 in the region 对应，而 essential 与 vial 同义替换，在原文中找到相关的人名为 Singh，本题答案为 B。

题号	解题关键词	题目解析
38	examining previous patterns of behaviour	题目：Examining previous patterns of behaviour may have long-term benefits. 译文：研究之前的行为模式或许有长期价值。 对之前行为模式的研究出现在文章G段，段首提到Petrie and Singh's team is now examining archeological records and trying to understand details of how people led their lives…，之后对他们具体的研究内容进行了描述。而H段中指出了考古学家在研究过去人们如何应对环境和气候变化时的特殊作用，以及对当今政府和公众的指导意义，这部分均是围绕Petrie的叙述，因此直接对应人名即可。本题答案为A。
39	the approximate length of a period of water shortage	题目：Rough calculations indicate the approximate length of a period of water shortage. 译文：粗略计算可以预估水资源短缺的大概时间长度。 关于水资源短缺的信息出现在文章E段，其中说到当时水的来源主要是夏季季风，而由于湖泊的蒸发量超过了降雨量，导致发生干旱，而Hodell还说到We estimate that the weakening of the Indian summer monsoon climate lasted about 200 years before recovering to the previous conditions，也就是夏季季风的减弱持续了大约200年，而由于夏季季风与降雨量之间的关系，所以该内容与题目表述是一致的。本题答案为D。
40	the decline of Harappan Civilisation	题目：Information about the decline of the Harappan Civilisation has been lacking. 译文：关于哈拉帕文明衰落的信息是缺乏的。 A段说到哈拉帕文明曾经非常繁荣，但关于他们自身的描述是缺失的。B段第一句中Cameron Petrie说到There is plenty of archaeological evidence to tell us about the rise of the Harappan Civilisation, but relatively little about its fall，这一信息与题目表述一致，对应文中人名确认答案，本题答案为A。

参考译文

哈拉帕文明发生了什么？

新研究揭示了一个古文明社会的消失

A 古巴基斯坦和印度的哈拉帕文明在五千年前非常繁荣，但是一千年后这里的城市便被废弃。哈拉帕文明曾是一个精细复杂的青铜时代社会，他们建造了许多"大型城市"并进行奢华工艺品的国际贸易，但似乎关于他们自身的描述几乎都没有留下。但是哈拉帕文明自身形象的缺失——在一个埃及人已经在庙宇中到处雕刻和绘制自身象征的时代——只是这个谜题的一部分。

B "有许多考古学证据可以告诉我们有关哈拉帕文明的崛起，但相比之下没有什么关于其没落的证据"，剑桥大学考古学家 Cameron Petrie 博士解释道。"随着人口增加，他们建立了在不同区域分布着大型浴场、工艺品工厂、宫殿和会堂的城市。房屋按照街区布置，有宽敞的大街和狭窄的巷子，很多有自己的水井和排水系统。这在很大程度上是一个'发展兴旺的'文明。"在公元前 2100 年左右，变化开始发生。街道不再清洁，建筑物开始被遗弃，仪式建筑也被废止使用。在它们最终衰落之后，过了一千多年真正的大型城市才再一次在亚洲南部出现。

C 一些人认为巨大的冰川河流改变了线路，对供水和农业产生了显著影响；或者城市无法应对增长的人口，资源被消耗殆尽，贸易经济体系受到破坏，或者它们毁于侵略和冲突；而有些人认为气候变化导致了环境变化，这种变化影响了食物和水资源供应。"不太可能是单一的因素导致了一种文明的衰亡，但事实是，迄今为止，我们在这一地区对一些关键要素没有什么确凿证据"，Petrie 说。"许多考古学的辩论只是一些论证充分的推断。"

D 一个由 Petrie 带领的研究团队，与贝拿勒斯印度教大学的 Ravindanath Singh 博士一起，在他们调查的早期发现许多考古学遗址并不位于人们假设的地方，这完全改变了人们过去对于这一区域位置的理解。当他们调查完更大地区的位置与水资源的关系，他们发现已发布的古老定居地点的地理位置存在着从几百米到几公里不等的误差。他们意识到使用现有数据进行的任何尝试可能从根本上就是存在缺陷的。经过几个季度的野外考察，他们完成了新的报告，发现了 198 个之前并不为之所知的定居位置，这非常令人惊讶。

E 如今，来自剑桥大学地球科学系的 Yama Dixit 博士和 David Hodell 教授发表的研究提供了第一个真凭实据，说明了气候变化对印度西北部平原的影响，而数百个哈拉帕定居点就位于这里。研究者们在一个古代湖泊的沉积物中发现了瘤拟黑螺的贝壳，并使用地球化学分析作为追溯该地区气候历史的方法。"像今天一样，湖泊中的水或许主要来自夏季季风"，Dixit 说。"但是我们观测到大约 4100 年前发生了突然的变化，当时湖泊的蒸发量超过了降雨量，这预示着干旱的发生。"Hodell 补充道："我们估计印度夏季季风气候的减弱持续了大约 200 年，之后才恢复成我们如今依然能够看到的那种环境。"

F 长久以来人们认为其他伟大的青铜时期文明也在相似的时间衰亡，并将全球范围的气候事件视为其衰亡的原因。尽管这些地区规模的事件或许存在联系，真正的考古兴趣在于理解这些全球范围的事件对不同环境和不同人群的影响。"考虑到哈拉帕文明的广大地域以及多变的天气系统，"Singh 解释道，"我们在摩亨佐达罗和哈拉帕这两座大型城市以及印度旁遮普周围的地区得到更多气候数据是非常重要的。"

G Petrie 和 Singh 的团队如今正在调查考古记录并试图细致了解人们五千年前是如何在这里生活的。他们分析当时培育的谷物，并试图发现它们是否种植在极端的水压环境下，以及人们是否根据不同的天气系统调整种植谷物的组合方式。他们同样关注人们使用的陶器种类，以及他们物质文化的其他方面，是特定区域独有的还是在更大的区域内类似的。这使得我们深入了解人们的交互模式，以及是否发生过变化。

H Petrie 相信考古学家在调查过去社会如何应对环境和气候变化方面处在独一无二的位置。"通过调查对环境压力和威胁的应对方式，我们可以向过去的人们学习，从而与公众和相关的政府及行政机关进行沟通，使他们将来在一些问题的处理上更有前瞻性，比如水资源的管理、城乡发展的平衡，以及文化遗产保护的重要性。"

Task 1

📓 题目要求

（见《剑桥雅思官方真题集 13：学术类》P73）

🖋 审题

题目翻译：下面的这张柱状图展示了 2014 年电量生产和消耗排名前十的国家。选取并汇报主要特征，总结信息，并在相关处进行对比。

十个国家：中国、美国、俄罗斯、日本、印度、加拿大、法国、巴西、德国、韩国

💡 写作思路

柱状图是雅思图表作文里考得最多的，大约占 40%。柱状图通常分为具有变化和进行比较的柱状图与纯粹进行比较的柱状图两种。本题主要考查的是在同一个年份，各个国家的电量生产和消耗的情况以及国家之间同类事物的对比。

☕ 考生作文

（见《剑桥雅思官方真题集 13：学术类》P130）

🔊 参考译文

从柱状图展示了 2014 年排名前十位的生产和消耗电的国家。从电的生产来看，排第一的是中国，有 53,980 亿千瓦时，第二名是美国，有 40,990 亿千瓦时，第三名是俄罗斯，有 10,590 亿千瓦时，第四名是日本，有 9362 亿千瓦时，第五名是印度，有 8910 亿千瓦时，第六名是加拿大，有 6189 亿千瓦时，第七名是法国，有 5612 亿千瓦时，第八名是巴西，有 5309 亿千瓦时，第九名是德国，有 5266 亿千瓦时，第十名是韩国，有 4851 亿千瓦时。从电的消耗来看，第一名是中国，有 53,220 亿千瓦时，第二名是美国，有 38,660 亿千瓦时，第三名是俄罗斯，有 10,380 亿千瓦时，第四名是日本，有 8569 亿千瓦时，第五名是印度，有 6988 亿千瓦时，第六名是德国，有 5825 亿千瓦时，第七名是加拿大，有 4999 亿千瓦时，第八名是法国，有 4629 亿千瓦时，第九名是巴西，有 4558 千瓦时，第十名是韩国，有 4495 亿千瓦时。

从信息。有最多生产量和消耗量的是中国。产量和消耗量最小的是韩国。

几乎所有的国家都有比消耗量多的生产量，除了德国，它的消耗量大于生产量。

☕考官点评

（见《剑桥雅思官方真题集 13：学术类》P130）

🌀参考译文

本文的回应比较机械化，因为它按生产和消耗电的顺序列出了国家，挑出了生产量和消耗量最大及最小的国家，并注意到了一个事实，即除了德国，所有国家都是生产量大于消耗量。不过，这篇文章有数据支持，尽管数字的部分描述有错误（对俄罗斯、印度和巴西的生产量数据描述是不准确的，对日本的消耗量的数据描述也有误）。组织结构有限，并且使用衔接关系的例子较少；同样，词汇量有限，仅够表达本文的内容。文中有简单句和复杂句混合使用的情况，但是复杂句都不太准确 [that have / has | Almost all the country have / Almost all the countries have]。

⚙️分析

本文得分 5 分。

接下来我们从评分标准的四个方面（任务完成情况、连贯与衔接、词汇、语法）对这篇考生作文进行详细分析。

任务完成情况

在任务完成方面 6 分作文的内容要求是：内容全面，有清晰的概述；描述了主要特征，但有些细节不得体或不准确。5 分作文的内容要求是：内容基本全面；机械叙述细节，缺少清晰的概述，可能没有具体数据支持；描述了主要特征，但涵盖不全，可能过于偏重细节。4 分作文的内容要求则是：内容不全面，缺失重要特征。

这篇文章包含了图表中的所有信息，在这方面接近 6 分作文的要求。但因为机械化地描述图表信息，如十个国家的生产量和消耗量分别从大到小排列，且数据的描述有错误，如对俄罗斯、印度和巴西的生产量数据及对日本的消耗量数据的描述不准确，导致最后只能得到 5 分的成绩。

第一段：介绍题目并将十个国家的生产量和消耗量分别从大到小进行排列。

第二段：挑出占比最大和最小的两个国家。

第三段：挑出德国与众不同之处。

连贯与衔接

在连贯与衔接方面，4 分作文信息安排杂乱，5 分作文则有一定的组织，但往往缺乏整体的连贯性和逻辑性。此外，5 分作文一般在使用衔接手段、指代和替换等方面存在问题。本文所使用的衔接关系很有限，只用到了顺序衔接，如排第一、排第二等，而且非常机械。另外，本文的分段也不够合理，没有明确的首段和尾段，考生还把大量的内容集中在同一段，很难分辨。而后面的两个段落又显得单薄，内容不够充实。

词汇

本文在词汇方面的运用相当匮乏。首先，考生照抄了题目，由此会被扣掉照抄内容的字数，而首段避免照抄的方式可以是同义词替换，如 countries 可以用 nations 替代，也可以改变语序，如 production and consumption of electricity 可以改成 how much electricity in billion kWh was produced and consumed，或通过拓展来避免重复，如 in 2014 可以改成 in the year of 2014。

其次，文中大量重复 rank 和 billion kWh 这两个表达，导致词汇部分的分数大幅下降。而这两类表达，可以通过词性的改变，如 the 1st rank is China 改成 China ranked the first，以及将单位放入首段对象的后面，如 how much electricity in billion kWh was produced and consumed，从而避免在文章中重复出现，或者用 the same amount / the similar proportion 等指示代词替换。

此外，本文主要描述的是对比，而考生并未使用像 account for（占据，占有），the most significant proportion（占比最大的），three times more than...（是……的三倍多）等表示对比的表达。

语法

在语法范围和准确性方面，6 分作文的特点是能使用简单句和复杂句结构，5 分作文的特点是句子结构有限，虽然尝试使用复杂句，但错误较多，而本文就存在这个问题，大部分复杂句都不够准确，如：

From the bar chart that show → The bar chart shows that

The 1st rank is China that have → The 1st rank is China that has（此类错误极多）

Almost all the country have → Almost all the countries have

From the information.（句号的不恰当使用）→ From the information, we can see that...

Task 2

📋题目要求

（见《剑桥雅思官方真题集 13：学术类》P74）

🖋审题

题目翻译：一些人认为历史是学校里最重要的课程之一。另一些人认为，在当今世界，科学和技术比历史更重要。讨论双方观点并给出你自己的看法。

本题在题材上属于教育和社会类话题的结合，题型为讨论型。

☕考生作文

（见《剑桥雅思官方真题集 13：学术类》P131~132）

🔄参考译文

在我看来，我认为每一门课程对我们来说都很重要。我们需要从我们的过去、现在和未来学习一切东西。一些人认为历史是学校里最重要的课程之一，这确实是真的，但它需要符合现代社会，即科学和技术。我们如何能在没有历史的情况下进步，那些在我们背后的人"始祖"是最有力量的、可以推着我们前进的人。他们教会我们如何点火，如何寻找食物，如何与其他人和动物共同生活，如何生存等等。没有他们我们当然不可能知道这些。科学和技术也很重要。它们给予我们与之共同前进的机会。没有科技，我们仅仅只是普通的人类。我们每天一无是处。没有它们我们没有电没有食物，我们没有任何舒适的东西。古人可能可以没有这些东西而生存。人类基于有限的管理创造出了无限的人们需要的发明。

请让我举一个科技发展的例子。这两个东西给予了我们一个成为 ASEAN "东南亚联盟"成员的机会我们可以与其他九个国家通过高科技交流。它帮助我们与另外九个国家通过团队合作来发展我们的国家。在交通、交流和合作等方面帮助我们。它绝对可以帮助我们在不久的将来紧紧抓住那个希望。

总而言之，经济可以最终达到。一个事实是成为 ASEAN 组织的成员有别于政治立场、文化和传统，但是它不是一个问题，有着我们的帮助，我知道，有一个光明的未来在等着我们所有人。这就是为什么历史、科学和技术一样重要的原因。

我们通过历史去学习他人，他们的文化、他们的传统，可以更好地了解彼此，而使用科技帮助我们、我们的国家、我们的世界前进，帮助每一个人，给予他们明亮的机会和未来，尤其是孩子，给他们机会学习，去上学，去获取知识，那么未来的十年、二十年以至于到新时代的来临他们可以帮助彼此把这些机会传递给其他孩子。

☕考官点评

（见《剑桥雅思官方真题集 13：学术类》P131）

🐌参考译文

作者回应了题目的要求并列出了为什么各种科目都是重要的，使用了相关的例子来证明这些想法。尽管结构安排有时令人感到混乱，但文章还是有一定的连续性并得出了明确的结论。有效地使用了衔接手段 [In my opinion | Of course | especially]。指示代词普遍比较准确 [we wouldn't know that without them | these things | that hope | that is a reason why]，但是有一处错误 [With this / these two things]。词汇的范围有一定的多样性 [go along with today's world | to move forward | daily life | transportation, communication collaboration etc. | political standing, culture and traditions]，尽管有一些错误 [every subjects / subject | normally / normal human beings | a bright chances / chance]，尽管所使用的指代词汇 [stuff and things] 体现了作者很难找到更恰当的词汇来表达意思。有简单句和复杂句混合的句子结构，包括各种从句的使用 [Some people say that... | ...which is science and technology | ...people who pushes / push us to | The / They taught us how to]，尽管有错误出现，但是它们通常不会造成歧义或理解困难。标点有时出错，尤其是句号的丢失。

⚙分析

本文得分 6 分。

接下来我们从评分标准的四个方面（内容、连贯与衔接、词汇、语法）对这篇考生作文进行详细分析。

内容

6 分作文的特点是文章涉及题目中的所有内容，不像 5 分作文有部分跑题的现象。而与 7 分作文相比，6 分作文往往论证不够充分。本题需要讨论的核心是哪一门学科更重要：历史还是科学和技术。

文章首段直接表明了作者观点，即这些学科一样重要，然后通过恰当的延展强调了历史的重要性，接下来强调了科学和技术的重要性。第二段继续通过例子说明了科技带给国家的好处。第三段总结了两者一样重要。第四段再次重申了观点。

从内容方面看，本文是 discuss 类型的文章，不应该在没有分析两种观点的情况下，先提出自己的观点。此外，本文虽然回应了题目的要求，但是作者对科技重要性论述的部分远远多于对历史重要性的论证，导致历史部分的延展性不够。

连贯与衔接

本文在整体结构安排上虽然有推进性和明确的观点，但是分段让读者觉得有些迷茫和混乱。尤其是在首段直接表明观点后，可以分别论述两种学科的重要性，而作者选择把它们放在一起论证，就会造成读者理解困难。

本文有效地使用了一些衔接手段：In my opinion / Of course / especially / while / overall，以及指示代词：we wouldn't know that without them / these things / that hope / that is a reason why / give a chance to them，但是有一处错误 With this two things → With these two things。

词汇

本文在词汇部分的使用有一定的多样性，如：go along with today's world / to move forward / daily life / transportation, communication collaboration etc. / political standing, culture and traditions / hold on to，但是仅够对本文内容进行论证，没有地道的表达，而且作者使用指代词汇 stuff and things 体现出他很难找到更恰当的词汇来表达意思。此外，文中经常出现小的拼写错误，如：every subjects → every subject，normally human beings → normal human beings，a bright chances → a bright chance，但不影响读者理解。

语法

本文在语法部分既有简单句又有复杂句及多种句子形式的组合。这是 6 分作文与 5 分作文的重要区别。5 分作文往往句子结构简单，即便有复杂句也会出现很多错误，影响理解。

本文使用了各种从句，如：Some people say that... | ...which is science and technology | ...people who pushes / push us to | The / They taught us how to...

出现明显错误的句子是：

第三段：it is a fact that the member of the member of the ASEAN have differences in term of political standing, culture and traditions but it's not a problem with our help I know that there're a bright future are waiting for all of us. 应改成：It is a fact that as the member of the ASEAN, we understand that there are differences among political standing as well as culture and traditions, and even with these differences, there should be no problem for us to look forward to seeing a bright future for all of us.

第四段：We use History to learn about others, their culture, their tradition to be understand each other more and more and using science and Technology to help us, our country, our world to be moving forward, to help each other and to give a bright chances and future for everyone, especially kids give a chances to them to study, to go to school, to get knowledge so the next ten years, twenty years to the new up coming year all of them can help each other to pass these chances to other kids go on and on. 应改成：We use History to learn about others, especially their culture and tradition, which could help us better understand each other, and we also use Science and Technology to help our country and the world move forward, giving a bright chance and future for everyone, especially kids who could be given a chance to study, to go to school, to get knowledge. So this help may continue to be passed on to many generations from now on.

本文的标点问题比较明显，尤其是句号的丢失和逗号的不恰当使用。此外，大小写的误用也是问题，逗号后面应该是小写，句号后面应该是大写。

Speaking

Part 1

在第一部分，考官会介绍自己并确认考生身份，然后打开录音机/笔，报出考试名称、时间、地点等考试信息。考官接下来会围绕考生的学习、工作、住宿或其他相关话题展开提问。

🔍 话题举例

Money

1. **When you go shopping, do you prefer to pay for things in cash or by card? [Why?]**
   Definitely by card. It's such *a hassle to* bring *a handful of change* with you all the time. Using a card, especially one with *Quick Pass*, can *save you a lot of time*.

a hassle to... 做……是件麻烦事	a handful of change 一大堆零钱
Quick Pass 闪付	save...a lot of time 为……节省大量时间

2. **Do you ever save money to buy special things? [Why/Why not?]**
   Yes, sometimes. I'm not making a lot of money since I'm still a student. So, whenever I *have my eye on* something which is a bit *out of my price range*, I'll certainly have to *save up* in order to buy it at a later time.

have one's eye on... 看上……	out of my price range 超出我能承受的价格范围
save up 存钱	

3. **Would you ever take a job which had low pay? [Why/Why not?]**
   Well, it really depends on whether there are *other incentives*. For example, if there was a job that provides great learning opportunities, I wouldn't be too worried if the pay wasn't handsome enough. After all, I'm not the *breadwinner* in my family.

other incentives 其他好处	breadwinner 赚钱养家的人

4. **Would winning a lot of money make a big difference to your life? [Why/Why not?]**
   Absolutely! I would be able to help my parents *pay off the mortgage*. With that money I could also attend a better university overseas, which would definitely change my life. And, of course, *a fancy diamond necklace* would really *put a cherry on top*!

pay off the mortgage 还清房贷	a fancy diamond necklace 精美的钻石项链
put a cherry on top 锦上添花	

Part 2

考官给考生一张话题卡（Cue Card）。考生有1分钟准备时间，并可以做笔记（考官会给考生笔和纸）。之后考生要作1~2分钟的陈述。考生讲完后，考官会就考生的阐述内容提一两个相关问题，由考生作简要回答。

> Describe an interesting discussion you had as part of your work or studies.
> You should say:
>   what the subject of the discussion was
>   who you discussed the subject with
>   what opinions were expressed
> and explain why you found the discussion interesting.

➡ 话题卡说明

这是一张比较常见的事件类话题卡，主要考查考生描述在工作或学习中进行过的一次有趣的讨论。作答时考生需注意，要充分拓展觉得这次讨论有趣的原因。题目中的 interesting 所指的"有趣"并不只限于"搞笑的、幽默的"，而应理解为"让人感兴趣的"，这样会有更多的拓展方向可供选择。可以和此话题串联的卡片包括 Describe an interesting lesson you attended，Describe a team project that you were involved in 等。

整体介绍	I'd like to talk about the discussion I had with my classmates on *Artificial Intelligence* when we were preparing for a group presentation for our science class in high school.
和谁讨论	There were 4 people in our group, two guys named Yang and Ming, a girl named Lan, and I. We were discussing what should be included in our presentation, and apparently the team members had rather different ideas as to what our conclusion should be.
观点表达	The guys were quite *adamant* that the benefits of AI are so *far-reaching* that any risks associated with it would seem *insignificant and negligible* in comparison. Lan and I were of the opinion that we should *tread really carefully* with AI, considering the possibility that one day we may reach the *technological singularity* which is known as the *turning point* when the intelligence of computers begins to *surpass* the *collective intelligence* of human beings.
为何有趣	The discussion was *riveting* in that we covered a number of interesting issues relating to AI, from its history to its recent development, and even to the possible future *depicted in* the famous *Matrix trilogy*. Different ideas were exchanged, and we kept challenging each other to come up with more powerful arguments. It was truly an awesome discussion because apparently both sides did their research to support their opinions. If there had been *a neutral bystander*, he or she would have had a hard time deciding who should have won. This *heated discussion* also gave us an idea as to how exactly we should deliver the presentation — *in the form of* a debate! And as you may have guessed, it turned out really great. I shall always remember this truly interesting discussion.

📖 重点词句

Artificial Intelligence 人工智能
adamant 坚决的
far-reaching 影响深远的
insignificant and negligible 无足轻重的
tread carefully 慎重行事
technological singularity 科技奇点
turning point 转折点
surpass 超越

collective intelligence 集体智慧
riveting 吸引人的
be depicted in... 在……中被描绘
the *Matrix* trilogy 《黑客帝国》三部曲
a neutral bystander 中立的旁观者
heated discussion 激烈的讨论
in the form of... 以……的形式

Part 3

第三部分：双向讨论（4~5 分钟）。考官与考生围绕由第二部分引申出来的一些比较抽象的话题进行讨论。第三部分的话题是对第二部分话题卡内容的深化和拓展。

🔍 话题举例

Discussing problems with others

1. **Why is it good to discuss problems with other people?**
   Well, *two heads are better than one*. Once you have shared a problem with others, they may be able to *offer some new perspectives*. Sometimes those who are closely involved may not see things so clearly, and it's necessary to look at the problem *with a fresh eye*. I suppose in some cases, *an in-depth discussion* may also *spark some new ideas* which in turn will help solve a problem. So if you're *stuck with a problem*, it's a good idea to discuss it with others.

Two heads are better than one. 三个臭皮匠，赛过诸葛亮。	offer new perspectives 提供新的视角
with a fresh eye 以全新的眼光	an in-depth discussion 深度讨论
spark new ideas 激发新的想法	be stuck with a problem 被问题难住了

2. **Do you think that it's better to talk to friends and not family about problems?**
   I suppose it really depends on what kind of problems you have and what your expectations are when you talk to these people. In most of the cases, family members can give you some *moral support* to make you feel better, and it may also be a good idea to *consult them with* some personal issues. However, if your problems are purely academic or professional, there's little they can do to help you. In such cases, *it's more advisable to seek the advice of* a friend who is more familiar with these issues.

moral support 精神上的支持	consult...with... 征求某人关于某事的建议或意见
it's advisable to... 做……是很明智的	seek the advice of... 寻求……的建议

3. **Is it always a good idea to tell lots of people about a problem?**
   Not really. When you *encounter a problem*, it's understandable that you want to share it with those who are close to you. However, it's not wise to trouble too many people with it. Telling different people

about the same problem doesn't *make it go away*. Another downside is that you may *strike people as* being *self-absorbed and whiny*. It's much better to focus on solving the problem rather than complaining about it.

encounter a problem 遇到问题	make a problem go away 解决问题
strike somebody as... 让某人觉得	self-absorbed and whiny 自恋且爱发牢骚

Communication skills at work

1. **Which communication skills are most important when taking part in meetings with colleagues?**
Well, you have to be able to express your opinions *succinctly above all things*. In order to communicate with others effectively, one usually needs to *put ideas and opinions in a few words*. You don't want your listeners to *run out of patience*. Aside from that, being an attentive listener is also important. An essential element of successful communication is *mutual respect*. By listening to your colleagues attentively, you show them that you respect them and their opinions are valued.

succinctly 简明扼要地	above all things 比其他都重要
put...in a few words 把……长话短说	run out of patience 耗尽耐心
mutual respect 互相尊重	

2. **What are the possible effects of poor written communication skills at work?**
If you cannot *convey meanings* clearly with your written works, there may be some serious problems. Poor *written correspondence* with colleagues could result in misunderstandings and an increase in the cost of communication. If your letters and reports to clients are not well written, your *company's name will suffer*. More importantly, no boss would appreciate an employee who is not skillful with paperwork. *All in all*, it's always wise to *practice and polish* your written communication skills.

convey meaning 表达含义	written correspondence 书面通讯
company's name will suffer 公司名誉会受损	all in all 总而言之
practice and polish 练习并打磨	

3. **What do you think will be the future impact of technology on communication in the workplace?**
There is no doubt that technology has brought and will continually *bring revolutionary changes* to the workplace. Development in certain technologies such as *voice recognition* and Artificial Intelligence will certainly *boost the efficiency* of communication in the future. People will no longer need to *type letters and messages out*. Instead, they can simply say things out loud and those words will be transcribed by a computer. This can certainly save us a lot of time on correspondence.

bring revolutionary changes 带来革命性的变化	voice recognition 语音识别
boost the efficiency 大幅提升效率	type letters and messages out 把信和消息的内容打出来

Listening

Section 1

📖 场景介绍

一位打算去 JPNW（公司）参加培训的女士电话询问一位曾参加过该培训的男士关于这个培训项目的一些事宜。咨询的内容包括部门的选择、薪资待遇以及面试的注意事项等。

🔤 本节必背词汇

apply	*v.* 申请	minimum	*adj.* 最小的，最低的
department	*n.* 部门	wage	*n.* 工资
initial	*adj.* 最初的	regular	*adj.* 定期的，有规律的
finance	*n.* 金融，财务	massively	*adv.* 巨大地
diploma	*n.* 文凭	variety	*n.* 种类；多样性
trainee	*n.* 接受培训者	tutor	*n.* 导师
loads of	许多	casual	*adj.* 休闲的，非正式的
organisation	*n.* 组织，机构	respond	*v.* 回应

🔤 词汇拓展

accounting	*n.* 会计，会计学	marketing	*n.* 市场营销
assistant	*n.* 助理	maximum	*adj.* 最大的
certificate	*n.* 证明；证书	receptionist	*n.* 接待员
degree	*n.* 学位	recruit	*v./n.* 招聘
dress code	着装标准	reference letter	推荐信
economics	*n.* 经济学	salary	*n.* 工资
enquiry	*n.* 询问	statistics	*n.* 统计学
informal	*adj.* 非正式的；日常的	venue	*n.* 地点；场地

⚙️ 文本及疑难解析

1. Because of its size you can work in loads of different areas within the organisation. 因为这家公司的规模很大，你可以在公司里的不同领域从事不同的工作。根据上下文的语境，此处 size 应该理解为"大的规模"。

2. I know you get a lower minimum wage than regular employees. 我了解到，你拿到的最低工资是低于正式员工的最低工资的。此处 regular employees 意为"正式员工"。

3. There's a lot of variety too. 还有其他各种（收获）。

4. So long as you're well prepared there's nothing to worry about. 只要你准备得好，就没有什么可担心的。so long as 的意思是"只要"。

5. It makes people respond better to you. 这（保持微笑）会让你得到更好的回应。

🌼 题目解析

第 1~10 题是 Section 1 典型的笔记填空题。

1. 原文中的 initial 替换题干中的 at first。本题需要考生注意时态，题干中的 at first 和 did 意指过去，而原文中的 customer services 表达现在，为干扰信息。

2. school 原文重现，用来定位。原文中的 I failed Maths（我数学挂科了）对应题干中的 didn't have a qualification，故 Maths 为答案。

3. 用 diploma 定位，考生容易误填 IT。本题解题的关键是读清题干，题干中的 should have done 为虚拟语气，表达想做而没有做的事。原文 I took the one on IT skills 为过去时，陈述过去的事实，故 IT 不是正确答案；but I wish I'd done that one instead 为虚拟语气，与题干对应，注意本句中的 that one 指代前文提到的 business skills，故 business 为正确答案。

4. 用 other trainees 定位，原文提到三个与年龄相关的数字，分别为 18、17、18~20。17 是其中最小的数字，对应题干中 youngest 的概念。

5. 本题可通过 training at JPNW, opportunities, size 和 organisation 多个信息进行定位。the same number of 对应题干中的 the same amount of，答案词 holiday 拼写难度不大。

6. 用 experience 和 confidence 定位，one day each month 对应题干中的 one day per month，结合上下文，答案为 college。

7. 用 company 定位，原文 the location's a real advantage（地理位置是一个很大的优势）与题干对应，答案为 location。

8. 用 interview 和 wear 定位，根据题干判断空格所填信息为名词。原文 nothing too casual — like jeans 中 jeans 为名词，符合题目要求。考生容易误填 casual，但 casual 为形容词，不符合题目要求。

9. 原文提到 they hate people who are late，也就是建议面试不要迟到。

10. 本题需要考生适当理解原文，原文说"我的经理在面试前给了我一条非常有用的建议，就是要微笑"，由此可判断本题答案为 smile。

Section 2

🔖 场景介绍

一个关于新西兰一家滑雪中心的介绍。主讲人讲解了该滑雪中心提供的活动，如越野滑雪、狗拉雪橇等，并详细说明了该滑雪中心各滑雪路线的特点。

📖 本节必背词汇

premier	*adj.* 最好的；第一的	melt	*v.* 融化；熔化
cross-country	*adj.* 越野的	slope	*n.* 斜坡，山坡
fairly	*adv.* 相当地	carpet	*v.* 覆盖，铺满
steep	*adj.* 陡峭的	ascent	*n.* 上坡路
mountainside	*n.* 山坡	summit	*n.* 山顶；顶点
trail	*n.* 小路，小径	hut	*n.* 棚屋，木屋
aerobic	*adj.* 有氧的	firewood	*n.* 木材，木柴
glide	*v.* 滑行	conserve	*v.* 节省，保护
scenery	*n.* 风景，景色	stormy	*adj.* 暴风雨的，暴风雪的
sled	*n.* 雪橇	beacon	*n.* 灯塔；灯标
relay	*n.* 接力赛	accessible	*adj.* 可到达的，可接近的
lap	*n.* （跑道等的）一圈	regardless	*adv.* 不管，不论
course	*n.* 跑道，比赛场地	scary	*adj.* 恐怖的，吓人的
expedition	*n.* 探险	master	*v.* 掌握，精通
miner	*n.* 矿工	shelter	*n.* 遮蔽物；庇护所
trace	*n.* 痕迹，踪迹	expose	*v.* 使暴露，使显露

📖 词汇拓展

baton	*n.* 接力棒	protective	*adj.* 保护的，防护的
blizzard	*n.* 暴风雪	resort	*n.* 度假胜地
fatal	*adj.* 致命的	snowboarding	*n.* 滑板滑雪
first-aid kit	急救箱	sprint	*n.* 短跑，冲刺
helmet	*n.* 头盔	tennis court	网球场
intermediate	*adj.* 中级的，中等的	waterproof	*adj.* 防水的
nasty	*adj.* 险恶的，危险的	weather forecast	天气预报

✿ 文本及疑难解析

1. Well, you've come to New Zealand's premier snow and ski centre, and we've a whole load of activities for you during your week here. 你们来到了新西兰最有名的滑雪中心，在（接下来的）一周里，我们为大家准备了很多活动。a whole load of 意为"许多，大量的"。

2. Most visitors come here for the cross-country skiing, where you're on fairly flat ground for most of the time, rather than going down steep mountainsides. 大多数游客来这儿是为了越野滑雪，在这儿的大部分时间里，你们都是在平坦的地面上滑行，而不是在陡峭的山坡上滑行。

3. You can go at your own speed — it's great aerobic exercise if you really push yourself, or if you prefer you can just glide gently along and enjoy the beautiful scenery. 你们可以按照自己的速度来，如果你使劲儿快滑的话，这会是一个很好的有氧运动；如果你悠闲慢滑的话，你可以欣赏沿途的美景。

4. For your final expedition, you'll head off to Mount Frenner wearing a pair of special snow shoes which allow you to walk on top of the snow. 作为最后一项探险活动，你会去往 Mount Frenner，你需要穿上一双特殊的、能够让你在雪上行走的鞋。

5. For washing, we recommend you use melted snow, though, to conserve supplies. 但是，如果有东西要洗的话，建议使用融化的雪水，这样可以节约供给。though 在这里表转折，意思相当于 but，结合上下文，本句意在表达"饮用水是由滑雪中心提供的，但是洗涤用水建议使用雪水"。

6. Don't stress about getting back here to the centre in time to catch the airport bus — they'll probably not be running anyway. 别急着赶回滑雪中心去乘坐机场巴士，（在这样的天气条件下）他们有可能根本就不会运营。这里的 stress 作动词，意为"紧张，焦虑"。

7. Then there's Pine Trail...if you're nervous about skiing, leave this one to the experts! 还有 Pine Trail（这条滑雪路线），如果在这条路线上滑雪你会很紧张的话，把它留给高手来滑就好了！

❁ 题目解析

11~16 题为单选题。

11. 用 cross-country skiing 定位，原文提到的 you can also leave these 对应 A 选项 get away from the regular trails。选项 B 可能会成为干扰选项，但原文中没有提及 stop 的概念。

12. this afternoon 和 dog-sled trip 原文重现，用来定位。原文指出如果你愿意，你可以有自己的 team，并且可以学习如何 drive them，这里的 them 指代 dogs，与 B 选项表述一致。本题也可以采用排除法，A 选项的主语是人，而原文中的主语是 dogs；C 选项说 one group member 可以成为 leader，与原文 following behind our leader 表达不符。

13. 用 relay event 进行定位，原文中提到每一个参与的人都可以获得一枚奖章，直接对应 A 选项。

14. snow-shoe trip 原文重现，用来定位。考生有可能会因为 ascent 和 steep 这样的生词影响对句子的理解，但本题可通过 get to the summit 和 climb to the top of a mountain 的同义替换直接得出答案。

15. 本题难度不大，用 hut 定位，原文 it's got cooking facilities, firewood and water for drinking 直接对应 A 选项。注意原文虽有提及"我们可以帮你拿行李"，但需要付 10 美金，不包含在住宿的费用里。C 选项 cooked meals 与原文"你可以自己做饭"相矛盾。

16. 本题需要考生一定程度上理解原文，原文说如果遇到暴风雪天气，你就待在 hut 里，通常情况下这种天气不会持续很长时间，跟 B 选项的等待天气好转表达同一意思。考生容易误选 C 选项，但原文指出 emergency locator beacon 仅在有人生病或受伤的紧急情况下使用。

17~20 题为配对题。

17. 题干定位。原文提到这个路线既适合 first-timers（初次滑雪的人）也适合 experts（滑雪高手），符合 B 选项"适合所有滑雪能力的人"的表达。

18. 题干定位。原文中的 techniques 同义替换 D 选项的 skill。

19. 题干定位。原文提到有一个 shelter（庇护所）你可以坐着休息，对应 A 选项的 a place to stop and rest。

20. 题干定位。原文提到如果下雪或者刮风，你要在出发前跟我们确认这个路线当天是开放的，暗指 E 选项"如果天气不好的话这个路线有可能会关闭"。

Section 3

🗂 场景介绍

男女学生讨论一份关于食品营养标签的报告。该讨论涉及了他们在完成作业过程中的心得和对两种不同标签系统的看法。

📇 本节必背词汇

nutritional	*adj.* 营养的	reliable	*adj.* 可信赖的，可依靠的
label	*n.* 标签	consistency	*n.* 一致性，连贯性
trace	*n.* 痕迹，踪迹	conclusive	*adj.* 结论性的，确凿的
allergy	*n.* 过敏	small-scale	*adj.* 小型的，小规模的
packaging	*n.* 包装	universally	*adv.* 普遍地，全体地
calorie	*n.* 卡路里	compulsory	*adj.* 强制性的，义务的
eye-opener	*n.* 令人大开眼界的事物	ridiculous	*adj.* 荒谬的，可笑的
transparent	*adj.* 透明的；显而易见的	consultation	*n.* 咨询，商讨
manufacturer	*n.* 生产商	reservation	*n.* 保留意见
intake	*n.* 摄入量	literacy	*n.* 读写能力
ingredient	*n.* 成分；（烹饪）原料	accessible	*adj.* 易理解的，易懂的

📇 词汇拓展

bitterness	*n.* 苦味	obese	*adj.* 肥胖的
carbohydrate	*n.* 碳水化合物	protein	*n.* 蛋白质
extract	*v.* 提取	raw material	原材料
refreshment	*n.* 茶点	salinity	*n.* 盐度
fibre	*n.* 纤维	seal	*v.* 密封
liquid	*n.* 液体	solid	*n.* 固体
mineral	*n.* 矿物质	sourness	*n.* 酸味
moderate	*adj.* 适度的	wrapping	*n.* 包装纸

1. I've still got loads to do for our report on nutritional food labels. 关于那份食品营养标签的报告，我还有很多事要做。

2. Well, I've always had to check labels for traces of peanuts in everything I eat because of my allergy. 因为我对花生过敏，所以我总是检查我吃的每一种食物的标签，看看有没有花生的成分在里面。本句中的 trace 本意为"痕迹，踪迹"，结合上下文，traces of peanuts 在此可理解为"花生的成分"。

3. I liked the traditional daily value system best — the one which tells you what proportion of your required daily intake of each ingredient the product contains. 我最喜欢传统的每日摄入量体系，因为这种体系告诉你该产品所包含的你每天所需摄入的各种成分的比例。

4. I think supermarkets like the idea of having a colour-coded system — red, orange or green — for levels of fat, sugar and salt in a product. 我觉得超市喜欢用颜色（红色、橙色、绿色）编码系统来显示产品中所含的脂肪、糖和盐的水平。

5. Hardly surprising that some of them are opposed to flagging up how unhealthy their products are. 一些厂商反对（用这种方式）让人关注到他们的食品有多不健康，这种做法不足为奇。flag up 在此意为"引起……关注"。

6. They should have focused on people with low literacy levels because these labels are designed to be accessible to them. 他们本应该关注那些文化水平低的人，因为这些标签就是为了方便这样的人的理解而设计的。

7. The thing that wasn't stated was how often they bought packaged food — all we know is how frequently they used the supermarket. （这里）没有说明的是他们多久买一次包装食品，我们所知道的只是他们多久去一次超市。

21~26 题为单选题。

21. 本题可利用题干中的原词 nutritional food labels 进行定位，但要选出正确答案需要考生理解原文。原文提到 Jack 因为对花生过敏所以会关注食品标签上的花生含量，对于产品是否健康这种事没有太多的关注。由此可以看出，Jack 除了关注食品标签上的花生含量，并没有读食品标签上的每一个信息，对应 A 选项。

22. 本题较难定位，没有明显的定位词。原文提到 Alice 过去总是相信包装上写的内容，但她现在意识到即使是"健康的"酸奶里面也含有大量的糖和很高的卡路里。可见她之前并没有意识到（was unaware of）某些特定的食物里具体包含了什么样的成分，对应 A 选项。原文虽有提到 C 选项中的 calories，但并没有与 calories 的数值相关的信息，为干扰选项。

23. 用题干中的 supermarket 和 pizza 定位。根据原文的表达，除非人们仔细阅读食品标签，不然他们不会发现一整个披萨上标注的营养数值其实是半个披萨的。这就起到了一定的误导作用，对应 C 选项的 misleading。

24. 用题干原词 daily value system 进行定位，原文提到"我不确定这个 daily value system 的体系是不是最好用的，但是至少你得到的信息是很全面的"，full story 字面意思为"整个故事"，结合语境可理解为"全面的"，对应 C 选项中的 comprehensive。

25. 用 flavour of crisps 定位。原文中 Jack 提到他就是不明白为什么那些被叫做鸡肉味的薯片里只是含有一些人工添加剂而已，而 Alice 也表示她至少希望这些薯片里能含有一小部分真正的鸡肉，可见这些产品里不含有任何真正的肉类，与 B 选项的表达相符。

26. 题干中的 research 在原文中被 study 同义替换，均表示"调查，研究"。根据原文中 those findings weren't that conclusive（这些结论不是那么的确凿），对应 A 选项"没有清晰的结论"。

27~30 题为多选题。

27~28. 用题干原词 traffic-light system 定位，注意本题的考点是学生们对哪两件事情感到 surprised。Alice 提到超市喜欢这个 colour-coded system，对应 B 选项超市愿意使用 traffic-light system，但 Jack 觉得该 system 还没有被普遍采用，对应题干中的 surprised，故 B 选项为正确答案。紧接着，Alice 提到 manufacturers，但她表示 hardly surprising（不足为奇），可排除 D 选项。最后，Alice 说 traffic-light system 是在没有足够的商讨情况下引入的，也就是 C 选项中的"没有足够的研究"，而 Jack 用 that is a bit weird 表示惊讶，对应题干中的 surprised，故 C 选项为正确答案。

29~30. 用题干原词 participants 定位，本题需要选出两个正确表述。原文提到 they should have focused on people with low literacy levels，这里使用了虚拟语气，表达他们本应该关注 low literacy levels，但事实上并没有，排除 A 选项。接着原文提到从 all socio-economic groups 那里得到了反馈，证明 all socio-economic groups 都参与了，由此判断 D 选项表述正确。然后原文提到 if they hadn't interviewed participants face-to-face，这里也使用了虚拟语气，表达与事实相反的情况，意思是他们确实是使用 face-to-face 的方式进行的采访，由此判断 E 选项表述正确。之后 Jack 问到这些人是自愿的还是被挑选的，Alice 回答说这些人是自愿的，可排除 C 选项。最后 Alice 说不能确定 customers 多久买一次 packaged food，与 B 选项的 regular customers（常客）相矛盾，故 B 选项不是正确答案。

Section 4

场景介绍

一个关于咖啡的课堂展示。该课堂展示涉及了咖啡的发展史，尤其是咖啡在经济和社会方面产生的重要影响。

本节必背词汇

documentary	adj. 文件的，文献的	monopoly	n. 垄断
originally	adv. 原来，起初	plantation	n. 种植园
court	n. 宫廷；法庭	colony	n. 殖民地
physician	n. 医生，内科医生	skyrocket	v. 剧增，飞涨
cultivate	v. 种植，栽培	slave	n. 奴隶
potentially	adv. 潜在地，可能地	peasant	n. 农民
destruction	n. 毁坏，破坏	taxation	n. 税金，征税
consumption	n. 消耗，消费	take over	接替，接管
perform	v. 履行，起……的作用	boom	v. 激增；使兴旺
enormous	adj. 巨大的，极大的	stimulant	n. 兴奋剂

alternative	*n.* 可供选择的事物	export	*v.* 出口
brew	*v.* 沏（茶），煮（咖啡）	import	*v.* 进口
caffeine	*n.* 咖啡因	grind	*v.* 磨碎
chain	*n.* 连锁商店	moderate	*adj.* 适度的，适量的
classify	*v.* 分类，归类	organic	*adj.* 有机的
commodity	*n.* 商品	roast	*v.* 烘，烤
decline	*v./n.* 减少，下降	substitute	*v.* 代替，取代
expansion	*n.* 扩张，扩展	supply	*n.* 供给量，供应量

文本及疑难解析

1. In my presentation, I'm going to talk about coffee, and its importance both in economic and social terms. 在我的课堂展示中，我要说说咖啡，以及它在经济和社会方面的重要性。

2. We think it was first drunk in the Arab world, but there's hardly any documentary evidence of it before the 1500s, although of course that doesn't mean that people didn't know about it before then. 我们认为是阿拉伯世界的人们最早开始喝咖啡的，但是基本上找不到任何 16 世纪前的文字记载，然而这当然并不意味着在那之前人们不知道咖啡这种东西。

3. However, there is evidence that coffee was originally gathered from bushes growing wild in Ethiopia, in the northeast of Africa. 然而，有证据表明，咖啡最初是从非洲东北部的埃塞俄比亚的野生灌木上采集到的。

4. In the late 1600s, the Yemeni monopoly on coffee production broke down and coffee production started to spread around the world, helped by European colonisation. 在 17 世纪末，也门在咖啡生产上的垄断地位被打破，咖啡生产在欧洲殖民化的影响下传播到了世界各地。

5. But whatever system was used, under the European powers of the eighteenth century, coffee production was very closely linked to colonisation. 但是不管是什么（劳动）制度，在 18 世纪欧洲列强的统治下，咖啡生产都与殖民化紧密相连。

题目解析

31~40 题为提纲填空。

31. 本题定位难度不大，可利用副标题中的 Arab world 和分论点中的 Ethiopia, 1522, Ottoman, medicine, 1623 和 Constantinople 多个信息定位，答案直叙，原文中的 demanded 替换题干中的 ordered，之后出现答案 destruction。

32. 用 17th century 和 coffee shops 定位，本题需要考生理解 compare to 意为"与……相似"，对应原文中的 a similar function to universities（与大学的功能相似），可得出答案 universities。

33. 利用题干中的并列结构判断空格处所填信息为形容词，原文中与 social 并列的形容词 political 即为答案。

34. 副标题中的 European colonisation，分论点中的 plantations 和 colonies 可以帮助定位。本题题干在原文中进行了一定程度的改写，原文中 names...were often taken from the port 可理解为"名字来自于

port", 对应题干中的"根据 port 而命名"。

35. Brazil 和 Caribbean 原文重现, 用来定位。题干中的 most（大多数）与原文中的 almost all 同义替换, 紧接着出现的 slaves 即为答案。考生需要注意 slaves 的拼写。

36. 用 Java 和 used as 联合定位。本题进行了简单的改写, 原文中的 a means of 替换题干中的 a form of, 之后的 taxation 即为答案。

37. 题干中的 as important as 原文重现, 之后的 sugar 即为答案。

38. 本题较难, 考查对原文的理解。原文提到英国从中国引进了茶, 茶开始变得非常受欢迎, 但是当美国从英国独立出来之后, 美国人认为茶等同于英国（they identified this drink with Britain）, 而咖啡仍然是美国人偏爱的饮料。由此可见, 英国从咖啡向茶的消费转变并没有发生在美国。答案为 tea。

39. 用 19th century 和 prices 定位, 原文中的 fall 同义替换题干中的 drop, because 原文重现, 之后的 transportation 即为答案。

40. 原文中的 industries 对应题干中的 industrial。原文提到有的时候工人需要工作到很晚, 咖啡对于他们来说很重要, 由此得出, 咖啡可以帮助工人在晚上工作, 本题答案为 night。

Reading Passage 1

📑 篇章结构

体裁	说明文
主题	卡蒂萨克号帆船
结构	第一段：19 世纪英国造船技术发生了巨大变化
	第二段：快速帆船是主要的贸易工具
	第三段：卡蒂萨克号名字的来历
	第四段：卡蒂萨克号的制造过程
	第五段：卡蒂萨克号速度快但并未达到主人的预期
	第六段：蒸汽船给快速帆船带来巨大威胁
	第七段：卡蒂萨克号开始承担一些并不重要的任务
	第八段：卡蒂萨克号船长的更换
	第九段：卡蒂萨克号被售卖并重新命名
	第十段：卡蒂萨克号恢复最初的名字
	第十一段：卡蒂萨克号最终被用于公开展览

🌐 解题地图

难度系数： ★★★

解题顺序： TRUE/FALSE/NOT GIVEN (1~8) → SENTENCE COMPLETION (9~13)

友情提示： 本篇文章主要描写卡蒂萨克号帆船历史上发生的事件，从其名字的来源到成功完成贸易，从衰败到几经辗转最终用于公开展览，与之相关的信息基本都有涉及。作为本套题的第一篇文章，全文基本以事实信息为主。共出现两组题目，由于题目本身都是顺序出题，因此按照正常顺序，先完成 TRUE/FALSE/NOT GIVEN，再完成 SENTENCE COMPLETION 即可。

🔤 必背词汇

1. transport *v.* 运输 *n.* 交通，运输

   Applicants must have their own *transport*. 申请人必须有自己的交通工具。

   Transport to and from the airport is included in the price. 价格中包括往返机场的交通费。

2. dominate *v.* 控制，支配

   The book is expected to *dominate* the best-seller lists. 这本书预计会占据畅销书排行榜的榜首。

   Sports, and not learning, seem to *dominate* in the school. 似乎是运动而不是学习在那所学校占重要地位。

3. ensure *v.* 保证，确保

Please *ensure* all lights are switched off. 请务必将所有灯都关掉。

Ensure that it is written into your contract. 确保把这一点写入合同中。

4. capacity *n.* 容量；能力

The theatre has a seating *capacity* of 2000. 那座剧院能容纳 2000 名观众。

Limited resources are restricting our *capacity* for developing new products.
有限的资源正制约着我们开发新产品的能力。

5. suspend *v.* 使暂停；推迟

Production has been *suspended* while safety checks are carried out. 在进行安全检查期间生产暂停。

The introduction of the new system has been *suspended* until next year. 新制度推迟到明年再行实施。

6. competition *n.* 竞争；比赛

I have to change my approach, the *competition* is too good now. 我得改变方法，现在的竞争对手太强。

There will be a chess *competition* next week. 下个星期有一场国际象棋比赛。

7. original *adj.* 原始的，最初的

The *original* plan was to hold an indefinite stoppage. 最初的计划是无限期停工。

The *original* settlers are the Indians. 最早在这里定居的是印第安人。

8. restore *v.* 恢复，修复

We will *restore* her to health, but it may take time. 我们会让她恢复健康，但可能需要一些时间。

The measures are intended to *restore* public confidence in the economy.
这些举措旨在恢复公众对经济的信心。

认知词汇

sailing	*n.* 航行，航海	route	*n.* 路线，航线
iron	*n.* 铁	ultimately	*adv.* 最后，最终
steel	*n.* 钢铁，钢制品	replacement	*n.* 更换；取代
vessel	*n.* 船，舰	incompetent	*adj.* 无能力的，不胜任的
clipper	*n.* 快速帆船	appoint	*v.* 任命，指定
propulsion	*n.* 推进，推进力	turnaround	*n.* 转变，转向
intact	*adj.* 完整的，未受损伤的	navigator	*n.* 航海家，领航员
display	*n.* 显示，陈列	hemisphere	*n.* 半球
chase	*v.* 追逐，追捕	iceberg	*n.* 冰山
prestige	*n.* 声望，声誉	life expectancy	预期寿命
maiden	*adj.* 初次的	profitable	*adj.* 有利润的，有收益的
misfortune	*n.* 不幸，灾祸	miscellaneous	*adj.* 各种各样的，混杂的
daunting	*adj.* 令人畏缩的	harbour	*n.* 海港
cargo	*n.* 货物	transfer	*v.* 转让；转移

佳句赏析

1. The nineteenth century was a period of great technological development in Britain, and for shipping the major changes were from wind to steam power, and from wood to iron and steel.

- 参考译文：19 世纪是英国发生巨大技术发展的时期，对造船而言主要的转变在于从风能转向蒸汽能，从木材转向钢铁。
- 语言点：本句是由两个分句构成的并列句，第一个分句为 The nineteenth century was a period of great technological development in Britain，第二个分句为 for shipping the major changes were from wind to steam power, and from wood to iron and steel。第二个分句指出 shipping 的两个主要变化：from wind to steam power 以及 from wood to iron and steel。

2. While stem ships could make use of the quick, direct route between the Mediterranean and the Red Sea, the canal was of no use to sailing ships, which needed the much stronger winds of the oceans, and so had to sail a far greater distance.
   - 参考译文：蒸汽船可以使用地中海和红海之间快捷、直接的线路，运河对帆船来说是没用的，帆船需要大海更强的风力，因此需要航行更远距离。
   - 语言点：本句首先出现 While 引导的让步状语从句：While stem ships could make use of...and the Red Sea，之后主句出现，需要注意 be of + n. 结构出现时，of + n. 部分起形容词的作用，之后出现 which 引导的定语从句，对 sailing ships 进行修饰。

3. As a sailing ship, Cutty Sark depended on the strong trade winds of the southern hemisphere, and Woodget took her further south than any previous captain, bringing her dangerously close to icebergs off the southern tip of South America.
   - 参考译文：作为帆船，卡蒂萨克号依靠南半球的强烈信风，Woodget 比之前历任船长将船只带到了更向南的地方，接近危险的南美洲南端的冰川。
   - 语言点：本句中第一个分句为 As a sailing ship, Cutty Sark depended on...southern hemisphere，第二个分句为 Woodget took her further south...the southern tip of South America，其中第二个分句的主句为 Woodget took her further south than any previous captain，修饰成分为 bringing her dangerously close to icebergs off the southern tip of South America。

❀ 试题解析

Questions 1~8

- 题目类型：TRUE/FALSE/NOT GIVEN
- 题目解析：

1. Clippers were originally intended to be used as passenger ships.

参考译文	人们最初希望使用快速帆船运送乘客。
定位词	Clippers, originally intend to
解题关键点	passenger ships
文中对应点	第二段第一句：The fastest commercial sailing vessels of all time were clippers, three-masted ships built to transport goods around the world, although some also took passengers. 关于人们建造快速帆船的目的，在第二段第一句已经有清楚的描述：built to transport goods around the world, although some also took passengers，也就是说主要目的是 transport goods around the world，而题目中提到的 as passenger ships 只是次要作用，题目的表述与原文信息相反，因此本题答案为 FALSE。

2. Cutty Sark was given the name of a character in a poem.

参考译文	卡蒂萨克号的名字来源于一个诗歌中的角色。
定位词	Cutty Sark, given the name
解题关键点	a character in a poem
文中对应点	第三段第一、二句: Cutty Sark's unusual name comes from the poem *Tam O'Shanter* by the Scottish poet Robert Burns. Tam, a farmer, is chased by a witch called Nannie, who is wearing a 'cutty sark' — an old Scottish name for a short nightdress. 关于卡蒂萨克号名字的来源出现在第三段,文中说到这个名字来自一首诗歌,而出现关键词时,文中表达为 wearing a 'cutty sark',破折号之后进行了进一步解释: an old Scottish name for a short nightdress,从这里可以看出 Cutty Sark 实际上是 a short nightdress 的名字,而不是题目中的 a character in a poem,所以根据原文信息判断,题目表述是错误的,因此本题答案为 FALSE。

3. The contract between John Wills and Scott & Linton favoured Wills.

参考译文	John Wills 和 Scott & Linton 的合同对 Willis 有利。
定位词	contract between John Willis and Scott & Linton
解题关键点	favoured Wills
文中对应点	第四段第二句: To carry out construction, Willis chose a new shipbuilding firm, Scott & Linton, and ensured that the contract with them put him in a very strong position. 从第四段第二句可以看出,Willis 确实与 Scott & Linton 签订了合同,并且在这个合同中处于 a very strong position,这一表述与题目中的表达一致,因此本题答案为 TRUE。

4. John Wills wanted Cutty Sark to be the fastest tea clipper travelling between the UK and China.

参考译文	John Wills 希望卡蒂萨克号成为英国与中国间运送茶叶最快的帆船。
定位词	John Wills , tea clipper travelling between the UK and China
解题关键点	the fastest
文中对应点	第五段第一句: Willis's company was active in the tea trade between China and Britain, where speed could bring shipowners both profits and prestige, so Cutty Sark was designed to make the journey more quickly than any other ship. 文中第五段首句说到 Willis 的公司在中国和英国的茶叶贸易方面非常活跃,而在这个领域,速度是至关重要的,因此 Cutty Sark was designed to make the journey more quickly than any other ship,这里的 more quickly than any other ship 与题目中 the fastest 的含义是一致的,题目中的句子实际上同义替换了原文中的信息,因此本题答案为 TRUE。

5. Despite storm damage, Cutty Sark beat Thermopylae back to London.

参考译文	尽管受到暴风雨的破坏,卡蒂萨克号仍早于 Thermopylae 号返回伦敦。
定位词	storm damage, Cutty Sark, Thermopylae
解题关键点	beat

	第五段第五、六、七、八句：On one occasion, in 1872, the ship and a rival clipper, Thermopylae, left port in China on the same day. Crossing the Indian Ocean, Cutty Sark gained a lead of over 400 miles, but then her rudder was severely damaged in stormy seas, making her impossible to steer. The ship's crew had the daunting task of repairing the rudder at sea, and only succeeded at the second attempt. Cutty Sark reached London a week after Thermopylae.
文中对应点	本段关于 Cutty Sark 和 Thermopylae 两艘船的描述出现在第五句，其中说到 Cutty Sark 和 Thermopylae 在同一天离开了中国的港口，第六、七句中重点描述了 Cutty Sark 在航程中遇到的状况，而第八句中则说明 Cutty Sark reached London a week after Thermopylae，也就是说 Cutty Sark 晚于 Thermopylae 回到伦敦，而题目中的表达则与文中信息相反，因此本题答案为 FALSE。

6. The opening of the Suez Canal meant that steam ships could travel between Britain and China faster than clippers.

参考译文	苏伊士运河的开拓意味着蒸汽帆船可以比之前的帆船更快地往返于英国和中国。
定位词	The opening of the Suez Canal
解题关键点	steam ships could travel between Britain and China faster than clippers
文中对应点	第六段第二、三、四句：In addition, the opening of the Suez Canal in 1869, ..., had a serious impact. While steam ships could make use of the quick, direct route between the Mediterranean and the Red Sea, the canal was of no use to sailing ships, ... Steam ships reduced the journey time between Britain and China by approximately two months. 文中第六段描述了苏伊士运河对快速帆船的影响。第二句说到苏伊士运河的开通 had a serious impact，第三句进行了具体的描述，第四句给出了其造成的结果，也就是 Steam ships reduced the journey time between Britain and China by approximately two months，这与题目中的表述是一致的，因此本题答案为 TRUE。

7. Steam ships sometimes used the ocean route to travel between London and China.

参考译文	蒸汽船有时使用远洋航线往返于伦敦和中国。
定位词	Steam ships, London and China
解题关键点	sometimes used the ocean route
文中对应点	第六段至第八段 第6题出现在文中第六段，而第8题中有比较明确的定位词 Captain Woodget，因此本题对应的文中位置是比较容易确定的，在文中第六至八段中，都无法找到 steam ships 是否使用了 the ocean route 往返于伦敦和中国，因此本题答案为 NOT GIVEN。

8. Captain Woodget put Cutty Sark at risk of hitting an iceberg.

参考译文	Woodget 船长使卡蒂萨克号处于撞击冰山的危险中。
定位词	Captain Woodget
解题关键点	at risk of hitting an iceberg

	文中对应点	第八段第二句：As a sailing ship, Cutty Sark..., and Woodget took her further south than any previous captain, bringing her dangerously close to icebergs off the southern tip of South America. 关于 Captain Woodget 的描述出现在文章第八段，本段第二句中说到 Woodget took her further south than any previous captain, bringing her dangerously close to icebergs off the southern tip of South America，这里的描述与题目中 put Cutty Sark at risk of hitting an iceberg 的说法是一致的，因此本题答案为 TRUE。

Questions 9~13

- 题目类型：SENTENCE COMPLETION
- 题目解析：

题号	定位词	文中对应点	题目解析
9	After 1880, most successful time	第七段第二、三、四句：In 1880, violence aboard the ship led ultimately to the replacement of the captain with an incompetent drunkard who stole the crew's wages. He was suspended from service, and a new captain appointed. This marked a turnaround and the beginning of the most successful period in Cutty Sark's working life, transporting wool from Australia to Britain.	定位词 1880 出现在文章第七段第二句，而本段第四句中说到 the beginning of the most successful period in Cutty Sark's working life, transporting wool from Australia to Britain，也就是说在这段时间，卡蒂萨克号负责将羊毛从澳洲运送到英国，文中 transported 与题目中 carried 同义替换，因此本题答案为 wool。
10	captain, Woodget	第八段第一句： The ship's next captain, Richard Woodget, was an excellent navigator, who got the best out of both his ship and his crew.	第八段首句提到 Woodget，而题目中对他的身份进行提问，captain 在原文中已经有所提及，本句中还说到他是 an excellent navigator，这与题目中的问题和结构一致，因此本题答案为 navigator。
11	Ferreira, Falmouth	第十段第一句： Badly damaged in a gale in 1922, she was put into Falmouth harbour in southwest England, for repairs.	第九段最后说到 Cutty Sark 被重新命名为 Ferreira，而第十段出现了定位词 Falmouth 以及题目中提到的 damage，本句中说到 Ferreira 在 gale 中受到 damage，这与题目问到的信息一致，因此本题答案为 gale。
12	between 1923 and 1954	第十一段第一句： Dowman used Cutty Sark as a training ship, and she continued in this role after his death.	本题问到 1923 到 1954 年期间，Cutty Sark 被用来做什么。根据上一题的信息，从第十段的 1922 之后，到十一段第二句 1954 之间，属于定位区域。通过阅读这部分文字，不难发现第十一段首句说到，这期间 Cutty Sark 主要被作为 a training ship，因此本题答案为 training。

题号	定位词	文中对应点	题目解析
13	twice been damaged, in the 21st century	第十一段第三句： The ship suffered from fire in 2007, and again, less seriously, in 2014, but now Cutty Sark attracts a quarter of a million visitors a year.	文中最后一段中提到，21 世纪 Cutty Sark 经历过两次火灾，时间分别是 2007 年和 2014 年，文中 suffered from fire 的表述与提问形式比较一致，因此本题答案为 fire。

∽ 参考译文

──────────── 卡蒂萨克号：史上最快的帆船 ────────────

19 世纪是英国发生巨大技术发展的时期，对造船而言主要的转变在于从风能转向蒸汽能，从木材转向钢铁。

史上速度最快的商业帆船是快速帆船，这种三桅船被用来在世界范围内运输货物，尽管其中的一些也运送乘客。从 19 世纪 40 年代到 1869 年，随着苏伊士运河的开通以及蒸汽动力逐渐替代船帆，快速帆船成为了世界贸易的主导。尽管人们建造了很多船只，只有一艘几乎被完整地保存下来：卡蒂萨克号，它如今陈列在伦敦东南部的格林威治。

卡蒂萨克这个有些特殊的名字来自苏格兰诗人 Robert Burn 的诗歌 *Tam O'shanter*。Tam 是一位农民，他被一名叫做 Nannie 的女巫追逐，女巫穿着"卡蒂萨克"，这是一种古老的苏格兰短睡衣的名字。女巫的形象被用作卡蒂萨克的船头雕像，也就是在古老帆船船头雕刻的女性人像。在传说以及 Burn 的诗歌中，女巫是无法穿过水域的，因此这个名字的选择确实非常奇怪。

卡蒂萨克号于 1869 年在苏格兰登巴顿为一家属于 John Willis 的航运公司建造。为了完成建设，Willis 选择了一家新的造船厂，Scott & Linton，并确保在与他们的合同中处于非常优势的地位。最终，这家工厂被迫破产，船只由一家竞争者建造完成。

Willis 的公司在中英两国间的茶叶贸易方面非常活跃，速度会给船主带来利润和声望，因此设计卡蒂萨克号就是为了使旅程比其他船只更快。她于 1870 年首航，从伦敦出发，带着大量货物到达中国。船只装载着茶叶返航，用了四个月时间回到伦敦。然而，由于恶劣的天气和各种不走运，卡蒂萨克号并没有达到主人的高预期。在 1872 年，有一次卡蒂萨克号和另一艘帆船 Thermopylae 在同一天离开中国港口。她们穿越印度洋，卡蒂萨克号领先 400 英里，但之后她的船舵在波涛汹涌的大海中严重损坏，使其无法驾驶。船员们不得不在海上修理船舵，并在第二次尝试中才取得成功。卡蒂萨克号晚于 Thermopylae 一星期到达伦敦。

随着速度和货物运载量的增加，蒸汽船给快速帆船带来的威胁越来越多。此外，苏伊士运河于 1869 年开通，这也是卡蒂萨克号建造完成的时间，运河的开通有很大影响。蒸汽船可以使用地中海和红海之间快捷、直接的线路，运河对帆船来说是没用的，帆船需要大海更强的风力，因此需要航行更远距离。蒸汽船将往返于英国和中国的航程缩小了将近两个小时。

到了 1878 年，卡蒂萨克号不再受到茶叶贸易者的青睐，相反，她承担起了一些并不重要的任务，在世界上任意两个港口间运送各种货物。1880 年，船只上的暴力最终导致船长更换为一位没有能力的醉汉，他拿走了船员们的薪水。他被禁止继续在这里工作，并任命了一位新的船长。这意味着转机的到来，并开始了卡蒂萨克号服役期间最成功的一段时期，船只负责将羊毛从澳洲运送到英国。一次这样的航行用时不到 12 周，比当年任何船只都节省了大约一个月。

船只的下一任船长，Richard Woodget，是一位出色的领航员，使他的船只和船员发挥了最充分的作用。作为帆船，卡蒂萨克号依靠南半球的强烈信风，Woodget 比之前历任船长将船只带到了更向南的地方，接近危险的南美洲南端的冰川。他的冒险得到了回报，卡蒂萨克号成为十年间进行羊毛贸易最快速的船只。

随着 19 世纪 90 年代蒸汽船竞争的增加，卡蒂萨克号到达了使用寿命的末期，她不再有那么强的盈利能力。她被卖到了一家葡萄牙工厂，并被重命名为 Ferreira 号。在之后的 25 年间，她又在世界范围内运送各种各样的货物。

她在 1922 年的一场大风中受到巨大破坏，被送到了英国西南部的法尔茅斯湾进行维修。一位拥有一艘训练船的退休船长 Wilfred Dowman 认出了卡蒂萨克号并想要购买她，但并未成功。她回到葡萄牙，被卖给了另一家葡萄牙公司。然而 Dowman 下定决心并给出高价，价格被对方接受，船只在之后的一年回到法尔茅斯湾并恢复使用最初的名字。

Dowman 使用卡蒂萨克号作为训练船，在他死后船只继续扮演着这样的角色。1954 年，她不再有航行任务，被改用作干船坞并在格林威治进行公开展览。卡蒂萨克号在 2007 年遭遇火灾，并在 2014 年再次经历了一次不太严重的火灾，如今她每年能吸引 25 万游客前去参观。

Reading Passage 2

篇章结构

体裁	论说文
主题	保护土壤的必要性和可能措施
结构	第一段：土壤破坏对人们有巨大的威胁
	第二段：人们对土壤重要性的理解在增加
	第三段：土壤的主要作用
	第四段：土壤破坏会导致微生物的破坏
	第五段：土壤破坏对农业的影响
	第六段：人们通过使用合成肥料保护土壤
	第七段：使用化肥带来的问题
	第八段：人们开发了一种混合物用以保护土壤
	第九段：人们希望获得土壤监控的全球地图
	第十段：需要用政府和大众容易理解的方式描述方案
	第十一段：需要解决对哪些土壤进行保护的问题
	第十二段：需要尽快采取行动解决土壤问题

难度系数： ★★★

解题顺序： SUMMARY (14~17) → MATCHING (18~21) → MATCHING (22~26)

友情提示： 本文针对土壤衰退现象带来的危害以及可能的解决措施进行分析，篇幅较长，信息量也比较大，但由于分段清晰，观点之间也没有太多复杂的关系，因此阅读和解题时，找准文中对应的区域即可。题目方面，首先完成 SUMMARY，这部分题目出题位置比较靠前，之后完成 MATCHING SENTENCE ENDING，最后完成乱序出题的 MATCHING INFORMATION。

📖 必背词汇

1. decline *n./v.* 下降；衰退

   The company reported a small *decline* in its profits. 公司报告其利润略有减少。

   An increase in cars has resulted in the *decline* of public transport. 汽车的增加导致了公共交通的减少。

2. sustain *v.* 维持，支撑；遭受（损失）

   Which planets can *sustain* life? 哪些行星可以维持生命的存在？

   The company *sustained* losses of millions of dollars. 公司遭受了数百万元的巨大损失。

3. recover *v.* 恢复

   The economy is at last beginning to *recover*. 经济终于开始复苏了。

   The skater stumbled but at once *recovered* himself. 滑冰的人绊了一下，但立刻恢复了平衡。

4. commercial *adj.* 商业的

   I work for a *commercial* radio station. 我在一家商业广播电台工作。

   British Rail has indeed become more *commercial* over the past decade.

   过去 10 年来，英国铁路确实变得更加商业化了。

5. manufacture *v.* 制造，加工 *n.* 制造；产品；制造业

   The date of *manufacture* of the jewellery has not been authenticated. 这些珠宝的制造日期尚未经证实。

   They make *manufactures* from their own raw materials. 他们用自己的原料制造产品。

6. classify *v.* 分类；分等

   It is necessary initially to *classify* the headaches into certain types. 首先，必须将头痛分为几个类型。

   Librarians spend a lot of time *classifying* books. 图书馆工作人员花许多时间将书分类。

7. approach *n.* 方法，途径 *v.* 接近，靠近

   We have a very communicative *approach* to teaching languages.

   我们在语言教学中非常强调交际教学法。

   He *approached* the question as a scientist. 他以一个科学家的眼光去处理这个问题。

8. conserve *v.* 保存，保护

   He writes on both sides of the sheet to *conserve* paper. 他在纸张的两面都写字以节省用纸。

   to *conserve* energy by insulating your home 对房屋做隔热处理来帮助节约能源

layer	*n.* 层，层次	fertile	*adj.* 富饶的，肥沃的
endangered	*adj.* 濒临灭绝的	synthetic	*adj.* 综合的，合成的
farmable	*adj.* 可耕种的	fertiliser	*n.* 化肥
degradation	*n.* 退化	release	*v.* 释放；发射
bacteria	*n.* 细菌	indiscriminate	*adj.* 任意而为的，不加选择的
microorganism	*n.* 微生物	acidic	*adj.* 酸的，酸性的
virus	*n.* 病毒	nourish	*v.* 滋养
fungi	*n.* 真菌；菌类	emerge	*v.* 出现；形成
decompose	*v.* 分解，腐烂	scale	*n.* 规模；比例
mineral	*n.* 矿物	accessible	*adj.* 可获得的，可进入的
antibiotics	*n.* 抗生素	vice versa	反之亦然
ally	*n.* 同盟，伙伴	neutrality	*n.* 中性，平衡
digest	*v.* 消化，吸收	agitate	*v.* 煽动，争论
property	*n.* 性质，特性	diversity	*n.* 多样性，差异
nutrient	*n.* 营养物	benchmark	*n.* 基准；标准

佳句赏析

1. Soil is also an ally against climate change: as microorganisms within soil digest dead animals and plants, they lock in their carbon content, holding three times the amount of carbon as does the entire atmosphere.

   • 参考译文：土壤同样可以帮助我们对抗气候变化：由于土壤中的微生物消化死去的动物和植物，它们可以留住动植物的碳成分，保存相当于整个大气层三倍的碳含量。

   • 语言点：首先出现主句 Soil is also an ally against climate change，冒号后面的部分对主句进行解释说明，这一部分中，主句是 they lock in their carbon content，前面的 as microorganisms within soil digest dead animals and plants 和后面的 holding three times the amount of carbon as does the entire atmosphere 都是状语成分，起修饰作用。

2. When they applied Floris's mix to the desert-like test plots, a good crop of plants emerged that were not just healthy at the surface, but had roots strong enough to pierce dirt as hard as rock.

   • 参考译文：当他们将 Floris 的混合物用在沙漠般的试验区时，长出的作物不仅表层是健康的，根系也发达到可以刺穿岩石般坚硬的泥土。

   • 语言点：本句中首先出现的是修饰成分 When they applied Floris's mix to the desert-like test plots，之后的主句部分中，比较重要的是 that 定语从句中包含了 not..., but... 结构。平时分析句子时，将主句与修饰成分划分清楚，同时看清句子结构起到的作用，对增强阅读能力会起到很大帮助。

3. Researchers from nine countries are working together to create a map linked to a database that can be fed measurements from field surveys, drone surveys, satellite imagery, lab analyses and so on to provide real-time data on the state of the soil.

   • 参考译文：来自九个国家的研究者们正在共同建立一张连接到数据库的地图，它可以获得来自实地考察、无人机考察、卫星影像、实验室分析等方式的测量数据，以提供关于土壤状态的实时数据。

- 语言点：本句出现的修饰成分比较多，from nine countries 作为后置定语对 researchers 进行修饰，linked to a database 对 a map 进行修饰，之后的 that 定语从句对 database 进行修饰，定语从句中 field surveys, drone surveys, satellite imagery, lab analyses and so on 这一并列结构是信息收集的具体方式，同时本句中出现了两次目的状语，分别是 to create a map 和 to provide real-time data on the state of the soil。

⚙ 试题解析

Questions 14~17

- 题目类型：SUMMARY
- 题目解析：

题号	定位词	文中对应点	题目解析
14	healthy soil, bacteria, microorganisms	B 第一段第三句：A single gram of healthy soil might contain 100 million bacteria, as well as other microorganisms such as viruses and fungi, living amid decomposing plants and various minerals.	本题针对健康土壤中的主要成分进行提问，文中 B 第一段第三句与题目中的句子有明确的对应关系。题目中说到了 bacteria, other microorganisms, plant remains，这些在原文中都可以找到对应的词汇，而原文中最后提到的 various minerals 与题目中的空格对应，结合题目中 one word only 的要求，本题答案为 minerals。
15	food, antibiotics, storing, climate	B 第二段第一、二句：That means soils do not just grow our food, but are the source of nearly all our existing antibiotics, and... Soil is also an ally against climate change: ..., they lock in their carbon content, holding three times the amount of carbon as does the entire atmosphere.	本题依然针对土壤的作用出题，根据句中说到的 food 和 antibiotics，可以将本句与原文中 B 第二段第一句对应，之后根据出题位置提到的 a significant effect on the climate，定位到本段第二句，本句说到可以 lock in their carbon content, holding three times the amount of carbon as does the entire atmosphere，这里的 holding 与题目中 storing 一致，本题答案为 carbon。
16	damage to property and infrastructure	B 第二段第三句：Soils also store water, preventing flood damage: in the UK, damage to buildings, roads and bridges from floods caused by soil degradation costs £233 million every year.	本段最后一句说到在英国，damage to buildings, roads, bridges from floods 所带来的损失，这部分与题目中 damage to property and infrastructure 的描述一致，土壤能够防止这些损失的发生，主要是因为原文中说到的 soils also store water，这里的 store 与题目中的 holds 同义替换，本题答案为 water。

题号	定位词	文中对应点	题目解析
17	microorga-nisms, special properties	C 第二段第一句： Agriculture is by far the biggest problem.	本题中说到如果 microorganisms 消失，土壤会失去其 special properties，这一表达与原文 C 第一段一致，而 C 第二段首句说明 Agriculture is by far the biggest problem，之后说明了为什么人类农业行为会破坏土壤的生态，而题目中问的是造成这种土壤退化现象的主要原因是人类的什么行为，本题答案为 agriculture。

Questions 18~21

- **题目类型**：MATCHING
- **题目解析**：

题号	定位词	文中对应点	题目解析
18	unused parts of harvested crops	C 第二段第三句： Humans tend not to return unused parts of harvested crops directly to the soil to enrich it, meaning that the soil gradually becomes less fertile.	本题问到关于 unused parts of harvested crops 的问题，可以在 C 第二段第三句中找到对应的表达。原文中说到 Humans tend not to return unused parts of harvested crops directly to the soil，也就是说这一部分往往不会被返还到土壤中，这与选项 C 中 may not be put back into the soil 一致，因此本题答案为 C。
19	synthetic fertilisers, the Haber-Bosch process	D 第二段第一、二、三句： But over the past few decades, it has become clear this wasn't such a bright idea. Chemical fertilisers can release polluting nitrous oxide into the atmosphere and excess is often washed away with the rain, releasing nitrogen into rivers. More recently, we have found that indiscriminate use of fertilisers hurts the soil itself, turning it acidic and salty, and degrading the soil they are supposed to nourish.	原文中 D 第一段说到了使用 Haber-Bosch process 来制作合成化肥的方法，而 D 第二段首句说到 it has become clear this wasn't such a bright idea，并在之后的两句话中具体解释了这种方法造成的影响，包括污染河流、加速土壤退化等，选项 E 中 may cause damage to different aspects of the environment 可以概括这里的描述，因此本题答案为 E。
20	a mixture developed by Pius Floris	E 段第四句： When they applied Floris's mix to the desert-like test plots, a good crop of plants emerged that were not just healthy at the surface, but had roots strong enough to pierce dirt as hard as rock.	E 段第四句的内容与本题题干一致，说明加入这种 mixture 对植物的生长有很大好处，选项 A 中 may improve the number and quality of plants growing there 与之一致，因此本题答案为 A。

题号	定位词	文中对应点	题目解析
21	zero net soil degradation	G 第一段第四、五句：Chasek and her colleagues have proposed a goal of 'zero net land degradation'. Like the idea of carbon neutrality, it is an easily understood target that can help shape expectations and encourage action.	关于 zero net soil degradation 的表述出现在原文 G 第一段第四句，根据上下文，可以了解到这是一种更容易被理解的说法，而第五句中也说到 it is an easily understood target，选项 D 的表述与之一致，因此本题答案为 D。

Questions 22~26

- 题目类型：MATCHING
- 题目解析：

22. a reference to one person's motivation for a soil-improvement project

参考译文	提到一个人进行土壤改善项目的动机
定位词	motivation for a soil-improvement project
文中对应点	E 段第一、二句：One of the people looking for a solution to this problem is Pius Floris, who started out running a tree-care business in the Netherlands... He came to realise that the best way to ensure his trees flourished was to take care of the soil, and has developed a cocktail of beneficial bacteria, fungi and humus to do this. 文章 E 段首句提到 Pius Floris 从事 tree-care business，并给一些土壤科学家提供了建议，而第二句中写到 He came to realise that the best way to ensure his trees flourished was to take care of the soil，因此他的 motivation 是希望 ensure his trees flourished，这部分表述与题目信息一致，因此本题答案为 E。

23. an explanation of how soil stayed healthy before the development of farming

参考译文	对于农业发展之前土壤如何保持健康的一种解释
定位词	how soil stayed healthy before the development of farming
文中对应点	C 第二段第二句：In the wild, when plants grow they remove nutrients from the soil, but then when the plants die and decay these nutrients are returned directly to the soil. C 第二段中说到自然环境下，植物生长时会带走土壤中的营养物质，但随着植物衰退腐烂，这些营养物质会直接返还到土壤中，而人类往往不会在农业行为中返回一些庄稼或作物，这一部分对比了大自然自身的生态循环方式和人类的行为，而前面一部分与题目中 how soil stayed healthy before the development of farming 的表述一致，因此本题答案为 C。

24. examples of different ways of collecting information on soil degradation

参考译文	关于收集土壤退化信息的不同方式的例子
定位词	different ways of collecting information on soil degradation

文中对应点	F 段第六句：Researchers from nine countries are working together to create a map linked to a database that can be fed measurements from field surveys, drone surveys, satellite imagery, lab analyses and so on to provide real-time data on the state of the soil. 文中 F 段提到为了评估保护土壤的措施，首先需要了解全球土壤的状况以及它们面对的问题，在这种情况下联合国建立了 Global Soil Map project，而为了收集信息，本段第六句列举了人们使用的方式，包括 field surveys, drone surveys, satellite imagery, lab analyses 等，这与题目中 different ways of collecting information on soil degradation 的表述一致，因此本题答案为 F。

25. a suggestion for a way of keeping some types of soil safe in the near future

参考译文	关于在不久的将来保持一些类型的土壤健康的建议
定位词	a way of keeping some types of soil safe in the near future
文中对应点	G 第二段第二句：Several researchers are agitating for the immediate creation of protected zones for endangered soils. 文中 G 第二段中提到了通过建立土壤保护区的方式，对一些类型的土壤进行保护，这与题目中 a way of keeping some types of soil safe in the near future 的表述一致，当然在本段第三句中，也提出了这种做法面临的困难，即如何界定在其中需要保护哪些土壤，因此本题答案为 G。

26. a reason why it is difficult to provide an overview of soil degradation

参考译文	很难提供土壤退化的整体概况的原因
定位词	difficult to provide an overview of soil degradation
文中对应点	F 段第四句：For one thing, there is no agreed international system for classifying soil. 文章 F 段提出为了评估保护土壤的措施，首先需要了解全球土壤的状况以及它们面对的问题，但是这并不容易：there is no agreed international system for classifying soil，也正是由于这个原因，联合国建立了 Global Soil Map project，所以这部分内容与题目中 why it is difficult to provide an overview of soil degradation 的描述一致，因此本题答案为 F。

参考译文

———————————— 保护土壤 ————————————

地球上超过三分之一的表层土壤面临威胁。我们星球最珍贵的资源是否还有希望被保护？

A 根据一项最近的联合国报告，世界上超过三分之一的土壤正在遭受破坏。如果我们不减缓这种衰退趋势，所有可耕种的土壤会在 60 年内消失。由于我们食物中的 95% 需要依靠土壤，并且土壤在其他更多方面维持人类生命，所以这是一个巨大的问题。

B 来自纽约卡瑞生态系统研究所的 Peter Groffman 指出在几十年间，土壤科学家一直针对地球上的土壤退化现象发出警告。与此同时，我们关于土壤对人类的重要性的理解也在提高。仅一克健康土壤中就可能含有一亿细菌，以及一些其他微生物，如病毒和真菌，它们存在于腐烂植物和各种矿物质中。这意味着土壤并不是只用来种植食物，而是几乎所有现存抗生素的来源，并且可能是我们对抗耐药性细菌的最大希望。土壤同样可以帮助我们对抗气候变化：由于土壤中的微生物消化死去的动物和植物，它们可以留住动植物的碳成分，保存相当于整个大气层三倍的碳含量。土壤同样可以贮存水分，防止洪水灾害：在英国，每年由于土壤退化而遭受洪灾的建筑物、道路和桥梁需要花费 2.33 亿英镑来修复。

C　如果土壤失去发挥这些功能的能力，人类会陷入巨大的麻烦。这种危险并不在于土壤会完全消失，而在于赋予土壤特殊性质的微生物将会消失。一旦这种情况发生，土壤需要几千年才可以恢复原有的状态。

到目前为止农业是最大的问题。自然环境下，植物生长时会带走土壤中的营养物质，但随着植物衰退腐烂，这些营养物质会直接返还到土壤中。人类往往不会将所收获庄稼的未使用部分直接返还到土壤中使其更加肥沃，这意味着土壤会逐渐变得越发贫瘠。过去我们使用各种方法避开这一问题，比如定期改变种植农作物的品种，或是在一个季度中不对田地进行耕作。

D　但是随着人口增加以及农业以更加商业化的方式进行，这些方法变得不再可行。20 世纪早期，随着制作硝胺酸的哈布二氏法出现，人们找到了一种解决方法。自此以后农民们将这种合成肥料用在自己的农场里。

但是在最近的几十年，人们发现这显然并不是一个非常明智的主意。化肥会向大气中释放污染性的一氧化二氮，过量部分则经常被雨水冲走，从而将氮元素带到河流中。最近，我们发现滥用化肥对土壤本身也有很大伤害，使其变成酸性且含盐度高，并且使那些本想被其滋养的土壤出现退化。

E　Pius Floris 在荷兰经营一家树木护理公司，他是寻求这一问题解决方法的人之一，现在他开始为一些世界顶级土壤科学家提供建议。他意识到保证树木得到滋养的最佳方式是保护土壤，并且开发了一种有益菌、真菌和腐殖质的混合物来实现这一目的。西班牙巴利亚多利德大学的研究者们最近给一些土壤使用了这种混合物，这些土壤由于过度使用肥料被破坏。当他们将 Floris 的混合物用在沙漠般的试验区时，长出的作物不仅表层是健康的，根系也发达到可以刺穿岩石般坚硬的泥土。而用传统肥料养成的对照区的植物，则细小而脆弱。

F　然而，这种方法并不足以解决全球土壤退化问题。为了评估我们在全球规模上可以采取的措施，我们首先需要关于每个地方的土壤种类以及它们所面临问题的精确描述。这并不容易。一方面，尚没有一致的关于土壤分类的国际通行体系。在努力统一不同方法的过程中，联合国建立了全球土壤地图项目。来自九个国家的研究者们正在共同建立一张连接到数据库的地图，它可以获得来自实地考察、无人机考察、卫星影像、实验室分析等方式的测量数据，以提供关于土壤状态的实时数据。在未来四年中，他们的目标是绘制世界范围内深度在 100 米以内土壤的地图，并将结果免费提供给所有人。

G　但这仅仅是第一步。我们需要呈现问题并使政府和更广泛的公众了解这一情况的途径，来自加拿大温尼伯国际可持续发展研究所的 Pamela Chasek 说。"大多数科学家说的并不是政策制定者们能够听得懂的语言，相反政府人员说的话他们也无法理解。"Chasek 和她的同事们提出了"零土地净退化"的目标。就像碳平衡的想法一样，这是一个非常容易被理解的目标，可以帮助人们描述预期并鼓励行动。

对处于衰退边缘的土壤，这些或许都为时已晚。几位研究者呼吁马上建立针对濒危土壤的保护区。这里的一个困难是界定这些地区应该保护什么：呈现出最高土壤多样性的地区？还是有未受破坏的土壤可以作为未来质量标准的地区？

无论我们做什么，如果我们希望土壤得以存活，我们需要当下就采取行动。

Reading Passage 3

📖 篇章结构

体裁	议论文
主题	积极心理学对社会发展的作用
结构	第一段：积极心理学的主要观点和作用
	第二段：哲学家关于人类幸福的探讨
	第三段：书中对 Bentham 的主要工作进行了描述
	第四段：关于如何量化幸福的讨论
	第五段：有的心理学家认为人的行为是可被塑造的
	第六段：政府应促进幸福这一观点与人类自由的矛盾

🌐 解题地图

难度系数： ★★★★★

解题顺序： MULTIPLE CHOICE (27~29) → SUMMARY (30~34) → YES/NO/NOT GIVEN (35~40)

友情提示： 本文属于书评性质，文中提到几个不同的描写对象，并对他们进行了评述。阅读时需要注意两点：一是在复杂的评述中，把握住评论者的主要态度是积极还是消极，支持还是反对，不要陷入复杂的句式和举例中；二是需要分清楚评论的对象，是对积极心理学，还是对《幸福产业》，或是对 Bentham。这篇文章相对来说难度较大，阅读时需要把握以上两个重点。题目方面可以首先完成 MULTIPLE CHOICE，然后完成 SUMMARY 和 YES/NO/NOT GIVEN，即没有乱序题的情况下，按照正常顺序解题即可。

🔤 必背词汇

1. ultimate *adj.* 最终的；极限的
   This race will be the *ultimate* test of your skill. 这次竞赛将是对你的技能的最大考验。
   He said it is still not possible to predict the *ultimate* outcome. 他说现在还无法预料最终的结局。

2. advocate *n.* 提倡者，支持者 *v.* 提倡，主张
   We do not *advocate* the use of violence. 我们不支持使用暴力。
   Many experts *advocate* rewarding your child for good behaviour.
   很多专家主张对小孩的良好表现加以奖励。

3. identify *v.* 确定，鉴定，识别
   First of all we must *identify* the problem areas. 首先我们必须找出问题所在。
   As yet they have not *identified* a buyer for the company. 迄今为止他们还没有为公司找到买主。

4. ethical *adj.* 伦理的，道德的

It is necessary to get the youth to have a high *ethical* concept. 必须使青年具有高度的道德观念。

Is it *ethical* to promote cigarettes through advertising? 通过广告推销香烟合乎道德吗？

5. adopt *v.* 采取，采纳，接受

All three teams *adopted* different approaches to the problem. 三个队处理这个问题的方法各不相同。

The council is expected to *adopt* the new policy at its next meeting.

委员会有望在下次会议上正式通过这项新政策。

6. tendency *n.* 倾向，趋势

There is a *tendency* for this disease to run in families. 这种疾病易在家族里遗传。

Prices continue to show an upward *tendency*. 物价呈继续上升的趋势。

7. apply *v.* 应用；申请

They may *apply* to join the organization. 他们可以申请加入该组织。

These regulations *apply* to everyone, without exception. 这些规章对谁都适用，没有例外。

8. establish *v.* 建立，创办

The School was *established* in 1989 by an Italian professor. 这所学院由一名意大利教授于 1989 年创建。

We had already *established* contact with the museum. 我们已经和那家博物馆建立了联系。

认知词汇

well-being	*n.* 幸福，康乐	confinement	*n.* 监禁；限制
external	*adj.* 外部的	sensation	*n.* 感觉
pronouncement	*n.* 声明，宣告	pulse	*n.* 脉冲，脉搏
summarise	*v.* 概括，总结	alternatively	*adv.* 二者择一地，或者
collective	*adj.* 集体的，共同的	quantification	*n.* 定量，量化
oblivious	*adj.* 遗忘的，不知道的	associate	*v.* 联想，联系
philosophical	*adj.* 哲学的	entangle	*v.* 使纠缠，使混乱
reconcile	*v.* 使一致，使和解	capitalism	*n.* 资本主义
metaphysics	*n.* 形而上学	integral	*adj.* 完整的，整体的
virtue	*n.* 美德，优点	malady	*n.* 弊病，疾病
lucid	*adj.* 明晰的，易懂的	founder	*n.* 创始人，建立者
arresting	*adj.* 醒目的，有趣的	behaviourism	*n.* 行为主义
banknote	*n.* 纸币	desirable	*adj.* 令人满意的
solitary	*adj.* 单独的；孤独的	pedigree	*n.* 血统；起源

佳句赏析

1. The only question is how to achieve it, and here positive psychology — a supposed science that not only identifies what makes people happy but also allows their happiness to be measured — can show the way.

- 参考译文：唯一的问题是如何达到这种状态，在这方面积极心理学会提供方法，这门所谓的科学不仅界定什么使人们感到幸福，也会使幸福能够被测量。
- 语言点：本句中，主句为 The only question is how to achieve it, and here positive psychology can show the way，句中出现了比较长的插入语，对前面的名词 positive psychology 进行解释，说明人们希望积极心理学不仅能够界定是什么为人们带来幸福，同时也使幸福可以被测量。

2. Those who think in this way are oblivious to the vast philosophical literature in which the meaning and value of happiness have been explored and questioned, and write as if nothing of any importance had been thought on the subject until it came to their attention.

- 参考译文：那些以这种方式思考的人并未了解丰富的哲学文献，在其中幸福的含义和价值已经被探究和问询，并且他们在写作时，就像在他们开始关心这一主题之前任何重要的事情都没有被思考过一样。

- 语言点：本句主语为 Those who think in this way，两个并列的动词分别是 are 和 write，因此第一个分句为 are oblivious to the vast philosophical literature in which the meaning...questioned，第二个分句为 write as if nothing of any importance had been thought...attention。

3. The Greek philosopher Aristotle may have identified happiness with self-realisation in the 4th century BC, and thinkers throughout the ages may have struggled to reconcile the pursuit of happiness with other human values, but for Bentham all this was mere metaphysics or fiction.

- 参考译文：希腊哲学家亚里士多德或许在公元前 4 世纪将幸福定义为与自我实现有关，这一时代的思想家们似乎在努力处理好对幸福的追求与其他人类价值之间的关系，但对 Bentham 而言这一切都只是形而上的或虚构的东西。

- 语言点：本句共包含三个分句，转折前的两个分句分别是 The Greek philosopher Aristotle...in the 4th century BC 和 thinkers throughout the ages may have...other human values，but 之后给出了 Bentham 对这种观点的态度，即 all this was mere metaphysics or fiction。

✿ 试题解析

Questions 27~29

- **题目类型**：MULTIPLE CHOICE
- **题目解析**：

题号	定位词	题目解析
27	the reviewer's attitude, advocates of positive psychology	题目：评论者对积极心理学倡导者的态度是什么？ A. 他们拒绝 Bentham 的观点是错误的。 B. 他们受到对 Bentham 理论研究的过度影响。 C. 他们对于人类幸福的观点有全新的方法。 D. 他们对自己应当考虑的观点一无所知。 分析：本题考查评论者对积极心理学倡导者的态度，原文第一段首先引出积极心理学及其主要观点，第二段开头开始进行评论性质的描述：an astonishingly crude and simple-minded way of thinking，之后进行了进一步解释：oblivious to the vast philosophical literature in which the meaning and value of happiness have been explored and questioned, and write as if nothing of any importance had been thought on the subject until it came to their attention，可以看出评论者对积极心理学的倡导者们忽略之前人们的讨论和研究的做法是不满意的，而在后文中也能找到类似的表述：without knowing anything much of him or the school of moral theory he established，D 选项的含义与之一致，因此本题答案为 D。

题号	定位词	题目解析
28	Aristotle	题目：评论者提到希腊哲学家亚里士多德是为了说明幸福_____ A. 或许不只是愉悦和无痛苦。 B. 不应当成为人类的主要目标。 C. 不是应当追求的东西。 D. 不只是一个抽象概念。 分析：文中第二段提到 Bentham 的观点：For Bentham it was obvious that the human good consists of pleasure and the absence of pain，之后提到亚里士多德：may have identified happiness with self-realisation in the 4th century BC，并指出这一时代的思想家们似乎在努力处理好对幸福的追求与其他人类价值之间的关系，而这些对 Bentham 而言只是形而上的或虚构的东西，可见亚里士多德对幸福的定义和思考与 Bentham 不同，选项中 A 的表达与此一致，因此本题答案为 A。
29	linking the price of goods to happiness	题目：对 Davies 而言，Bentham 将商品价格与幸福紧密联系的观点很重要是因为_____ A. 这是评估幸福的第一种成功方式。 B. 这建立了工作和心理学间的联系。 C. 这是心理学研究的第一个成功案例。 D. 这考虑到了消费者的权利。 分析：文章第四段中提到了将商品价格与幸福进行联系的观点：money could be used as the standard for quantification，之后 Davies 对 Bentham 这一主张的评价是：set the stage for the entangling of psychological research and capitalism that would shape the business practices of the twentieth century，而 B 选项 it established a connection between work and psychology 与这一观点一致，因此本题答案为 B。

Questions 30~34

- 题目类型：SUMMARY
- 题目解析：

题号	定位词	文中对应点	题目解析
30	1790s, government	第三段第五句： In the 1790s, he wrote to the Home Office suggesting that the departments of government be linked together through a set of 'conversation tubes', and to the Bank of England with a design for a printing device that could produce unforgeable banknotes.	题目中首句说到 Bentham 在哲学之外的领域也非常活跃，这一表达在原文中第三段出现，并具体讨论了 Bentham 提出的建议。题目问到在 1790s，为不同政府部门建议的 type of technology 对应本段第五句，这里提到的 a set of 'conversation tubes' 是为了促进不同部门间的交流，本题答案为 F。

题号	定位词	文中对应点	题目解析
31	printing banknotes	第三段第五句： In the 1790s, he wrote to the Home Office suggesting that the departments of government be linked together through a set of 'conversation tubes', and to the Bank of England with a design for a printing device that could produce unforgeable banknotes.	题目中说到 He developed a new way of printing banknotes，这一表达同样出现在第三段第五句，原文中说到 a design for a printing devices that could produce unforgeable banknotes，可见这一做法的目的是为了让纸币无法被伪造，从而提高其安全性，选项中 security 与原文含义一致，本题答案为 B。
32	food	第三段第六句： He drew up plans for a 'frigidarium' to keep provisions such as meat, fish, fruit and vegetables fresh.	本题问到关于 food 方面的做法，原文中第三段第六句中提到了 provisions such as meat, fish, fruit and vegetables，这部分与 food 含义一致，而 Bentham 希望让它们 keep fresh，选项中的 preservation 与原文含义一致，本题答案为 G。
33	prison	第三段第七句： His celebrated design for a prison to be known as a 'Panopticon', in which prisoners would be kept in solitary confinement while being visible at all times to the guards, was very nearly adopted.	本题问到与 prison 有关的内容，原文中第三段第七句说到 prisoners would be kept in solitary confinement while being visible at all times to the guards，也就是说守卫可以随时看到犯人的情况，因此这与对犯人的 observation 有关，本题答案为 E。
34	researching happiness, suggested some methods	第四段第一、二句： Bentham was also a pioneer of the 'science of happiness'. If happiness is to be regarded as a science, it has to be measured, and Bentham suggested two ways in which this might be done.	文中第四段开头说到幸福作为一门科学，需要能够被测量，Bentham 提出了两种不同的方法，这与题目中的表达一致，Bentham 关注的是对幸福的 measurement，本题答案为 A。

Questions 35~40

- **题目类型**：YES/NO/NOT GIVEN
- **题目解析**：

35. One strength of *The happiness Industry* is its discussion of the relationship between psychology and economics.

参考译文	《幸福产业》一书的优点之一是它讨论了心理学和经济学之间的关系。
定位词	*The happiness industry*
解题关键点	discussion of the relationship between psychology and economics
文中对应点	第五段第一、二句：*The Happiness Industry* describes how the project of a science of happiness has become integral to capitalism. We learn much that is interesting about how economic problems are being redefined and treated as psychological maladies. 第五段首句出现了《幸福产业》这本书，并说明本书写到了 how the project of a science of happiness has become integral to capitalism，并在第二句说明用心理学的方式定义和解决经济学问题是本书的特点，题目表述与原文一致，因此本题答案为 YES。

36. It is more difficult to measure some emotions than others.

参考译文	对一些情绪的测量比另一些更难。
定位词	to measure some emotions than others
解题关键点	more difficult
文中对应点	第五段第三、四、五句：In addition, Davies shows how the belief that inner states of pleasure and displeasure can be objectively measured has informed management studies and advertising. The tendency of thinkers...was that human beings could be shaped, or manipulated, by policymakers and managers. Watson had no factual basis for his view of human action. 本题的表达中含有比较关系，因此需要在文中对应位置判断是否将 some emotions 和 others 进行了对比。37 题考查华生的行为主义，并且有定位词 1915，结合上一题的位置，可以判断本题位于第五段第三至五句，在这一部分表述中，并没有提到一些情绪比另一些情绪更难测量，因此本题答案为 NOT GIVEN。

37. Watson's ideas on behaviourism were supported by research on humans he carried out before 1915.

参考译文	华生关于行为主义的理论得到了他 1915 年之前对人类研究的支持。
定位词	Watson's ideas on behaviourism, 1915
解题关键点	supported by research on humans
文中对应点	第五段第六句：When he became president of the American Psychological Association in 1915, he 'had never even studied a single human being': his research had been confined to experiments on white rats. 定位词 1915 出现在第五段第六句，关于华生，句中说到 had never even studied a single human being，并且 his research had been confined to experiments on while rats，说明华生的研究并不是针对人类的，而题目中 supported by research on humans 的表述与之相反，因此本题答案为 NO。

38. Watson's ideas have been most influential on governments outside America.

参考译文	华生的理论对除美国之外的政府影响力最大。
定位词	Watson's ideas
解题关键点	most influential on governments outside America
文中对应点	第五段第七句：Yet Watson's reductive model is now widely applied, with 'behaviour change' becoming the goal of governments: in Britain, a 'Behaviour Insights Team' has been established by the government to study how people can be encouraged, at minimum cost to the public purse, to live in what are considered to be socially desirable ways. 关于华生研究的影响力，文中第五段第七句中说到 now widely applied，并且行为改变也成了 goal of governments，之后举了英国的例子，说明华生的理论是如何应用的，但是并没有描述题目中所说的 most influential，英国的例子也无法完全代表题目中的 governments outside America，因此本题答案为 NOT GIVEN。

39. The need for happiness is linked to industrialisation.

参考译文	对幸福的需求与工业化有关。
定位词	The need for happiness
解题关键点	linked to industrialisation
文中对应点	第六段第一句：Modern industrial societies appear to need the possibility of ever-increasing happiness to motivate them in their labours. 本句提到的modern industrial societies和need the possibility of ever-increasing happiness与题目中的industrialisation和the need for happiness对应，题目表述与原文一致，因此本题答案为YES。

40. A main aim of government should be to increase the happiness of the population.

参考译文	政府的主要目的应当是增加人们的幸福感。
定位词	a main aim of government
解题关键点	to increase the happiness of the population
文中对应点	第六段第二句：But whatever its intellectual pedigree, the idea that governments should be responsible for promoting happiness is always a threat to human freedom. 第六段首句首先说明了社会中通过幸福感来激励工人是非常普遍的，但是第二句中通过转折说明了认为政府应当负责增进人们的幸福并不是一件好事，题目表述与原文相反，因此本题答案为NO。

参考译文

--------- 书评 ---------

《幸福产业》：政府和大公司是如何向我们兜售幸福的

"幸福是最终的目标，因为它本身毫无疑问是有益的。如果我们被问到为什么幸福很重要，我们不用给出进一步的外部原因，很明显幸福是很重要的。"作为一名经济学家和"积极心理学"的支持者，Richard Layard 的这一说法概括了当今很多人的想法。对 Layard 和其他与之类似的人来说，很明显政府的目的是促进一种共同幸福的状态。唯一的问题是如何达到这种状态，在这方面积极心理学会提供方法，这门所谓的科学不仅界定什么使人们感到幸福，也会使幸福能够被测量。他们说，在这门学科的帮助下，政府可以用一种之前从未有过的方式来保障社会幸福感。

这是一种令人吃惊的粗糙和简单的思考方式，并且正是由于这一原因变得越发流行。那些以这种方式思考的人并未了解丰富的哲学文献，在其中幸福的含义和价值已经被探究和问询，并且他们在写作时，就像在他们开始关心这一主题之前任何重要的事情都没有被思考过一样。哲学家 Jeremy Bentham（1748~1832）比其他任何人都更应为这种思考方式的发展负责。对 Bentham 而言，很明显人类的幸福包括喜悦和无痛苦。希腊哲学家亚里士多德或许在公元前 4 世纪将幸福定义为与自我实现有关，这一时代的思想家们似乎在努力处理好对幸福的追求与其他人类价值之间的关系，但对 Bentham 而言这一切都只是形而上的或虚构的东西。这些积极心理学的倡导者们由于受到教育和确定信念的影响，在思想史方面是无知的，他们对 Bentham 和他建立的道德理论学派一无所知，这些积极心理学的倡导者们跟随着他的足迹，拒绝追溯那些对人类幸福的伦理反映，在他们看来这是不合时宜又无关紧要的。

但是正如 William Davies 在他最近的《幸福产业》一书中指出的那样，认为幸福只是理所当然有好处的想法，实际上是一种对道德追问的限制。这本书内容丰富，观点明晰并且非常有趣，它的优点之一在于它将如今对幸福的狂热置于一个定义清楚的历史框架之中。Davies 恰如其分地从 Bentham 开始他的写作，指出他绝不仅仅是一位哲学家。Davies 写道，"Bentham 做的是那些或许我们今天会和公共部门管理顾问联系在一起的事情。"在 18 世纪 90 年代，他写信给内政部建议政府部门通过一系列"通话管"联系在一起，并建议英格兰银行设计一种印刷装置来生产无法被伪造的纸币。他起草了"冷藏室"计划来保持肉类、鱼类、水果和蔬菜等储存物的新鲜。他设计了著名的"圆形监狱"，在这里犯人会被单独囚禁并随时可以被守卫看到，这一设计几乎被政府采纳（Bentham 并不仅仅希望他的"圆形监狱"作为监狱的范例，他同样希望其作为一种管控工具在学校和工厂中应用，令人吃惊的是，Davies 并没有讨论这一事实。）

Bentham 同样是"幸福科学"的先驱。如果幸福要被作为一门科学，它就需要被测量，Bentham 建议了两种方式使之可能被实现。可以将幸福视为一系列愉快的情感，他提出幸福可以通过测量人的脉搏率得到量化。或者，金钱可以被用作量化标准：如果两种不同的商品价格相同，就可以说它们为顾客带来了相同程度的愉悦感。Bentham 更喜欢后一种测量方式。通过将金钱与内在体验如此紧密地建立联系，Davies 写道，Bentham "为心理学研究与资本主义的结合提供了舞台，这会塑造 20 世纪的商业实践。"

《幸福产业》描述了幸福科学是如何成为资本主义的一部分的。我们看到了很多有趣的现象，关于经济问题是如何被重新定义并被作为心理问题对待的。此外，Davies 揭示了内心的愉快或沮丧状态可以被客观测量这一观点是如何影响管理研究和广告的。像行为主义的创建者华生这一类思想家，认为人类是可以被政策制定者和管理者们塑造或控制的。华生关于人类行为的观点并没有事实基础。当他在 1915 年成为美国心理协会主席时，他"从未研究过任何一个人"：他的研究局限在关于小白鼠的实验上。但随着"行为改变"成为政府的目标，华生的还原模型如今被广泛应用：在英国，政府建立了一个"行为洞察团队"来研究如何以最低成本的公共资金来鼓励人们用一种社会认可的方式生活。

现代工业社会似乎需要不断增长的幸福可能性来激励劳动者。但无论知识的流派如何，政府应当负责促进幸福的观点一直是对人类自由的一种威胁。

Task 1

📖 题目要求

（见《剑桥雅思官方真题集 13：学术类》P94）

✒ 审题

题目翻译：以下的规划图展示了一所大学的体育中心现在的布局及将来改造后的样子。选取并汇报主要特征，总结信息，并在相关处进行对比。

💡 写作思路

非数据类图表一般分成两种：一种是流程图，另一种是地图。本图属于地图题，描述的关键在于体育中心改造后，哪些原有的设置消失了，出现了哪些新的东西或者面积的增加，以及还有哪些保持不变。

消失：东西两侧的户外球场 (outdoor courts)。

新增：西边休闲泳池 (leisure pool)，西南角和东南角的更衣室 (changing room)，南边接待处 (reception)的面积扩大，设置了商店 (sports shop) 和咖啡厅 (cafe)，北面的健身房 (gym) 也扩容了，一直延伸到最东边新建的两间舞蹈教室（dance studio），东边的户外球场 (outdoor courts) 改成了体育馆 (sports hall)。

保持不变：坐落于中心的泳池 (25m pool)，泳池西边的更衣室 (changing room) 及东边的座位 (seating)。

本题由两幅地图组成，写作时可以分成四段。第一段可以通过改写题目的说明性文字交代两幅地图的主要内容。第二段和第三段分别描述体育中心改造前后的情形。第四段总结两幅地图的主要区别。

☕ 考生作文

（见《剑桥雅思官方真题集 13：学术类》P133）

🔄 参考译文

以下的规划图展示了一所大学的体育中心现有的布局及重建后的样子。

根据新的布局，重建后的体育中心将变得更大。首先，健身房变大了且一个额外的更衣室将出现。除此之外，在接待处的区域还会有一个运动商店和咖啡厅。此外，两间舞蹈教室将在健身房的对面出现。最后，体育中心还将有一个新的休闲泳池。它将位于原本户外球场所在的位置。从新的布局图中可以看到，两个户外球场都将被重建后的体育中心的其他设施所取代。此外，一个体育馆将出现在大学体育中心里。从第二张图还能清晰地看到重建后的体育中心完全是室内的。

☕ 考官点评

（见《剑桥雅思官方真题集 13：学术类》P133）

参考译文

    本文回应了体育中心改造后的主要特征，但如果它能对该中心目前的情况有一个大致的介绍就会更好了。另外一个可以改进的地方是展示各个设施之间相对的方位关系：从本文的描述，读者很难了解健身房、休闲泳池和舞蹈教室将位于哪里。不过，本文的词汇范围高于平均水平（illustrate | reconstruction | redeveloped | additional | replaced by other facilities | renovated），展示了灵活度和准确性。有多种复杂结构的使用，如动词的现在时和将来时、被动形式和关系从句（the place where... | it is also clear...that）。可以用更多不同的方式来表示将来时：going to 用得太多了。

分析

    本文得分 6.5 分。

    接下来我们从四个评分方面（任务完成情况、连贯与衔接、词汇、语法）对这篇考生作文进行详细分析。

任务完成情况

    任务的完成情况主要是看图表中的核心信息是否被清晰有效地呈现。7分作文的要求是涵盖题目要求，清晰呈现并说明核心信息，但可以进行更加充分的扩展。而 6 分作文的要求则是呈现并说明核心信息，但细节可能不够相关、不合适或不准确。本文在内容方面符合 6 分作文的要求，没有描述体育中心现在的布局，且没有清晰地呈现方位，如东、南、西、北，导致读者无法想象布局的位置。

    第一段话介绍了图表的基本信息，对题目的内容稍加改写。

    第二段话直接描述了重建后所有的变化，包括更衣室、商店、咖啡馆、体育馆、舞蹈教室等。还总结了总体面积的增加及场馆全部变成室内的特征。

连贯与衔接

    连贯与衔接主要看两个方面：文章整体组织架构的连贯性、逻辑性，以及衔接手段的合理运用。

    整体的连贯性：本文的组织架构比较清晰。先说明有两张图，再指出具体的变化，最后总结两图最大的差异：面积增加及场馆全部变成室内。但是，如果可以分成四段：首段说明题意，主体段一陈述现有布局情况和方位，主体段二描述产生的变化及保持不变的设施，尾段总结体育中心设施在两个阶段中设置的差异。这样，整体架构就更清晰，且更易传递内容。

    衔接手段的运用：时间关系（at the present moment / after a reconstruction）、顺序关系（first / besides / apart from that / finally / furthermore）、对比关系（according to the new layout / it is also clear from the second layout that）

词汇

    本文的用词正确率非常高，没有拼写错误，并且有一些有灵活度和准确性的表达，如 illustrate / reconstruction / redeveloped / additional / replaced by other facilities / renovated。但是和7分作文要求的词汇相比，本文只是使用了恰当范围的词汇，但缺乏一些不太常见的表达，如在表达变化的时候，可以用 modification 而不是使用简单的 change，在表示预测的时候可以使用 be predicted to do 来表示 be going to。

语法

    6分作文在语法方面的要求是能使用简单和复杂的句子结构，语法和标点出现一些错误。7分作文在语法方面的要求是首先能使用各种复杂的句子结构，其次文章的大多数句子都没有错误。本文除了高频使用 be going to 是语法部分的弱点以外，语法结构的多样性和准确性是本文的亮点。

    复杂结构举例：

    It is going to be located in the place where the outdoor courts used to be. 本句运用了被动语态、从句及过去形式的表达。

    It is also clear from the second layout that... 本句使用了从句。

Task 2

📔题目要求

（见《剑桥雅思官方真题集 13：学术类》P95）

🖋审题

题目翻译：尽管农业有了很大的进步，全世界有许多人仍然在挨饿。分析这个问题的原因并提出相应的解决方法。

💡写作思路

本文属于问题题型。应该在文章开头提出问题，在主体段落分析问题出现的原因，在结尾提出解决问题的方法。

☕考生作文

（见《剑桥雅思官方真题集 13：学术类》P134~135）

🐚参考译文

现在，很多国家被试图发展先进的可以解决食物短缺的东西，顺便说一句为什么全世界还有很多人挨饿呢。就我而言，我认为是"资本主义"。

根据美国在 1970 年（冷战）指定的"世界秩序"把全世界的国家分成了三组，1）第一世界如美国、英国、日本这些，2）第二世界如苏联，3）第三世界是一些发展中国家。我不认为资本主义是不好的，我认为它导致了一些问题，如贫困国家的食物匮乏。

根据经济学，发达国家有绝对的权力从发展中国家中用最便宜的价格、最艰苦的工作、危险的环境而获取资源。因此在发展中国家生活的人没有机会去改变他们的地位。他们拿着最低的工资相反去生产很贵的产品，例如一个发达国家的工人一天挣 1 美金，但卖了 100 美金的产品，有大概 99 美金的资本就到了居住在发达国家的雇主手里。

为了解决这个问题，我认为每个国家的政府应该保证他们的公民有基本的权利，如食物、干净的水和教育。那些由于高价而导致人们无法购买食物的情况，政府应该控制价格保证食物不会太贵。

在解决这个问题的长期过程中，政府将给予更多的教育经费使之为大众免费，因为我绝对相信教育可以改变社会地位，当人们有好的教育，他们就有好的就业机会。然后政府应该保证房价也不会太高。那人们就会花更多的钱。当人们花更多的钱，他们就有更多的钱，我们应该一起解决这个问题，不仅是一些国家的责任，这个问题将从全世界被根除。最终我们将有解决它的希望，而不是失望。

☕考官点评

（见《剑桥雅思官方真题集 13：学术类》P134）

参考译文

本文造成了读者的阅读困难。文中试图回应题目的第一个问题（Why is this the case?）但没有足够的支持，而对于第二个问题（What can be done about this problem?）的回答缺乏重点，因为提到了教育、清洁水源、社会流动性和食物。与此同时，可以看出作者有一定的想法，但是语言的缺乏使他无法令人满意地将想法表达出来。观点分段表达，文章有一定的延续性，使用了准确的衔接手段（Nowadays | According to | for example），但还是有一些不准确的表达（Hence | in the long team / term）。对拼写和词性转换的控制很弱，频繁出现错误，如（itmes | opioin | Captialism | divied | countris | resouse | develping），导致了进一步的阅读困难。有试图使用简单和复杂的句子形式，但是整体出错率较高，即使是简单句也会出错（I think it made many problem | the people will be expenditure more）。标点的使用也是经常出错。

分析

本文得分 6 分。

接下来我们从四个评分方面（任务完成情况、连贯与衔接、词汇、语法）对这篇考生作文进行详细分析。

任务完成情况

6 分作文的特点是文章涉及题目中的所有内容，不像 5 分作文有部分跑题的现象。而与 7 分作文相比，6 分作文往往论证不够充分。本文是问题题型，需要分析的是导致人们挨饿的原因及对应的解决措施，而解决措施与原因不仅应该在内容上呼应，还应该在数量上呼应，即一个原因对应一个解决措施，或两个原因对应两个解决措施。如果按作者的思路，原因是资本主义导致人们挨饿，那么解决措施就是改变资本主义导致人们挨饿这个现象即可，而不需要再提到除了食物以外的干净水源和教育。所以，本文既没有满足内容一致，也未达到数量相匹。

连贯与衔接

本文使用了一些衔接手段，但是因为一些频繁的错误导致读者的迷茫和混乱。

衔接手段：Nowadays / According to / for example

错误的表达：in my opioin → in my opinion / becaus → because / fainally → finally / in the long team → in the long term / by the way → but

本文有分段，在整体结构安排方面有推进性和明确的观点，尽管有的段落论证不够充分。5 分作文一般没有分段，或者分段混乱。总体的信息组织是否有延续性是区分 5 分与 6 分作文的一个标志。而 7 分作文在分段的逻辑性和衔接的有效性上做得更好。

如果本文可以变成四段式的结构，在整体结构安排方面会更清晰：首段改写题目，提出目前的问题是什么，主体段一提出导致这个问题的原因，主体段二论证对应的解决措施，尾段重申问题及解决方法。或者，首段内容不变，主体段两段分别提出两个原因，尾段直接写解决方法即可。

词汇

5 分作文的词汇量是有限的（limited），6 分作文是适当的（adequate），7 分作文是丰富的（sufficient）。本文的词汇基本能够满足题目，拼写和构词法出现一些明显的错误。

文中错误举例：

第一段：itmes → items / opioin → opinion

第二段：divied → divided / in to → into / devopling → developing

第三段：develped → developed / a → an / advantage → advantage / resouse → resource/ develping → developing / oppunities → opportunities / moblisation → mobilise / product → produced

第四段：guranted → guarantee / restrize → restrict / bare → remove / pices → prices

第五段：thie → the / civilan → civilian / becaus → because / mobilisatim → mobilisation / bare the free of household → decrease the fee of household / wild → world / fainally → finally

语法

本文在语法方面虽然尝试使用简单句和复杂句的形式，但是连简单句都会出现频繁的错误，此外，大写、冠词以及标点的任意或错误使用，都给读者造成了阅读障碍。

文中错误举例：

第一段：Nowadays, many countries has been tried to develop the Advances itmes to Solves the lack of food → Nowadays, many countries have been trying to develop the advanced items to solve the problem of food shortage

第二段：the third world was a devopling countries → the third world was some developing countries / I think it made many problem → I think it caused many problems

第三段：the people who live in the develping countires has no oppunities to moblisation their status → those who live in these developing countries have no opportunities to mobilize their status / the high price of their item product → the high price of the item produced / to be selled → to be sold / the cap is approximate 99 dollar US goes to the owner who live in the deveoped countries→ the capital is approximately 99 US dollars which go to the owners who live in the developed countries

第四段：The solve of this problem → To solve this problem / the government on each countries should guranted their citizen to have a basic rights → the government of each country should guarantee their citizens to have basic human rights

第五段：I absolutely think Education comes with mobilisatim the social status when the people has a high Education comes with a hire in a high working. → I absolutely think education comes with the mobilization of social status as when they have a higher educational background, they may have the opportunity to be hired by a great company. / When the more expenditure the people have, the more money they have we have to solve this problem together, Not the duty of some countries, the problem will be eradicated from the wild. fainally we have to have a hope to solve it, Not despair yet. → The more money people have, the more they will spend and we will solve this problem together as this is not only for some countries, but also for the world. When it is eradicated, we will not have any despair, but hope finally.

Speaking

Part 1

在第一部分，考官会介绍自己并确认考生身份，然后打开录音机 / 笔，报出考试名称、时间、地点等考试信息。考官接下来会围绕考生的学习、工作、住宿或其他相关话题展开提问。

🔍 话题举例

Animals

1. **Are there many animals or birds where you live? [Why/Why not?]**
   Yes, I suppose. I live in a *residential community* in the city. I can often see some people *walking their dogs* in the morning or after dinner. However, there aren't many birds there. The cleaners would *chase away* any birds *in sight*.

residential community 居民区	walking the dogs 遛狗
chase away 赶跑	in sight 目光所及

2. **How often do you watch programmes or read articles about wild animals? [Why?]**
   Well, not so often these days. When I was a kid I used to watch documentaries about animals all the time, but now I simply don't have the time for that. I suppose I'm no longer the *wide-eyed child* who has *innate curiosity* for everything.

wide-eyed child 天真的孩子	innate curiosity 天生的好奇心

3. **Have you ever been to a zoo or a wildlife park? [Why/Why not?]**
   Sure, I have been to several zoos in different places, but none of them compares to the *night safari park* I visited in Singapore. Never had I visited a park after dark before. It was the *experience of a lifetime*!

night safari park 夜间野生动物园	experience of a lifetime 一生难忘的经历

4. **Would you like to have a job working with animals? [Why/Why not?]**
   As much as I would love to say yes, I have to say no. Most mammals have *an overpowering smell* and I don't think my *sensitive nose* can take that. I mean, I'm happy to *watch animals from afar*, but not when I have to get really close to one.

an overpowering smell 强烈的气味	a sensitive nose 敏感的鼻子
watch...from afar 远远地看着……	

Part 2

考官给考生一张话题卡（Cue Card）。考生有 1 分钟准备时间，并可以做笔记（考官会给考生笔和纸）。之后考生要作 1~2 分钟的陈述。考生讲完后，考官会就考生的阐述内容提一两个相关问题，由考生作简要回答。

> Describe a website you use that helps you a lot in your work or studies.
> You should say:
>> what the website is
>> how often you use the website
>> what information the website gives you
> and explain how your work or studies would change if this website didn't exist.

➡ 话题卡说明

这是一张比较常见的虚物类话题卡，主要考查考生描述一个对工作或学习有帮助的网站。作答时考生需注意，要充分拓展如果这个网站不存在的话，将会对你造成什么样的影响。这是一个虚拟的情况，所以作答的时候要注意虚拟语气的使用。可以和此话题串联的卡片包括 Describe a useful APP on your mobile phone or computer, Describe a book recommended by others 等。

整体介绍	Well, the website that I can think of immediately is the one called LexisNexis. It's arguably the biggest legal research database online.
使用频度	Since I'm a law student I need to use it all the time. I love using it because the information it contains is *comprehensive* and the *operating features* such as the search engine are rather *user-friendly*.
所含信息	It contains all the legislation, cases and commentary that I need for my studies. Whenever I need to search for a case referred to in our casebooks, I will log onto this website to find the judgment and other relevant *case law authorities*. The commentary there can also help me understand the cases better.
如果没有这个网站会怎样	*It would be unthinkable* how I should locate these *invaluable learning materials* if this website didn't exist. No other website can provide such a complete collection of cases at all levels of courts. Looking for hard copies of the cases would be *a complete nightmare*. Without the commentary it would take a much longer time for me to thoroughly understand the judges' *reasoning process*. Since the database also shows whether a judgment has been *overturned* by an *appellate court* or in a later case, I can always be sure that the cases I cite in my essays are the *leading authorities*. I can't even begin to imagine how my life would be if this website was not there with each and every step of my studies of law. I'm so thankful that my university allows students to use it for free.

🔲 重点词句

comprehensive 全面的
operating features 操作特点
user-friendly 易于使用的
case law authorities 权威案例
it would be unthinkable... ……是难以想象的
invaluable learning materials 宝贵的学习材料

a complete nightmare 一场噩梦
reasoning process 推论过程
overturn 推翻
appellate court 上诉法院
leading authorities 顶级权威

Part 3

第三部分：双向讨论（4~5分钟）。考官与考生围绕由第二部分引申出来的一些比较抽象的话题进行讨论。第三部分的话题是对第二部分话题卡内容的深化和拓展。

🔍 话题举例

The internet

1. **Why do some people find the internet addictive?**
   Because of the crazy amount of information there is! No matter what you *are into*, you can always find relevant information on the internet. If you keep searching, the amount of information is *overwhelming*! Another reason is that many websites are designed to *get you hooked*. For example once you have finished watching a video, a window will *pop up* to ask if you are interested in some similar ones. If you don't *have enough self-restraint*, hours will have passed before you realise that you have watched many videos you didn't originally plan to.

be into... 对……感兴趣	overwhelming 压倒性的
get you hooked 让你感兴趣	pop up 弹出
have enough self-restraint 有足够的自制力	

2. **What would the world be like without the internet?**
   Well, it depends on whether you mean it had never existed or that it would *cease to exist*. If it had never been invented, the world would be quite different running at *a much slower pace*. News would not travel half as fast and communication would be a major issue for many. If for some reasons the internet ceased to exist, it would definitely be *a huge retrograde step* and the result would be *devastating*. The overall *human productivity* would decrease so much that the whole world would *go into panic mode*.

cease to exist 不复存在	a much slower pace 慢得多的速度
a huge retrograde step 巨大的倒退	devastating 灾难性的
human productivity 人类生产力	go into panic mode 陷入恐慌

3. **Do you think that the way people use the internet may change in the future?**
   Yes, this I can say for sure. The fact is that the way people use the internet has been constantly changing in the last few decades, so it's only natural that it will continue to evolve in the future. *There is every reason for me to believe* that internet will play an even more significant role in our lives, *seeping*

into every detail of our daily routines from household chores to medical care. In this age of *Big Data Revolution, the sky is the limit*.

There is every reason to... 有充分的理由……	seep into 渗透到
Big Data Revolution 大数据革命	The sky is the limit. （发展）无可限量

Social media websites

1. **What are the ways that social media can be used for positive purposes?**
   There have already been cases where people use social media to help *find missing persons*, to seek assistance on certain problems and to *call for donations* for those in need. All in all, social media is quite useful when it comes to matters which require *the collective input* of a large number of people within a limited period of time. It allows news to travel faster, which in turn *facilitates any urgent action* that needs to be taken.

find missing persons 找到失踪的人	call for donations 呼吁捐赠
the collective input 集体的投入	facilitate any urgent action 促成任何紧急行动

2. **Why do some individuals post highly negative comments about other people on social media?**
   Well, it's really hard *to pinpoint* why any given individual would do something like that. My guess is that while some may do it *purely out of malice*, others just want to reduce the pressure within. *In this day and age*, people are suffering more stress from their workplaces and schools than ever. Such stress *keeps accumulating* and people are *in desperate need to* let it out. Many people may also find it easier to say harsh things online because of the *anonymity*, which means they don't have to *face the other party in person* and there is usually *little consequence* for them.

to pinpoint... 准确指出	purely out of malice 纯粹出于恶意
in this day and age 在现在这个年代	keep accumulating 不断积累
in desperate need to... 急切需要……	anonymity 匿名性
face...in person 本人直接面对……	little consequence 几乎没有什么后果

3. **Do you think that companies' main form of advertising will be via social media in the future?**
   There is no doubt that social media will play an increasingly important role in advertising, but I wouldn't go so far as to say that it would become the *main medium*. I reckon that TV stations and video websites would still *take the lion's share of advertising-generated revenue* among all *media platforms*. After all, online videos and TV shows such as TV series and reality shows still *draw in* the biggest number of audience, which is unlikely to change *in the foreseeable future*.

main medium 主要媒介	take the lion's share of... 占……的最大份额
advertising-generated revenue 广告收入	media platform 媒体平台
draw in... 吸引……来	in the foreseeable future 在可预见的未来